P9-DMX-009

THE ANGUISH OF INDIA

By the same author

THE TOKOLOSH
POLITICAL AFRICA
AFRICAN PROFILES
INTO EXILE

BY *Ronald Segal*

ᔕᗞ

THE ANGUISH

OF INDIA

STEIN AND DAY / *Publishers* / New York

Copyright © 1965 by Ronald Segal
First published in the United Kingdom by Penguin Books
under the title THE CRISIS OF INDIA, 1965
Library of Congress Catalog No. 65-20473
All rights reserved

Stein and Day/Publishers/7 East 48 Street, New York, N. Y. 10017

S
80.84
.S38

To Susan, my wife

102797

EMORY AND HENRY LIBRARY

ACKNOWLEDGMENTS

Acknowledgments are gratefully made to the following:

for permission to quote passages from *Caste and Communication in an Indian Village* by D. N. Majumdar, to the author and Asia Publishing House, Bombay;

for maps based on the maps 'India in the Reign of Aśoka' and 'India in the Twentieth Century' from the *Oxford History of India* by V. A. Smith, third edition, edited by Percival Spear, to the Clarendon Press, Oxford; and for a map based on the *Oxford History of India* map 'India, 1836', after *An Historical Atlas of the Indian Peninsula* by C. C. Davies, to the Oxford University Press, Bombay;

for allowing the map 'Food and Population' to be reproduced, to the Food and Agriculture Organization of the United Nations, and the *Unesco Courier*, Paris;

for permission to quote passages from *Blossoms in the Dust* by Kusum Nair, to the author and Gerald Duckworth & Co. Ltd, London;

for permission to quote passages from *The Twice Born* by G. Morris Carstairs, to the author, to the Hogarth Press, London and to the Indiana University Press, Bloomington, Indiana;

for passages from *Hinduism*, edited by Louis Renou, to Prentice-Hall International Inc., London;

for permission to quote from an article by Vinoba Bhave, to *Amrita Bazar Patrika*, Calcutta;

for passages from *Jawaharlal Nehru: An Autobiography*, (published in America as *Toward Freedom: An Autobiography*, copyright © 1941 the John Day Company), to The Bodley Head, London, and to the John Day Company Inc., New York;

for a map based on the *Oxford History of India* map 'The Indus Civilization' after *The Indus Civilization* by Sir Mortimer Wheeler, to the Cambridge University Press, Cambridge;

and for permission to include a map based on the map 'Language Regions of India' from *India: The Most Dangerous Decades* by Selig S. Harrison, to Princeton University Press, Princeton, New Jersey.

CONTENTS

TABLES

MAPS

THE ANGUISH OF INDIA

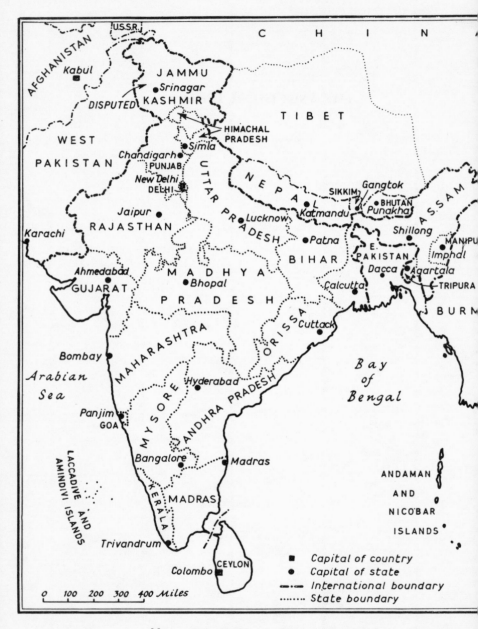

Map 1   THE POLITICAL DIVISIONS OF INDIA

CHAPTER ONE

A VISITOR TO INDIA

THE intention of my publishers in commissioning this book was that someone with some experience of other poor societies but none of India should visit the country and write an account of his impressions. I had spent most of my life in South Africa and much of the last few years there in political contact with the poor non-white bulk of the population, and since leaving South Africa had studied and written on political developments in Africa. I would, therefore – or so at least the argument ran – approach India with an African neutrality and without the standards and preconceptions of someone accustomed only to the rich white societies of the West. The prospect of visiting a country as significant as India, not more than a few years away from colonial subjugation and now by far the largest independent democracy in the world, dedicated to shaping a socialist society, enormously excited me. Besides, India is one of the great human centres, containing a sixth of the world's total population, and an ignorance of India seemed to me then, as it seems to me now, ignorance of humanity itself.

A few days before I left London, I went to see a journalist whom I had met during his stay in South Africa and who had then been stationed for a year or two in India. In South Africa he had emotionally identified himself with the political struggle of the non-whites, displaying a sharp appreciation of the issues involved, and I accordingly anticipated from him a sympathetic and astute introduction to the India he had subsequently visited. After ten minutes of his reminiscing, I suggested nervously that he didn't seem to have liked the Indians very much. 'Liked them? I hated them!' he cried. 'They are a dirty and submissive lot, with no flame or fight in them, swaddled in superstition and apathy and a meaningless arrogance. The rich are ravenous and corrupt, and the poor are drained dry almost of the will to survive. The government is muddled and ineffectual, the country is in a hopeless mess, and calamity of one kind or another is unavoidable.'

After three months and seven thousand miles of travelling in India, I found myself able to understand the journalist's rage. I, too, hated the dirt and the submission, the superstition and apathy, the greed and the corruption and the endless, astonishing and affronting poverty. It was all there, as he had promised it would be, just as there was also an almost obsessional cleanliness of the individual, an extraordinary grace of manner, a delicacy of form and of movement, a closeness to the rhythms of time and of place, a sense of mystery and drama, an intricate intelligence, a pervasive gentleness that showed itself as a longing for peace and an awe of life itself.

Much, if not most, of what I write may be considered hostile and even hurtful to the Indian people. I do not mean it to be so. If there is that in Indian tradition, culture and politics which I find repugnant, it is because I believe it to be hostile and hurtful to the Indians themselves, fortifying the ugly and cruel and destructive in their lives. Were I asked today by someone, 'Do you like the Indians?' I would only answer, 'I like people – people are all I really believe in.' And that is the excuse for this book. Of course the ugly and cruel and destructive are as I measure them, and it would be silly of me to suppose that other visitors to India, with far more searching an experience of the country and its people, may not measure differently. I can see why others may believe it more important to be holy than to be fed, but I cannot believe it. I am an unregenerate materialist and in my view no sense of mystery or grace of manner, no delicacy of movement and form, can compensate for the massive damage done by Indian hunger. That is my limitation, and the consequent limitation of this book.

Every country is, of course, unique: because they have been for long stretches of time politically or economically related, some are more and some are less like others; but each is indistinguishably itself, and it requires not only courage but impudence for a native of one to attempt interpreting another. All countries are unique, but some are more unique than others; and amongst the more unique, India must certainly be numbered. It has, to begin with, in Hinduism a religion of indetermin-

able age and vast contemporary devotion, which has never left
India at all except in the blood of emigrant communities. France
is not Catholicism – there are many other Catholic countries;
Pakistan is not Islam – there are many other Muslim states;
India is Hinduism.

To the visitor from another country, then, it is inevitably her
religion which sets India, first and finally, apart. For Hinduism
is not a furtive persuasion, seen from a corner of the visitor's
eye, an activity of forbidden temples or private murmuring. It
pervades the sounds and the sights of India like the ubiquitous
sunlight. The white humped cattle ambling with sophisticated,
even supercilious, ease through busy city streets; the oxen, with
painted horns and necklaces of flowers or beads, drawing their
creaking carts along white dusty tracks; the sudden jangle of
peasants in fancy dress, cavorting with red and silver tinsel
banners and brass pots through the many miles of their pilgrimage to the sacred river; the colour and size of the sari, its folds
and design, that a woman wears; the gold bangles on the thin
wrist of a ragged child; the predatory beggar with mutilated
limbs; the garish painted idols, twice human size, by a desolate
roadside; the shrill vivid women selling vegetables, and the
whitewashed merchants squatting in concentrated silence over
their account-books in the bazaar; the student touching his fore-
head with the dust of his teacher's sandals; the interminable
washing – in rivers, and at pumps, and from small brass pots at
a sudden turning in the road, with the unregarded filth of Indian
gutters; the variety and monotony of face and function: all are
manifestations of that Hinduism which belongs to India as the
blood to the body.

For Hinduism is the flow of India's life, as Catholicism was the
flow of life in medieval Europe, informing the market-place no
less than the cathedral, giving to power its shape, to labour its
content, and to society its meaning. Hinduism in India today is
the subject of popular music – Indian songs deal more frequently with the characters of Hindu epic and folklore than
with the personal pronouns of their Western equivalents – as it
is the theme of films, the bedtime stories of children. The character of the bazaar, the division of rural labour, the government
of village and state, no less than the intricate formalities of birth
and marriage and death, are all aspects of Hinduism. And as

Hinduism conditions the relationship of the individual to his society, prescribing his multitude of rights and obligations, it qualifies his relationship to his wife, to his parents, to his children and, above all, to himself. Hinduism influences not merely how an Indian acts, but how he thinks, not merely what he believes but how he feels.

Yet, for the visitor, India is unique not only in what is altogether her own, but also in what she has in common with other countries. For India has, too, a singular poverty. There is want and there is squalor even in the smug societies of the industrialized world; and certainly, in the countries of what is comfortably called the underdeveloped world – in Africa, in Asia, Central and South America – even in the fringe societies of Western Europe like Spain and Portugal, there is a kind of poverty that devours the human condition. But one slum is not very much like another; poverty, no less than pain, has its gradations, with death itself the only bottom, and Indian poverty, to many who have an acquaintance with poverty in similar societies, is unique. It is unique in its depths, which seem incapable of supporting life at all; unique in its blatancy, for it is everywhere, in city and village, not concealed among chimneys or trees, not isolated – like an epidemic – in an inaccessible slum, but everywhere, on the pavement at one's feet, always somewhere in the circle of one's sight; unique in its sheer magnitude, for in India the poor are not to be numbered in hundreds of thousands, but in hundreds of millions; unique in the quality of its submission, which registers a kind of glazed pride.

The religion and poverty of India are her two primary materials, out of which the whole structure of her society has been – and is still being – built. In relation to them, other considerations seem flippant, though each is significant enough in producing the singularity that is India, and some are intrinsic to these great twin facts of Indian existence. India is a vast but crowded country. With some one million square miles of territory she has 450 million people, and not merely in a few large cities is the pressure of humanity evident, as it is evident in the capitals of Western Europe and North America. India is fundamentally her villages, some six hundred thousand of them, in which eighty per cent of the total population lives. They differ enormously in size, in shape and in character. In the south they may be gather-

ings of palm-leaf-roofed huts interspersed with languorous coconut trees; in the centre they may be a series of mud houses that
seem to have grown gradually out of the earth itself; in the far
north, in Kashmir, they may be a cluster of boats lapping the
still water. Some have only a few hundred inhabitants; others,
a few thousand. But they are never far from each other – in
the main a mere mile or two away – and they make of India a
vast stretch of humanity rather than of land. The countryside
of overcrowded England is often, off the main roads and away
from the huge urban masses, deserted; there are few parts of
India, outside of the mountainous northern extremity, which
do not reveal someone – a young boy on a buffalo by a pool,
an old man sleeping to the rhythm of his bullock cart, women
lining up like still trees at a well, a lonely bent figure behind a
plough or a scattering of loin-clothed men jerking towards and
away from their reflections in a rice field – somewhere in the
landscape. And there are parts of rural India, like Kerala in the
south-west, which seem to seethe constantly with people, moving
along the sides of country roads with the jostling density of city
streets.

The villages of India have, in the main, no core; they are not
built around a temple or a well or a shop, as villages in Europe
seem to have gathered round a church or a pump, and villages
in North America around a general store. They are diffuse, not
cohesive, with a pattern of internal division rather than unity.
Each village, however small, consists as it were of suburbs without a town, each suburb corresponding to a different major
caste group. Since the life of a Hindu is largely governed by the
avoidance of ritual pollution, by the countless yet clear caste
formalities with their inflexible rules of how and where and
when and with whom to eat and drink and wash and work, these
village divisions are not only convenient but vital; they embody
in India a living principle – indeed, *the* living principle – of
social behaviour. The high-caste agriculturists will live together,
almost in a village of their own, perhaps with their own well
and their own small temple; the middle-caste carpenters or
potters will have their own cluster of houses, as will the low-
caste watchmen and washermen. The outcaste carrion-eating
basket-makers will have their special outlying suburb and, if
they are fortunate, a well for water. The whole village, with its

careful design, seems as permanent and ageless as the distinctions which have given it its shape.

If the Indian village has no core, it also has no 'rings' to define its development. Most villages in Europe or North America seem to grow chronologically, spreading from the core outwards through the years, like the rings in a tree trunk. The Indian village is denied a centre by its social formation, and a history by the materials of its structure. The mud or wooden walls crumble or decay, and are replaced; in the few villages where a stone or brick building was raised barely a century ago in this country of uncountable centuries, it is a source of pride and wonder to the villagers themselves. And yet the Indian village denies any impression of newness; the houses seem old at the moment they are built, with the oldness of the earth itself. To the visitor the Indian village is not new, and yet – unlike a village in France or England – it has no age, no beginning so that one can say: 'From the date on that, the oldest building, there, this village has six hundred years of history behind it.' India as it is today seems to be India as it has always been, not sixty years or six hundred years in becoming, but an immeasurable past away.

Poverty, of course, is less evident – except at times of flood or famine – in the village than in the city; earth and growth blur or disguise the effects of want, and it is difficult to believe that the peasant family in the small hut cuddled by coconut trees is as starved or diseased as the family squatting day and night in the naked squalor of a Calcutta street. It is, in any event, impossible for the normal visitor to enter the experience of Indian poverty; the experience of permanent hunger is as incomprehensible to someone who has always had enough to eat as is the experience of a cripple to someone with ordinary limbs. Yet it is easy and reasonable to suppose that the poverty of the village is not only less evident, but also less cruel than the poverty of the city. The Indian village may be crackled with caste divisions, but each division has its own cohesion and all the divisions together have a single shape. The formal distribution of different caste rights and obligations gives poverty its place and its support in the village structure. The upper castes are served by the lower ones and traditionally repay them not only in commodities or cash, but with help at times of special distress. Furthermore, the caste itself has a family character, so that one member may properly call upon others for help. This is not to romanticize poverty in the Indian village – poverty is no less poverty for the provision of sporadic benefits by patronage or caste kinship, and starvation is no less physically destructive for being shared within caste walls; but the poor of the Indian village belong to each other and to the village itself, whereas the poor of the Indian cities belong to no one and to nothing. For the labourers and their families who stream into Delhi and Bombay and Calcutta in the endless search for food, leaving the known caste relationships of the village behind them, there is seldom more than the terrible isolation of the makeshift and meaningless slum.

Even more terrible is the poverty too great for shelter even in the slums, the hundreds of thousands who eat and sleep and love and die in the streets. No one knows how many there are altogether or in any one city. A Communist trade-union organizer in Bombay told me that 700,000 of the city's 4,500,000 people lived on the pavements. A senior journalist on the *Times of India* estimated the figure at somewhere between 200,000 and 300,000. Lay opinion usually settles on 450,000 for Bombay and 550,000 for Greater Calcutta, or one in ten of the total population in each city. Yet – and what more merciless comment could there be? – no one knows. And, after all, it doesn't seem to matter.

For one comfort survives the transition from village to city: the doctrine of *dharma* or duty at the heart of Hinduism itself. Since the essence of virtue and the hope of reward – either in a better birth after death or, best of all, in a final state of union with God – lie in absolute acceptance of one's condition and absolute obedience to the rules of conduct which that condition requires, poverty becomes a preparation and not a despair. And so the fatalism of the Indian poor is different from the apathy, almost the atrophy, that is the mark of the poor in so many other places, just as the unconcern of the Indian rich is different from the callousness of the rich elsewhere. In the India of the village and the India of the city alike, what the poor display is not so much listlessness as indifference, a quality of dissociation from their surroundings that is something like pride. And the rich show less a callousness than a fatalism as well, an acknowledgment of their irresponsibility for the suffering of others.

India, of course, is more a continent than a country; indeed, British rule maintained as one of its excuses that India did not

exist at all except as an entity of government. It was this very
claim that made the resistance movement of Congress concentrate upon nourishing the national struggle with a national awareness, through the projection into the past of a unity which never
existed. India today is largely a union of linguistic states, and
the states themselves bear witness to the abundance of different
peoples, customs, languages and traditions that now compose one
country. The differences themselves are stark at the extremes.
The northern peasant and the southern are different in size, in
shape, and in colour, as well as in diet, costume, speech and
tradition. To the visitor, the long-limbed, heavy-featured light-
brown Bihari, with his Aryan ancestry, seems to belong to a
different country altogether from the shorter, delicately featured,
almost blue-black Tamil from Madras, with his Dravidian past.
The south, where the heat is more protracted and intense, where
even the curry burns more brightly, where rice is a desired diet,
where the trees and flowers have a tropical exuberance, appears
more than mere mileage away from the north, with its cold
winter nights, its wheat-fields, its dry dusty roads, its relatively
muted colours and growth.

The division of colour alone, which dates back some four
thousand years to the invasion and settlement of northern India
by the light-skinned Aryan-speaking peoples of central Asia,
remains a living reality. The ruling newcomers, whose warrior
religion was to fuse with the ancient cults of the darker-skinned
indigenous peoples to make traditional Hinduism, imposed not
only the dominion of the Brahmin priest caste, with the whole
traditional caste pattern, but simultaneously the hierarchy of
colour, the superiority of light over dark; and though in India
today there may be found priests with dark skins and sweepers
with light ones, in general the upper castes are light and the lower
castes dark. One of the basic and ubiquitous facts about present-
day India is that the country is planted deep in its past – and not
the recent past of British rule, a period which has naturally had
far more effect on the small moneyed and educated class than
on the masses, as much as the far, still largely unknown past of
Hinduism's very beginning. The battles fought so many thousands of years ago between native and invader are being fought
again in India today, not only in the matrimonial columns of the
newspapers, where caste and colour are more often than not the

conditions of suitability, but more directly, in the refusal by the Dravidian south to accept Hindi – the Aryan derivative – as the only official language of the country.

The extremities of north and south, however, are far from constituting all the significant differences and sources of internal conflict that give India its continental or multi-national character. The political history of the country from the Aryan invasions to the British conquest developed distinctions which British rule merely concealed for a time and which reappeared with renewed force in the wake of alien withdrawal. The horizontal flow of major rivers in a vertical land-mass break up India into three main physical divisions: the north, the south, and, in between, the Deccan table-land, over which north and south gave through the centuries intermittent battle for political and cultural control. Yet even these three areas were not individually united except under occasional expansionary dynasties, and within each one, regional entities, with their own political and linguistic characters, took gradual shape around centres of agricultural wealth.

The pre-eminent complex of regional entities was that of the north, centred in the Ganges basin, the richest agricultural area in India, and the one which the Aryan invaders made their heartland as 'Aryavarta', the setting of subsequent sacred Sanskrit texts. Cut off in the north by the Himalayas and to the south by the forest and desolate stretches of central India, this vast expanse of fertile soil sustained a thriving population and lent itself naturally to economic and political consolidation. Empire after empire rose somewhere in the Gangetic plain to spread its power throughout the north and then disintegrate; but since such power was final rather than pervasive, its withdrawal left the outlying areas culturally unabsorbed. The huge Hindi-speaking heartland of today – the states of Bihar, Uttar Pradesh, Madhya Pradesh and Rajasthan – with more than a third but significantly less than a half of India's total population, comprised the solid centre of imperial power in the north; but though their proximity allured the expansion of each Gangetic empire as it arose, the present-day states of Assam, West Bengal and Gujarat reasserted their independence when that imperial power declined, and developed their own cultural – and strong linguistic – identities. The Punjab itself, with the medi-

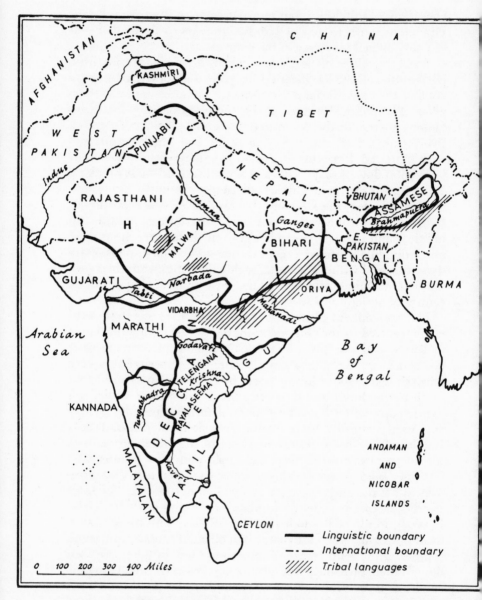

Map 2 THE LANGUAGE REGIONS OF INDIA

(based on the map 'Language Regions of India', from *India: The Most Dangerous Decades* by
Selig S. Harrison, Princeton University Press and Oxford University Press, 1960, p. 18)

eval Mogul conquest and the subsequent genesis of the Sikh religion, became in time the arena of a complex cultural and religious struggle, among Muslims, Hindus and Sikhs – a struggle now reduced, with the creation of Pakistan and the partition of the Punjab, to the issue of a separate Sikh state. Bengal had sufficient cohesion of its own to preserve a powerful independence for centuries at a time and even under the Pala kings (c. A.D. 750 to 1050), to produce a dominant north-Indian empire. Assam, with its strong Mongoloid infusion, was too distant for serious and consistent assault by Gangetic empires, but was constantly subject to pressure from neighbouring Bengal, and tension between the two states persists to this day. Gujarat on the western seaboard, with its maritime wealth providing a perpetual temptation to conquest, was vulnerable to both Gangetic and Deccan expansionism; but it had, too, its periods of dynamic independence, and under the Solanki dynasty (A.D. 961 to 1297) – a reservoir of contemporary regional pride – exercised sway over large areas to the south and north.

In the Deccan, or central India – comprising the four present-day states of Maharashtra, Mysore, Andhra Pradesh and Orissa – geography promoted four distinct political and linguistic entities. Jungle waste separates Orissa on the eastern seaboard from its neighbours; in the west, the lava-enriched black cotton land of Maharashtra ends at the borders of Mysore in the south and Andhra in the east; while the high southern part of the Deccan plateau divides the central states of Mysore and Andhra from each other. From time to time, as in the north, empires arose to dominate the whole area; but with their decline, as again in the north, the regional entities reasserted themselves. Each of the four had its own imperial age, providing it today with a precedent for regional assertiveness, and each regional language – Marathi in Maharashtra, Oriya in Orissa, Kannada in Mysore, and Telugu in Andhra – assumed separate shape before the thirteenth century, to develop a significant literary tradition. The Deccan itself, maintaining contact at times of united imperial rule with both the northern and southern cultures of India, became a passage-way for cultural transmission between the Indian extremes and so itself a process in the evolution of a coherent Hindu civilization. Maharashtra and Orissa are today, linguistically and culturally, nearer to the north than to the south, while Mysore and Andhra are nearer to the south than to the north; indeed, the linguistic battle against Hindi as the national language of India has been spear-headed by the two southern states of Madras and Kerala together with their still largely Dravidian neighbours, Mysore and Andhra Pradesh.

Of all the states in India, Madras – or Tamilnad, the land of the Tamils – possesses the strongest separatist movement, an organized political party which, until such agitation was made illegal during the national emergency over the border fighting with China, demanded the establishment of a separate Tamil state independent of India. Whether or not, as some Tamil propagandists would have it, Tamil culture is the developed remnant of one which covered all India till the time of the Aryan conquest, there can be no doubt that Tamilnad was the home of an ancient and self-sufficient civilization. Though Tamil kings at times attempted imperial expansion to the north – the eleventh-century Rajendra sent his war elephants through Orissa to Bengal – for the most part they ignored even the neighbouring Deccan, because their position on the great east–west ocean trade route gave them the wealth of a great maritime power. The sandalwood, peacocks and rice shipped to Babylon as long ago as the seventh century B.C. bore Dravidian rather than Sanskrit names; while during the Christian era, Tamilnad carried on a vast trade, to the west with imperial Rome, and to the east, for a thousand years or more, with Indonesia, Malaya, Viet-Nam and Cambodia. On the basis of this maritime wealth and the vast agricultural fertility of the Kaveri delta, a long civilization produced works of art – poetry, sculpture, and architecture – in tropical profusion.

Separating Kerala in the south-west from Tamilnad is the mountain barrier of the Western Ghats, which provide a climatic boundary as well as a political and so cultural one, since they block the monsoon from the Arabian Sea and so produce an abundance of rain along the whole coastal strip. The state enjoys today – as it has throughout recorded history – a fertility more luxuriant than either the Gangetic basin or the Kaveri delta, permitting the highest population density in rural India, with only five acres of land sufficient for a family's subsistence. Enjoying a sustained prosperity as a result of its considerable trade with countries across the Arabian Sea, the region of what is now Kerala suffered only intermittent conquest by the rulers of Tamilnad and, by the time of Pallava power in Tamilnad, from about A.D. 600 to 900, was breaking away altogether from its Tamil connections. As far back as the fourth century B.C., the Tamil spoken in Kerala was a distinct dialect, and by the tenth century A.D. it had become a separate language – Malayalam – which, within another two hundred years, would produce its own literary tradition.

It was Hinduism, with its sacred books, its ritual and, above all, its formalized caste structure, which imposed a strong cultural unity upon all these various political fragments, even in the south; but, ironically, the very growth of nationalism and the accomplishment of Indian independence have nourished regional differences and stimulated regional allegiances at the expense of national cohesion. It was the Congress struggle against British rule and, under Gandhi's leadership, the parallel struggle against caste rigidities which together first loosened the Brahmins' cultural hold and so inevitably the dominance of Sanskrit as India's only cultural language. Then, with the victory of Indian nationalism and the British withdrawal, increased schooling facilities and adult literacy campaigns, under the control of the various states, vastly expanded the public for newspapers and books in the regional languages; the country's huge cinema industry fed the appetite for vernacular films and, in feeding, further sharpened it; while the political agitation for linguistic states, which culminated in the redrawing of most state boundaries along linguistic lines in 1956, gave the different cultural allegiances of India conscious form and expression.

Whether in consequence 'India stands the risk of being split up into a number of totalitarian small nationalities,' as threatened by Professor S. K. Chatterji of the Official Language Commission,[1] must be one of the most formidable questions for the future to answer. Certainly, the differences between one region and another have in the past assumed violent form – as in the linguistic agitation which led to the division of Bombay State into Gujarat and Maharashtra at the beginning of April 1960 – and popular antagonisms are revealed in the stereotypes with

[1] Minority Report in the *Report of the Official Language Commission* (Government of India Press, Delhi, 1957), p. 313.

which people in one state associate people in another. An Indian social psychologist in 1953 studied the attitudes of Marathi-speaking university students and slum housewives, to discover that they gave the same descriptions, in the main derogatory, when asked to characterize other regional groups. Tamils, for instance, were despised as 'dark'; Gujaratis, as 'fat' and 'spineless'. An American researcher, conducting similar investigations in the same year, at the Hindi-speaking centre of Lucknow, met an identical readiness amongst those he interviewed to stereotype critically people from other linguistic regions, a greater readiness indeed than to stereotype people from foreign countries like Britain.[1]

The visitor to India is, at first, overwhelmed by the impression of unity – the everywhere inescapable manifestations of Hinduism as a living religion, the submissive ubiquitous poverty, the underlying similarity of so much that is alien – and he is easily enough misled into confirming this impression through his contacts with authority. It is not merely that the buildings of government in each state look like each other, and all of them like small replicas of the part-Mogul, part-Edwardian, bureaucratic cathedrals of New Delhi. But the governors themselves project an image of identity. Whether in Madras or Bihar, Maharashtra or West Bengal, the major politicians in opposition as well as in government, the civil servants, the social leaders, the heads of industry and commerce, the academics, the doctors and the lawyers and the architects, the writers and newspapermen, generally speak English by preference and share an experience of Western, if only British, culture. Yet, after some time and travel in the country, the visitor begins to recognize the enormous gulf that divides governor from governed in India. It is as though India consisted of two quite different peoples: one constituting less than a hundredth of the total, yet possessing all the power, with its own way of life, its own language, even its own press and entertainments, its separate aspirations; and the other, the masses of India, with an altogether different form of communication and set of allegiances. And if India appears to be

[1] Selig S. Harrison, *India: The Most Dangerous Decades* (Princeton University Press and Oxford University Press, 1960), p. 12. This book is an excellent study of regional rivalries in India and the dangers that they threaten to the future of the country.

not just a religious or cultural unity, but an economic and political whole as well, the image is projected in major measure by the governors rather than the governed. It is they who give 'Mother India' its political and economic meaning, rather than the peasant and urban masses, who seem rather more aware of 'Mother Maharashtra' or 'Mother Madras'.

Even during the national emergency that followed the outbreak of border fighting with China, when all instruments of communication – the press, the radio and the public platform – were employed to arouse popular patriotism, regional loyalties continued unabated and, on the major issue of India's official language, flared into sporadic dispute. A state governor who gave his opening address to a Hindi-speaking legislature in English, as permitted by the constitution, was persistently interrupted and then faced with a walk-out by Socialist members for not having spoken in Hindi; even the distinguished President of India, a southerner, was heckled in Parliament by a few opposition members from Hindi-speaking areas – and passionately defended by members from other linguistic regions – for delivering his address in English. Articles in the vernacular press dealt frequently with the glories of the particular region's past; where a popular theatre, for contemporary plays, existed at all – in West Bengal and in Kerala – it was a vernacular one; and the concerts of traditional music were devoted to regional tradition. Even so international an issue as the doctrinal dispute between China and the Soviet Union within the world Communist movement had regional overtones in India, with the party in West Bengal overwhelmingly opposing the pro-Soviet stand of the national leadership, while the party in Maharashtra, for instance, overwhelmingly supported it. The emergency, indeed, with its blow to India's military self-assurance and international serenity, had substantial internal repercussions, the extent of which was concealed by the need for displaying a united front to the enemy; there seemed a heightening popular awareness, if not everywhere to the dangers which India faced – the war in the Himalayas was a far cry from the problems of peasant poverty in Orissa or Madras – at least of the growing isolation of government, the gulf between 'us' and 'them'.

The visitor to India, aware of the enormous problems which

the country faces and unimpressed by the progress towards appropriate solutions that he is able to register, may find himself impatient with the laborious, sometimes seemingly self-defeating processes of democratic rule, may catch himself longing – and supposing that many Indians long as well – for a ruthless government that would, however authoritarianly, tackle at least the crises of poverty and over-population, superstition and separatism, official corruption and the crude self-seeking of the commercial classes, head on. Indeed, he may find it surprising that signs of a drift towards totalitarianism are so faint and so few, exceptionally so in a former colonial world of so many authoritarian – many of them military – regimes. He is inclined to suspect the credentials of Indian democracy altogether, and see the government of Congress as a disguised, if rather benign, one-party despotism popularly imposed.

Democracy in India is doubtless inadequate and inefficient – in how many countries of the world which practise democracy is it neither? – because so many of the voters are illiterate, ill informed, largely indifferent to the procedure by which laws are delivered down to them from the intimidating seats of authority in the state capitals and high New Delhi itself. Certainly on the village level, despite the government's diligent if distant sponsorship of democratic experience through local elected councils, the traditional pattern of power, with the upper castes dominating the lower ones, still in the main prevails; elections for village councils may be duly held, but their results merely confirm the existing forms of control. On the state and national level, however, popular participation in political choice is undeniably significant, displaying meaningful swings and regional or district variations in voting patterns. In an electorate of some 200 million – an electorate, moreover, overwhelmingly rural, with primitive communications in most areas and little access to the organs of normal political campaigning – a poll of over 52 per cent as registered at the 1962 elections is astonishingly high, and little less than that usually achieved in the far more practised democracy of the United States. Nor does Congress itself enjoy an undisputed rule. Though it is the party which so successfully led the struggle for independence and which still carries the prestige of Gandhi's long association with it, it has persisted in receiving less than half of the total vote. Voting patterns have changed; the Communist Party has tripled its vote, from 3·3 per cent in 1951–2 to 9·96 per cent in 1962; the right-wing Hindu traditionalist Jana Sangh has more than doubled its own, from 3·1 per cent to 6·44 per cent; and the vote for the two Socialist parties has dropped by more than a third, from 16·4 per cent to 9·33 per cent. The shift in popular allegiance has been even more marked on the regional level; in the state legislature of Madhya Pradesh, the Congress share of the total 288 seats fell from 232 in 1957 to only 142 in 1962, while substantial advances were made by the Praja Socialist Party and the Jana Sangh; in Maharashtra, the Congress share of the seats in the state legislature rose from 136 out of 262 in 1957 to 215 out of 264 in 1962, at the expense of the Communist Party, the Praja Socialist Party and other opposition groups; in the Punjab, the Congress share dropped from 120 out of 154 in 1957 to only 90 in 1962, as a result of organized opposition support for a separate Sikh state. The Indian electorate, therefore, votes neither blindly nor predictably; it distinguishes between parties and policies along both regional and national lines.

The press – vernacular and English – is free to say largely what it likes (the national emergency introduced some minor restraints) and generally it does so, though its democratic function is open to dispute, since it is owned in the main by the Indian industrialists and ruthlessly reflects their views. The opposition parties are free to campaign against the government and do so vigorously (though here again the national emergency allowed some particular – and major – restraints, for the government detained a number of Communists and made it treasonable to agitate, as the D.M.K. in Madras was doing, for secession from the Indian Union). Above all, the tenets of a liberal democracy are observed by government in most of India – the state of Kashmir is a constant and deeply embarrassing denial, while the dismissal of the Communist government in Kerala followed the letter but not the spirit of the Constitution – at the cost, one may not unreasonably suspect, of furthering a real popular democracy. For political democracy is hollow without economic democracy, and while the Indian government is so careful of individual rights – where the rights involved are those of the country's relatively few and socially irresponsible rich – it can do little to eradicate vast economic inequalities. Yet the people ultimately select their own government at regular intervals, and do so without pressure from, and beyond the threat of, the military. This is no small accomplishment. Pakistan, not so long ago part of undivided India, stands with its military regime, the embodiment of an alternative, across a disputed frontier. Yet even during the emergency, in the midst of military setbacks which were shrilly proclaimed in the Indian press as national humiliations and indications of government exhaustion, unpreparedness and equivocation, there was no danger – despite the fearful hope of some old India hands abroad – that the military was either willing or able to assume power. In India the civil authority is supreme, and under present circumstances it seems improbable that the peasant and urban masses would submit to any change. A smaller and more cohesive society than India, with similar problems of poverty and a religious doctrine of resignation, would doubtless be more vulnerable; but the very size and regional variety of India, which pose such difficulties for its centralized control, constitute the most effective obstacles to a military coup and the destruction of civil authority.

India too, despite the pervasive importance of Hinduism and the influence of a religiously militant political party like the Jana Sangh, despite – above all – the temptations to religious fervour, indeed frenzy, offered by the country's hostile relations with the constitutionally Islamic state of Pakistan, is secular. Much of the credit for this must unquestionably go to the leadership which Gandhi gave to Congress during the struggle against British rule and to the subsequent ascendancy of Nehru, a declared agnostic. Yet it remains unlikely that modern India would be a secular state if it were not for the tradition of tolerance so fundamental to Hinduism. It is not merely that Hinduism does not recognize heresy, that a Hindu born remains a Hindu whatever he believes, but that Hindu society as a whole has historically displayed tolerance towards religious minorities. It is no accident that a community of sun-worshipping Parsees, originally from Persia, with strange – and to most Hindus probably repugnant – ways of disposing of their dead, should have been permitted in peace to establish themselves as a prosperous community in India. Jewish settlement and prosperity in Europe have encountered very different treatment. Indeed, the small community of Jews in Cochin, on the western seaboard of India, received for several centuries substantial hospitality, with grants of land, from the Hindu rulers in the area, to suffer sudden persecution, including the destruction of their synagogue, with the arrival in the fifteenth century of the Portuguese.

If this record of Hindu tolerance was marred at the time of partition and sporadically since then, in violence against the property and persons of Muslims, it must be remembered that communal hysteria was intense on both sides of divided India, that Hindu violence was bitterly condemned by the political and religious leaders of India alike, and that it seldom stretched beyond the partitioned provinces themselves. It says much for Hindu and Indian tolerance that the country, with few and limited manifestations of communal hostility, despite continuingly tense relations with Pakistan, contains in general peace and security over forty million Muslims, or some ten per cent of the total population.

Article 25 of the Indian Constitution ensures to all persons equally freedom of conscience and the right freely to profess, practise and propagate any religion, subject only to the demands of public order, morality and health. Construing the Article, the Indian Supreme Court has declared:

> Subject to the restriction which this Article imposes, every person has a fundamental right under our Constitution, not merely to entertain such religious belief as may be approved by his judgment or conscience but to exhibit his belief and ideas in such overt acts as are enjoined or sanctioned by his religion and further to propagate his religious views for the edification of others.[1]

Further, under Article 26, every religious denomination has the right: (a) to establish and maintain institutions for religious and charitable purposes; (b) to manage its own affairs in matters of religion; (c) to own and acquire movable and immovable property; and (d) to administer such property in accordance with the law. Under Article 27, no person may be compelled

---

[1] G. N. Joshi, *The Constitution of India* (Macmillan & Co. Ltd, London, 1961), p. 97.

to pay taxes the proceeds of which are used for the promotion or maintenance of any particular religion or religious denomination, while under Article 28, compulsory religious instruction in educational institutions maintained by the State, or recognized or aided by the State, is prohibited. Indeed, both the theory and practice of religious tolerance in India compare favourably not just with twilit European countries like Spain and Portugal, but even those like France and Italy in the full blaze of Western civilization. It is no small manifestation of the liberal and secular democracy that independent India is dedicated to being that, despite the overwhelming allegiance of most citizens to Hinduism, there exist so many minorities, some of them substantial, pursuing their various faiths in such abundant freedom. The Hindu temple may be the most evident symbol of religious India; but there are symbols too in the mosques of Malabar, the Roman Catholic churches of Trivandrum, the Anglican cathedrals of Mysore and Madras, the towers of silence in Bombay where the Parsees abandon their dead.

This tolerance is not a marginal quality of Indian culture, like prohibition – sporadically promoted in the past during ascetic phases, employed by Congress under the leadership of Gandhi as a technique of boycott in the struggle against British rule, and now become a moral imperative, legally enforced, in some states, or some districts of some states, for all of the time or on some days of every week. (But then Indian tolerance allows aliens and self-proclaimed alcoholics to buy liquor, and even drink publicly in dry states, or on dry days in wet states, on the production of a permit, and permits are generally so easy to obtain that the rate of self-proclaimed alcoholism staggers belief.) Tolerance is of the very material from which the Indian character is formed. How has it arisen? Is it all, with so much else, no more – and there are visitors to India who leave in this belief – than a lethargy which comes from the consuming heat, day after day and month after month of it, till any effort under that harsh blue sky seems to demand an extraordinary will? The north has a few weeks of relief when the rains come; but the south, as the southerners say, has two hot months and ten hotter ones. Is tolerance no more than an indifference to anything that anyone needlessly does in the endless Indian summer? Is it the climate of India that has produced the resignation at the heart of

Hinduism, the acceptance of life and so other people's lives, without protest or desire, and the resignation, in turn, which has produced the tolerance?

Yet the climate is merely one of the calamities from which Indians have in their countless centuries suffered. There is no society which displays more massively the records of so many conquests, so much battle and plunder, so much submission for so long. If the resignation taught in Hinduism, with the tolerance that is a part of it, has a natural genesis, the genesis is all of Indian history, a record written not only into the stone of a multitude of monuments, but in the faces of the Indian peasantry. If Indians exhibit a generic resignation and tolerance, these are the final attributes of self-defence.

The visitor who was impressed first by the cultural unity of India, and then discovered the varieties of peoples, languages, traditions, customs, manners, and the conflicts between one and another, must return eventually to where he began. Tamils and Biharis may be improbably unlike each other, but they are more like each other than anyone beyond the Indian borders. Whatever else separates them, Hinduism unites them, and Hinduism is not merely a religion of sabbaths and holy days, but a whole code of social and family and individual commandments, operating for every alert moment of an Indian's life. No one – Muslim or Parsee, Christian or Sikh – who lives in Hindu India is unaffected by Hindu doctrine and traditional conduct, whether through the adoption of caste, or the obsession with ritual cleanliness, or fundamentally the resignation, the submission to the duty of one's condition. But as Hinduism provides India with its greatest strength, the whole skeleton of its national unity, it constitutes too India's greatest weakness. For if India is ever to escape its agelessness of material degradation, of want and pain, it must do more than merely endure. If the people of India are ever to accomplish that progress which their struggle for nationhood promised them, they must learn to refuse as well as to accept.

CHAPTER TWO

CASTE, RELIGION AND HISTORY

Caste

I T is the pervasive importance of caste that more than anything else characterizes India. There may be other societies where caste exists in a rudimentary form, but nowhere outside India is caste the very structure of social survival. And in India caste is ubiquitous. It is overwhelmingly Hindu in operation, but it is not exclusively so. Muslims, Christians, Jews have all, in varying degrees, succumbed to its influence. Caste is not a mere custom, like table manners, or a measure of social status, like accent and dress. It is in India the fundamental rhythm of life itself.

A caste is a group of people traditionally pursuing a common occupation and inhabiting a linguistically limited region who may marry each other and eat together without ritual offence and who, in consequence of their common occupation and habits, possess a generally accepted place in a basically religious hierarchy. Caste penetrates every aspect of living. It conditions how and when and what and where a person eats and washes and talks and prays; from whom specific foods and drinks and specific utensils may be taken, or to whom offered; the way the hair is worn, the kind of clothes, the shape of ornaments, the form of funerals, the frequency of sex (orthodox Brahmins in Tanjore only make love on Fridays).[1] Increasingly, despite the secular commitment of the Indian republic, caste selects candidates and determines votes, no less in national elections than in village ones.

Caste cannot be properly understood in isolation from Hinduism, for it is Hinduism that provides caste with its sanctions and gives to the whole system its moral meaning. Hinduism itself is the most spacious of all religions, with comfortable accom-

[1] Taya Zinkin in *Caste Today* (Oxford University Press, 1962), p. 23.

modation for the disciples of one god, many gods and no god at all, for the worship of animals, ancestors and ideas. Yet there are certain beliefs held by almost all Hindus, and it is these that together morally underpin caste. *Samsara* (rebirth), *karma* (trans-migration – the repayment for an individual's deeds in the condition of his next life), *papa* (sin), *punya* (merit), *moksha* (salvation) and *dharma* (duty) are all concepts intrinsic to the sustenance of caste. And of them all, *karma* and *dharma* are the twin essentials, for *karma* proclaims that the Hindu is born into a particular caste because of his deeds in a previous life, and *dharma* demands that he should accept his condition without protest, performing as well as possible the functions appropriate to it.

The word *dharma* means in essence a natural attribute. It is the *dharma* of a river to flow, the *dharma* of a pond to stand still. And just as a river or a pond possesses its *dharma*, so does every human being. The *dharma* of a shoemaker is to make shoes, the *dharma* of a soldier is to fight. The *Bhagavadgītā*, perhaps the most cherished of Hindu sacred texts and the one which Gandhi himself regarded as supreme, delivers the message clearly. When the warrior Arjuna is about to give final battle to his enemies, he is 'overcome by pity' and 'much depressed in mind'. But his chariot companion Krishna, god incarnate, persuades him to fight, resolving all his doubts, for Arjuna is a warrior and the duty of a warrior is to fight.

'It is better to die in [performing] one's *dharma*. The *dharma* of others is dangerous.'[1]

'Even if one's *dharma* seems mad, its performance brings blessing, rather than the assumption and pursuit of another's *dharma*.'[2]

The *Dharmasutras* (aphorisms on *dharma*), sacred texts which belong to the period between the sixth and the third centuries B.C., proclaim that if a man does good deeds in conformity with his *dharma*, he will be born again into a high caste and will be well endowed; but if he does bad deeds, flouting his *dharma*, he will be born again as the member of a low caste or even as an animal.

---

[1] *Bhagavadgītā*, canto 3, verse 35, quoted in *Hindu Society – An Interpretation* by Irawati Karve, Deccan College, Poona, India, 1961.

[2] Ibid., canto 18, verses 45–7.

The progress and retrogression of a soul goes on until it attains salvation, the nature of which is differently conceived in the different sects, but all have this in common, that the perfected soul is released from the necessity of continual birth and death, and that it either lies in intimate and perpetual contact with God or is absorbed in Him. Birth in a particular caste becomes, therefore, an index of a soul's progress towards God.[1]

It is not sufficient, however, for a man merely to pursue his *dharma*; he must do so without desire or ambition, in a mood of detachment, with a calm sense of duty. It is better, of course, to be born in a high caste than in a low caste, but it is best not to be born at all, to find final release from the cycle of birth and rebirth in union with Brahman, the disappearance into God. By the theory of *karma*, every human act has a positive or negative worth, and at death there is always an accumulated capital of positive and negative values. The soul must pay for both, since divine accounting does not cancel out a negative value with a positive one. 'Thus one and the same being can live in heaven for some time and in hell for some time for the good and the evil one has done and be born as a human being to start the account over again.'[2] The recompense of heaven and hell is not a final one. The ledger has not been closed. It is merely that a page has been turned, with the credit or debit balance carried forward to the next in the form of the new incarnation. A king or priest, therefore, is a soul that has already lived in heaven and in hell, and joins humanity again with a balance of good deeds to his credit. A butcher or a woman – the two share a similar abasement – will have committed more bad deeds than good ones in the previous life and be born with a debit balance. It is such moral accountancy that provides the justification for all the graduated inequalities of caste. The butcher has a duty to feed the priest because the former life of the butcher was, on balance, a bad one, while the former life of the priest was, on balance, good. Yet the priest and the butcher are both outside of God, even if the distance of each from God is different. Both are condemned, by the doing of good and evil, to an

[1] M. N. Srinivas, *Caste in Modern India and Other Essays* (Asia Publishing House, 1962), p. 151.
[2] Irawati Karve, *Hindu Society – An Interpretation*, p. 92.

eternity of lives. If the butcher does more good than evil, he will be born again, as a king perhaps, or a priest. And if the priest does more evil than good, he will be born again, as a butcher perhaps, or a woman. Release from rebirth can only come from the deliberate failure to collect any moral balance – credit or debit – at all, to end life with a zero and so be gathered into Brahman. Since good and bad actions do not cancel each other out, each action itself, accordingly, must be neutral, and neutral actions are only possible in the absence of desire. It is the senses which corrupt, with their interminable emphasis on 'I', separating the soul from the Absolute, confining it in the ever insatiable demands of a purely human fulfilment.

'When a man dwells in his mind on the objects of sense,' proclaims the Blessed Lord, Krishna, in the *Bhagavadgītā*, 'attachment to them is produced. From attachment springs desire and from desire comes anger. From anger arises bewilderment, from bewilderment loss of memory; and from loss of memory, the destruction of intelligence and from the destruction of intelligence he perishes. But a man of disciplined mind, who moves among the objects of sense, with the senses under control and free from attachment and aversion, he attains purity of spirit.'[1]

Living is acting, and no one alive can escape from the need to act. The road to release lies in the pursuit by each man of the duties to which he was born, without love or hatred.

'A man', says Krishna to the warrior Arjuna in the *Bhagavadgītā*, 'does not attain freedom from action merely by not engaging in action; nor does he attain perfection by mere renunciation. For nobody remains even for an instant without performing some action; since the qualities of nature constrain everybody not having free will [in the matter], to some action. The deluded man who, restraining the organs of action, continues to think in his mind about objects of sense, is called a hypocrite. But he, O Arjuna! who restraining his senses by his mind, and being free from attachments, engages in devotion [in the shape] of action, with the organs of action, is far superior. Do you perform prescribed action, for action is better than in-

[1] *The Bhagavad-Gītā*, canto 2, translated by S. Radhakrishnan (Allen & Unwin, 1949).

action, and the support of your body, too, cannot be accomplished with inaction ... Therefore always perform action, which must be performed without attachment. For a man, performing action without attachment, attains the Supreme ... If I did not perform actions, these worlds would be destroyed. I should be the cause of caste-interminglings; and I should be ruining these people ... One's own duty [*dharma*], though defective, is better than another's duty well performed. Death in [performing] one's own duty is preferable; the duty of others is dangerous.'[1]

Traditional behaviour, performing the duties of one's caste and station, is thus raised to the highest moral principle. And such performance, in sacred literature, provides extraordinary powers (*siddhi*), as well as offering complete union with God after death. The *Mahābhārata*, a huge epic poem, the first written form of which belongs somewhere between the third century B.C. and the first century A.D., describes the relentless war between the descendants of Bhārata. But the story is every now and then interrupted by political and moral digressions, short pointed episodes which illustrate and proclaim basic Hindu values. One such anecdote[2] emphasizes the power to be obtained by the proper performance of one's duty.

A holy Brahmin (priest) was sitting in contemplation under a tree when he was spattered with bird droppings. He looked up in great anger at the two birds responsible, and they died at once. He then started on his daily round to beg food in the city, and, coming to a certain house, called loudly that he had arrived. The housewife, busy cleaning her pots, asked him to wait and then, because her husband had come home, abandoned her pots, washed her hands, brought food for her husband and served him. Only after her husband had finished eating did she remember the Brahmin standing outside and bring him food, begging his pardon for the delay. The Brahmin was angry and abused her, asking whether she thought it right to keep a Brahmin waiting. But she replied calmly to him that she was a married woman, and that her first duty was towards her husband, and that in any event a Brahmin should not get angry

---

[1] *The Bhagavad-Gītā*, canto 3. Translation from *The Sacred Books of the East*, ed. Max Müller, vol. viii.

[2] Quoted by W. Norman Brown in 'The Basis for the Hindu Act of Truth', *Review of Religion*, November 1940, vol. v, no. 1.

and go about killing birds. The Brahmin was astonished and asked her to tell him more about duty, but she said that she had no time and directed him instead to a butcher in the city of Mithila. Having walked for days, the Brahmin at last reached the city and stood outside the butcher's shop, waiting. The butcher saw him, hurriedly approached, bowed at his feet, took him home, and having worshipped him, spoke to him of the dead birds and the dutiful housewife. Amazed, the Brahmin asked how a man doing such work as the butcher did could possess such spiritual powers. And the butcher replied: 'What I do is because of the deeds of my past birth. I cannot help it. But I do it from a sense of duty alone. I serve my parents and gods, give to Brahmins and live without untruth and cruelty.'

This system of specific functions, sanctioned by religion and encompassing every human activity, promoted a society at the same time stagnant and secure. The ruling castes, with an assurance as strong as – and much longer-lived than – that of the white empire-builders in Africa, accepted as proper their superiority and the privileges which accompanied it. They believed their power to be not only necessary but right, and those whom they ruled generally shared the belief; for when rebellion is not merely dangerous but sinful, carrying consequences far beyond the grave, submission becomes not merely discreet but natural. Throughout the centuries in India, the streets have been even more devout than the palace. Such scepticism as has arisen has been almost entirely aristocratic, and religious revolutions like Buddhism – promoted by the throne itself during the reign of Aśoka (273–232 B.C.) – have speedily collapsed. The hierarchical dispensation of Hinduism has survived every buffeting, to go on providing its comfort and its refuge.

Caste is comfortable. It informs each person of his precise place and duties, giving to all but the lowest of outcastes – for the outcastes, too, have their degrees – some measure of superiority, together with an opportunity to accomplish salvation. For a people devoted to salvation – and the multitude of shrines in every Indian village testifies to the extent of popular devotion – such a system has manifest attractions. The prescribed pursuit of duty offers an easy escape from the terrors of doubt and the puzzles of individual interpretation that for so long distracted – and still distract – European Protestantism. Furthermore, caste provides a refuge. A butcher is primarily not an individual but a member of the butcher caste, and his relations with other members of his caste are accordingly close. A caste is more like an extended family than a social or occupational class, and like a family, it nourishes and protects its members. Such social welfare as traditionally exists in India is rooted in caste. Not only do castes build their own schools and community centres, establish libraries and scholarships, but they also shelter their members in times of sudden distress. When, after heavy rains, two dams in Maharashtra broke and the city of Poona was swept by floods on July 12th, 1961, hardly a quarter of those whose homes were submerged sought protection in public places. The rest found shelter with others of their caste and kin, sometimes at substantial distances from the city, elsewhere in the state.

As the relations of those within the same caste are comfortably regulated, so – differently but still comfortably – are the relations between members of different castes. And these inter-caste relations are not merely exclusive, erecting ritualistic barriers against social contact. They are also inclusive, promoting a clearly defined association of caste with caste in a pattern of patronage (*jajmani*), by which members of one caste serve members of another, in a traditional relationship for payment sometimes in cash but usually in kind. In a village like Mohana[1] in the Uttar Pradesh, a particular member of the Thakur (former landlord, agriculturist) caste will employ particular members of the Lohar (blacksmith), Barhai (carpenter), Kumhar (potter), Nai (barber), Pasi (watchman and messenger), Dhobi (washerman), Bhaksor (basket-maker) and other castes as occasion demands, rewarding the services he receives with gifts of food and clothes – generally at harvest time – or, less often, with money. Nor is the direction of the patronage downwards. The Brahmin, traditionally at the top of the caste scale, will have his own patrons among members of the lower castes, receiving gifts in cash and kind for performing his myriad ceremonial functions. The patronage survives from generation to generation, fortified by accumulated loyalties and the very

[1] D. N. Majumdar, *Caste and Communication in an Indian Village* (Asia Publishing House, 1962).

barter nature of the relationship, which makes it difficult for
those receiving payment in kind to risk a sudden independence.
Barbers and blacksmiths do not seek out more generous patrons,
and patrons do not seek out more skilful blacksmiths or barbers.
'The relationship is both implicit and hereditary.'[1] Patronage
is not limited to the village, or to personal service. A washerman
will be attached to a particular family in the town and, when he
is not himself available, will hand over his duties to a relative
as of right, while sweepers will clean village streets and ponds,
and remove dead cattle, to be rewarded for their communal
service on special begging days. The whole *jajmani* system
strengthens, of course, the hierarchical character of caste, but
it does so by providing for returns often greater than the state
in its present form is able or willing to supply. Measures of rural
reform, like the fixing of a minimum wage for agricultural
labour – 1·5 rupees (a little less than 2s. 3d.) for men and 1
rupee (just under 1s. 6d.) for women, a day in Kerala – offer
less, in many instances, than the traditional relationship. Kusum
Nair, in her book on planned state development and the rural
communities, quotes one large landowner in Kerala. 'My
labourers are still working for me as before, on the same terms.
They did ask for more. So I gave them the minimum but withdrew the other facilities – clothes, loans, and gifts on births,
deaths and festivals. Then they came back to me of their own
accord and told me and the local revenue official that they
wanted to continue the old system.'[2] And she comments: 'This
is, it seems, a fairly common occurrence.'

Such a society is easy to rule but difficult to change. The castes,
each of them helpless on its own, are together self-sustaining,
possessing in every village a citadel, and in every few villages
grouped around a market town, a state, that can withstand the
siege of centuries. Conquerors have come and gone or stayed
to be absorbed, but their command has seldom reached below
the surface of order. In the village, the father has controlled the
family, the elders have controlled the caste, and the upper castes
have controlled the lower castes in a rhythmic rite of authority.
Relations within the village, between one village and another,
between the village and the officials representing outside power,

[1] Taya Zinkin, *Caste Today*, p. 30.
[2] Kusum Nair, *Blossoms in the Dust* (Duckworth & Co., 1961), p. 42.

have been regulated by the village council. New rulers have supplanted old ones in the distant capitals, and new officials – or the old officials serving new masters – have continued to collect revenue and organize compulsory labour on certain customary days every year. But the villagers have hardly cared who the new rulers are, provided that their own traditions are left untouched and that the exactions of power are not exceptionally harsh. If ever conditions become unendurable, whole villages will migrate to areas of more congenial jurisdiction, and it is therefore in the interests of the rulers not to tax the village communities too far. Rural life in India has always been hard, but it has possessed – and possesses still today – extraordinary powers of survival.

Pre-Aryan Culture

It was for long assumed that the basic structure of Indian society had its foundations in the Aryan conquest which took place in the middle of the second millennium B.C. But recent archaeological research into the pre-Aryan period, based on the city-sites of Mohenjo-daro and Harappā in what is now West Pakistan, has uncovered traces of a civilization that lasted a thousand years, from roughly 2500 to 1500 B.C.; and possessed features closely paralleled in the traditional culture of India. At Mohenjo-daro the initial street-plan of the city was preserved from first to last, with scarcely any encroachment on the building-lines of houses where they faced upon main streets or subsidiary lanes, showing that, whatever changes in authority occurred, the continuity of government, in a static civic pattern, was assured.

While it is dangerous to make deductions from the evidence with any confidence, one can nevertheless suggest that such a continuity over generations is likely to have been enforced by religious sanctions, and that, in its remarkable conservatism and scrupulous preservation of even the details of everyday life intact for centuries, the texture of the Harappā civilization has a strongly theocratic tinge, and surely implies a social system wherein the unchanging traditions of the temple were of more account than the ambitions of an individual ruler or the secular instability of the court, and in which the form of land tenure was dictated by the priestly hierarchy.[1]

Moreover, when the existence of special housing quarters for workmen of specific trades, very near the location of their work, is considered alongside the static street-plan of the cities throughout a thousand years, the possibility that a caste-structure, occupational and hereditary in basis, had already taken shape long before the arrival of the Aryans, cannot easily be dismissed as unreal.

The Harappā civilization possessed numerous and striking similarities to aspects of contemporary popular Hinduism. Research into the related prehistoric Kulli culture, from a site at Kolwa in South Baluchistan (now part of West Pakistan), has revealed the frequent presence of baked clay figurines of women and of cattle. The female figurines may well have been deities in household shrines or votive offerings, uses to which such clay objects are commonly put in village India today, and their abundance of ornament, necklaces and bangles, heralds the decoration – and even perhaps the search for security – of modern Indian women. The clay figurines of humped cattle have painted eyes and are further decorated with large vertical stripes across the body and short horizontal strokes down the shoulders and forelegs. Such adornment might have been no more than a conventional design for toys, but it is at least equally conceivable that the adornment implied a prehistoric custom of painting the real animal, as Indian villagers paint, and garland, their Brahmini bullocks on festival occasions today.

The clay figurines of women found at Kolwa and Harappā suggest worship of a Mother-Goddess very like the one adored, in various guises and under various names, throughout modern India, from the teeming Kali Ghat in Calcutta to the most remote village shrine. But religious resemblances do not end there. Several seals found at Mohenjo-daro and Harappā portray a male god, horned and three-faced, sitting in the attitude of a *yogi*, with his legs bent double, heel to heel, while one seal represents him as surrounded by four animals, the elephant,

---

[1] Stuart Piggott, *Prehistoric India* (Penguin Books, 1950), pp. 150–1.

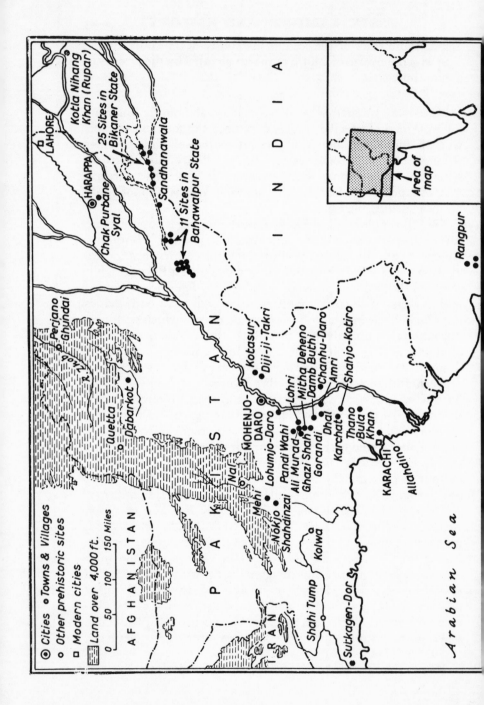

the tiger, the rhinoceros and the buffalo, with two deer at his feet. It is the prehistoric form of the great god Śiva as Lord of the Beasts and Prince of *Yogis*. There is also some evidence of phallic worship, widely practised today in Shaivite temples, where the god is present as a *lingam*, or phallic emblem, a short pillar or black stone, bare or engraved, around which the rites of devotion are performed. Harappā seals frequently depict a deity in the branches of the *pipal* or fig tree, still regarded as a sacred tree, and holy animals, especially the humped bull, which wanders its unhindered way through the markets and city traffic of India today.

Traditional Hinduism is obsessed with fear of pollution and the need for ritual washing. The centres of Harappā civilization possessed an intricate system of drains, while almost every house contained a bathroom, with a well-paved brick floor and an outlet drain in one corner. Evidence suggests that baths were taken then, as they are taken in India now, by pouring water over the body from a large jar. Skilfully constructed wells, lined in brick, supplied the water for both Harappā and Mohen-jo-daro, and while some were for the private use of individual houses, others served the public, like the *piau* or water-stall of contemporary India. Countless fragments of cheap mass-produced little clay cups have been found around the well-heads, as though the traditional Hindu taboo on drinking twice from the same cup was already established, and the cups were deliberately broken or discarded after use.

The fundamental stagnation of Harappā culture is nowhere more evident than in the flat mediocrity of the articles that have survived. Chisels, knives, razors, spears, bronze and silver vessels, pottery, all display a competence without delicacy or daring. What Stuart Piggott writes of Harappā is largely true of India today.

The dead hand of conservatism in design, rather than in technique, lies heavy on all the Harappā products. Complex technical processes were known, well understood, and admirably organized for production, but the output suffered from standardization and an almost puritanical utilitarianism. Working within such narrow limits of traditional forms, fossilized over the centuries into a rigid, inescapable

mental prison, the artist or craftsman could have found little
outlet save in developing technical virtuosity.[1]

Constituting the basic element in the population of the
Harappā empire were dark-coloured people, small in stature,
with wavy or curly hair, long heads, broad flattish noses and
protruding lips. Their cities had been safe for centuries –
though, on present evidence, it seems that they possessed little
military organization for attack or defence – and they could
hardly have expected the calamity that was soon to overwhelm
them. But massing in the north-west meanwhile were people
who called themselves *Aryas* or Aryans, a term originally meaning no more than 'kinsmen' though shortly to take on the implication of nobility and be contrasted with *Anāryas*, or the ignoble.
Linguists and archaeologists apparently agree on placing the
probable area of Aryan origin as somewhere between the Danube
and the Oxus, among the earliest agriculturists of the South
Russian steppes and the lands lying eastwards to the Caspian
Sea. Certainly by 2000 B.C. there was a loose confederacy of
tribes, who spoke closely related dialects within the Indo-
European framework, stretching from the south of Russia to
Turkistan and poised to attack their neighbours. Each tribe
was a group of families, with the father as master of each family,
governed by a *Rājā* whose powers were limited by a tribal
council, and though the various tribes fought with one another
as profitable occasion arose, they combined in hostility to those
whose wealth and lands they coveted.

Indo-Aryan Culture

The Aryan invaders of India grew grain and pastured sheep
and goats, but they were primarily cattle-breeders, with a warrior
aristocracy that roamed in search of battle and plunder. They
had evolved no city civilization and knew the use of only copper
and bronze, not iron; but they had domesticated the horse and
possessed in the two-horsed, two-wheeled chariot – from which
the warrior, accompanied by a charioteer, would wield his
bow or spear – a weapon of swift effect against their enemies.
Unlike the Hindus of the last two thousand years, they had no

[1] *Prehistoric India*, p. 200.

scruples about sacrificing bulls, cows and horses at weddings or on other ceremonial occasions and then eating the meat. Their dwellings were of wood, rectangular and thatched, and their amusements – apart from eating and drinking, both of which they generally, it seems, did to excess – included dancing, music, chariot racing and gambling with dice. They worshipped at turf altars, with animal sacrifices, and addressed their gods frankly, offering gifts and songs of praise in return for favours. Indeed, they saw their gods as they saw themselves magnified, with their war-god Indra the apotheosis of the Aryan warrior – huge, strong, tawny bearded, with an appetite for other people's cattle as insatiable as his appetite for food and drink, especially the intoxicating and sacred *Soma*. Indra is *puramdara*, the destroyer of forts, the conquering hero of the tribes in their assault upon the ill-guarded and effete empire of the *dasyus* or *dāsas*, the black-skinned noseless (anāsa) ones, with their strange worship and their heaps of gold.

At first the tribes raided rather than invaded, for there is evidence at the excavated Harappā sites of disturbance before disintegration. At Mohenjo-daro hoards of jewellery and copper tools, carefully hidden from marauders, have been found in the later levels, while street frontages seem to have been less strictly maintained, brickwork become shoddy, and large houses are split into flats with far poorer amenities. Pottery kilns appear within the city – one even in the middle of a street – and the residential areas show signs of decaying into industrial slums. Then, some short time before 1500 B.C., plunder gave way to conquest, and the cities collapsed in a sudden terror of violence that left huddles of contorted skeletons in the ruins behind. Amongst the rubble of the Harappā empire the Aryans built their rough houses, and from the Punjab – the 'land of the five rivers' – swept slowly south-eastwards till, about A.D. 200, the whole area between the Himalayas and the Vindhyas, from sea to sea, was *Aryāvarta*, or Aryan territory. The Vindhya belt of hills and Narbadā river at India's waist obstructed any large-scale tribal penetration of the Peninsula, but Aryan emissaries began conducting a peaceful invasion of the south many centuries before the birth of Christ, and though their influence did not defeat all aspects of the rich Dravidian civilization that they found – to this day the languages of the south are unrelated to the Sanskrit of the Aryans – they imposed many of their social, legal and religious concepts.

The most ancient surviving literature of the Indo-Aryans is collectively called *Veda* or knowledge, and the term is extended to the four sacred books or *Vedas* which are regarded by most orthodox Hindus today as *Śruti* or inspired revelation, as opposed to the later books of *Smriti* or traditional learning. Of all four the *Rigveda* – in length approximately equal to the *Iliad* and the *Odyssey* together – is the most ancient and the most important, since the other works presuppose its existence and in large part consist of commentaries upon it. An anthology of over a thousand poems, arranged into ten books, it is a strange assemblage, containing epic chants, prayers, hymns of praise, magic spells, fragments of popular song, and even some philosophical speculation, in a hotchpotch of the good, the bad, and the indifferent. Written in a very archaic form of Sanskrit, it was compiled somewhere about 1500 and 1200 B.C. and gives a vivid picture of the Aryans in the flush of their Indian conquests.

The *Rigveda* reflects the aims and circumstances of the upper social classes in a society which, like other Indo-European communities, was formally divided into Kṣatriyas, Brahmins and Vaiśyas – the warriors, priests and artisans. These groupings were not castes, they were ranks or orders, and the Kṣatriyas appear in early Vedic times to have been dominant, with the Brahmins regarded more or less as clients, composing the hymns and conducting the ritual mainly on behalf of the warrior aristocracy. Ritual was generally domestic and centred on the hearth, revolving for the most part around fire-worship; indeed, of all the gods, conceived as the personified powers of nature, Agni or Fire was, with Indra, the god of thunder and battle, the most important. But conquest was to change the conquerors no less than the conquered. The people whom the Aryans attacked were not savage tribesmen but heirs to an ancient and rich civilization, which could not have failed to affect the thought and manners of its despoilers. Gradually Harappā ideas permeated Aryan society. The anthropomorphic nature-worship of the Aryans gave place to a much more mysterious and intricate religion, depending on elaborate ceremonies and highly skilled priests. The Harappā empire had been theocratic, and in the new Aryan empire the power of the Brahmins grew as that of the Kṣatriyas declined. Fire became less, and water more, significant in ritual.

Slowly through the centuries a new religious vision took shape, of the universal soul or *Brahman*, to which the *atman*, or individual soul, was identical. The *Satapatha Brahmana*, or Brahmanical exegesis of the Hundred Paths, was the first great Vedic work written altogether in prose, and dates from about the tenth century B.C. In it appears the first speculation on *Brahman*.

Now, man here, indeed, is possessed of understanding, and according to how great his understanding is when he departs this world, so does he, on passing away, enter yonder world. Let him meditate on the Self, which is made up of intelligence, and endowed with a body of spirit, with a form of light, and with an ethereal nature, which changes its shape at will, is swift as thought, of true resolve, and true purpose, which consists of all sweet odours and tastes, which holds sway over all the regions and pervades this whole universe, which is speechless and indifferent; ... even as a smokeless light, it is greater than the sky, greater than the ether, greater than the earth, greater than all existing things; – that self of the spirit is myself; on passing away from hence I shall obtain that self. Verily, whosoever has this trust, for him there is no uncertainty.[1]

With the *Upanishads* or Approaches, which date from about the eighth century B.C., the Aryan nature gods have given place altogether to the universal soul. One *Upanishad – Kena –* even tells in allegory of the anthropomorphic defeat, with Fire, Wind and Indra himself, the greatest of the Vedic gods, unable to seize or control 'It'. 'It' is *Brahman*, and knowledge of 'It' is immediate, intuitive, interminable, the cry of astonishment at a flash of lightning, the cause of repeated remembrance. All human suffering and the frustrations imposed by desire come from *avidyā* or ignorance; man must seek knowledge, with which hatred, injury and greed are incompatible. The world of

[1] J. Eggeling, *The Satapatha-Brāhmana*, quoted in *Hinduism*, ed. Louis Renou (Prentice-Hall International Inc., 1961) pp. 83–4.

appearance is *maya*, illusion, full of contradiction and deceit. 'When to a man who understands, the Self has become all things, what sorrow, what trouble can there be to him who once beheld the unity?' (*Iśa Upanishad.*)

In one of the most important and widely quoted of the *Upanishads*, the woman Maitreyī questions her husband Yāj-ñavalkya about immortality. In his reply he says:

Lo, verily, with the seeing of, with the hearkening to, with the thinking of, and with the understanding of the Soul, this world-all is known...It is – as of all waters the uniting-point is the sea, so of all touches the uniting-point is the skin, so of all tastes the uniting-point is the tongue, so of all smells the uniting-point is the nostrils, so of all forms the uniting-point is the eye, so of all sounds the uniting-point is the ear, so of all intentions the uniting-point is the mind, so of all knowledges the uniting-point is the heart ... It is – as a lump of salt cast in water would dissolve right into the water; there would not be any of it to seize forth, as it were, but wherever one may take, it is salty indeed – so, lo, verily, this great Being, infinite, limitless, is just a mass of knowledge. Arising out of these elements, into them also one vanishes away. After death there is no consciousness ... For where there is a duality, as it were, there one sees another; there one smells another, there one hears another; there one speaks to an-other; there one thinks of another; there one understands another. Where verily, everything has become just one's own self, then whereby and whom would one smell? then whereby and whom would one see? then whereby and whom would one hear? then whereby and to whom would one speak? then whereby and on whom would one think? then whereby and whom would one understand? Whereby would one understand him by whom one understands this All? Lo, whereby would one understand the understander?[1]

Death, for the man who is absorbed by *Brahman*, is a dreamless sleep of satisfied desire.

[1] R. E. Hume, *The Thirteen Principal Upanishads*, quoted in *Hinduism*, pp. 92–4 (*Brhad-Āranyaka*, 11, 4).

As a falcon, or an eagle, having flown around here in space, becomes weary, folds its wings, and is borne down to its nest, just so this person hastens to that state where, asleep, he desires no desires and sees no dream ... As a man, when in the embrace of a beloved wife, knows nothing within and without, so this person, when in the embrace of the intelligent Soul, knows nothing within and without. Verily, that is his true form in which his desire is satisfied, in which the Soul is his desire, in which he is without desire and sorrow. There a father becomes not a father; a mother, not a mother; the worlds, not the worlds; the gods, not the gods: the Vedas, not the Vedas; a thief, not a thief. He is not followed by good, he is not followed by evil, for then he has passed beyond all sorrows of the heart.[1]

The philosophy of the *Upanishads* – summed up in the phrase *tat tvam asi*, or 'that art thou' – is commonly called the *Veda*, implying that it constitutes the final frontier of knowledge. Certainly it formed the centre-piece of Hindu metaphysics, but with and around it developed a whole social, political, economic and religious system, the skeleton of which was caste. The first written references to any division, however – they appear in the *Rigveda* – allude not to caste at all but to the three Aryan orders or ranks of Kṣatriya, Brahmin and Vaiśya, and these are then found – in the latest, tenth book – together with a fourth rank, the Śūdra, traditionally composed of peasants, labourers and servants. The *Puruṣa Sūkta*, or Hymn of Man, portrays creation as the consequence of immolating and dis-severing Puruṣa or Original Man, regarded as embodied spirit, the source of the universe, the animate principle in all living things. The sun, moon and elements, animal and man, are seen as having come from that 'great general sacrifice' made by the gods.

When they divided Puruṣa, how many portions did they make? What do they call his mouth, his arms? What do they call his thighs and feet?
The Brahman was his mouth, of both his arms was the Rājanya [Kṣatriya] made.

[1] Ibid., p. 95 (*Brhad-Āranyaka* IV, 3).

His thighs became the Vaiśya, from his feet the Śūdra was produced.[1]

The *Satapatha Brahmana* describes these four orders as *varnas*, and *varna* means colour. Indeed, the term was first employed to distinguish the light-skinned Aryans from the dark Dasyus of Dasas, the conquerors from the conquered, and whether or not the conquered only in part constituted the fourth and lowest order – there is no reason to suppose that Aryan peasants and servants did not comprise a distinct rank, below the warriors, priests and artisans – the early Vedic differentiation between Arya and Dasa soon gave place to the differentiation between Arya and Śūdra.[2] The upper three orders came to be called the 'twice-born', since men who belonged to them were entitled to put on the sacred thread at the Vedic rite of *upanayana*, while men of the Śūdra order were not. Beyond the four orders altogether, not even composing a fifth *varna* but existing outside the established Hindu communion, were various unassimilated tribes and those with occupations like sweeping which were generally regarded as unclean. Such were the outcastes, the untouchables, whose very shadows would be held to convey by their contact a ritual pollution.

Mankind was accordingly classified under four general heads, with the most esteemed profession, which had come to be that of the priest rather than the warrior, assigned the most honourable symbolic origin, and the least esteemed, that of the labourer and servant, relegated to the symbolic origin of Puruṣa's feet. Precisely how and when caste itself – with its specific hereditary occupations and regional limits – developed, cannot be established, but the stratification of Harappā society suggests that a caste-pattern may well have existed in India long before the Aryan invasion and that the conquerors simply adopted, with appropriate changes, the form of social organization which they found. Certainly the pronounced and proved resilience of Indian institutions would make this not at all improbable. The Vedic division of society into *varnas* would then have been used to impose an Aryan outline on an already existing detailed design,

---

[1] *Hindu Scriptures*, ed. Nicol Macnicol, quoted in *Hinduism*, p. 65.
[2] G. S. Ghurye, *Caste and Class in India* (Bombay, 1950), p. 47.

providing a religious rationalization for any necessary change to a generally accommodating social, political and economic system. The Aryan conquest did not produce centralized rule – it would take more than a thousand years to generate another Indian empire – and the caste system, disciplined by the Aryan hierarchy of *varnas*, gave some form of control over the multitude of minute units, each of which had its own semi-detached way of living, together constituting the people of India.

Whether the Aryans did, in fact, adopt the institution of caste from the culture they conquered, or originated it themselves, they clearly promoted it as a method of pervasive control. The Brahmins, assisted by the theocratic traditions of Harappā in establishing their supremacy, evolved through the centuries extremely strict rules to secure their own position from the dangers of undesirable contact. Elaborate taboos restricted marriage, diet, travel, visiting and eating or drinking with others. Inevitably, too, those belonging to the lower orders of society sought to emulate those at the summit and acquired their own rules and taboos, their own special *dharmas*, till each *jati* or caste possessed its own exclusive code of conduct, asserting its uniqueness and its superiority to all those it considered inferior by exercising an ever greater caution against ritually defiling associations. Meanwhile, alongside particular caste *dharmas*, there developed a general Hindu *dharma*, a common rule of morality for all Hindus that exacted, among other things, reverence towards Brahmins and respect for all animal life, especially horned cattle and chiefly the cow. Anyone who disregarded this general *dharma* was considered, however exalted his worldly rank and however vast his wealth, to be a barbarian beyond the Hindu communion or *mlēchchha*. As the British would one day discover, conquest might command deference but not hospitality, a bow but not a hand-shake, from the orthodox. From the King Emperor himself to the most junior official, the new rulers were all outcastes and untouchable.

In the process of cultural mingling which followed the Aryan conquest, many Aryan practices disappeared, and Dasa ones – unsubdued – asserted themselves. Above all, the doctrine of *ahimsā*, or respect for life, promoted wide-scale changes in diet and innumerable consequent caste distinctions. The sacred

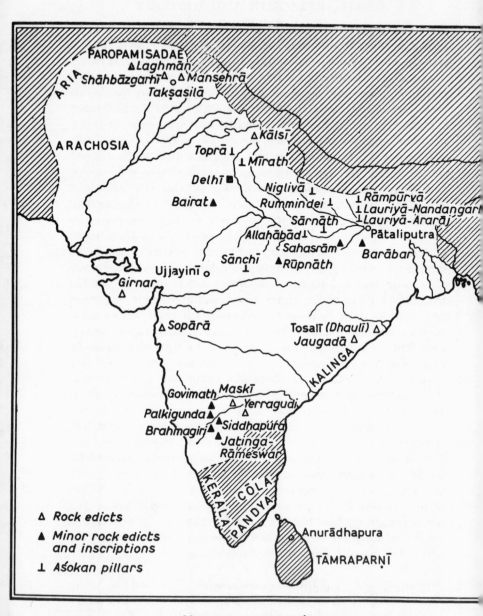

Map 4 INDIA UNDER AŚOKA

(based on the map 'India in the reign of Aśoka', from the *Oxford History of India*, third edition, edited by Percival Spear, p. 127)

character of certain animals, particularly the humped bull, in Harappā culture must have exercised some influence on the beliefs and customs of the Aryan invaders, for certainly no change could have been more dramatic than that from a cattle-raising, cattle-consuming people, whose ritual involved animal sacrifice, to a people who considered the killing of animals, particularly cattle, to be a revolting impiety and raised the ordinary cow to a level of sanctity. The *Mahābhārata*, the vast epic poem which was cast in its present shape about A.D. 200 but clearly composed over many centuries, depicts such practices as cow-killing with approval in some early passages, and with horror in other, later, ones. Doubtless some communities and individuals must have found it difficult to alter their customs and diet so radically, and they would accordingly have fallen in the caste scale beyond the more scrupulous and devout of their neighbours. Certain Aryans may have refused to renounce their habits and slid in general esteem below indigenous peoples who adopted – or observed – strict *ahimsā*. Indeed, if the doctrine was indigenous – as the less Aryanized and more rigorously vegetarian south of India would suggest – then the India which the Aryans invaded, vulnerable as it was to conquest, possessed a very long arm none the less.

The propagation of *ahimsā* was given powerful impetus by Jain and Buddhist teachers from about 500 B.C., when the new – or very old – creed received state sanction from the Buddhist Emperor Aśoka. His first Rock Edict,[1] which dates from 256 B.C., illuminates one significant moment in the long and largely hidden history of India's religious development.

> Formerly, in the kitchen of His Sacred and Gracious Majesty the King, each day many [hundred] thousands of living creatures were slaughtered to make curries. But now, when this pious edict is being written, only three living creatures are slaughtered daily for curry, namely, two pea-cocks and one antelope – the antelope, however, not invariably. Even those three living creatures henceforth shall not be slaughtered.

[1] Quoted in the *Oxford History of India*, third edition, ed. Percival Spear, p. 65.

The Jain and Buddhist sects may have spread support for *ahimsā* and furthered the already evident revulsion from ritual sacrifice, but they did little to change the essential character of Brahminical Hinduism. Buddhism, indeed, was to grow out of Indian soil into a world religion, sending out roots, like the banyan tree, to thrive in China and Japan, south-east Asia, Ceylon and Tibet, while withering in India itself. Both Mahā-vīra, the founder of Jainism, and Gautama the Buddha, who lived in the latter half of the sixth and the first half of the fifth centuries before Christ, rejected the authority of the *Vedas* and condemned caste. Neither succeeded in sapping the strength of Vedic sanctity or the caste system, and certainly the modern Jain in India is as caste-bound as the most orthodox Hindu.

The Jains denied the Hindu doctrine of the universal soul and defined God as 'only the highest, the noblest and the fullest manifestation of all the powers latent in the soul of man'. They taught that not humans and animals alone, but also plants, such minerals as were capable of growth, air, wind and fire possessed *jīvas* or souls endowed with varying degrees of consciousness and vulnerable to pain, and their first principle was, conse-quently, an *ahimsā* that went far beyond Brahminical or Bud-dhist beliefs, to respect for any kind of life, however low the stage of its evolution. Jains, however, never denied their Hindu parentage, and most today consider themselves to be Hindus, describing themselves as such in census returns. They continue the practice of their forefathers and employ Brahmins as domestic chaplains for the performance of birth and death ceremonies and even sometimes for temple worship. Unlike the Buddhists, they never developed a really independent existence and for that reason more than any other, perhaps, made no converts beyond the borders of India.

Buddha himself, like Mahāvīra, can hardly have intended to establish a new religion. He accepted the traditional Hindu theories of *karma* and rebirth, and laid special emphasis on the virtues of truthfulness, reverence towards superiors, and respect for animal life. He regarded discussion on the nature of God or the soul as finally unprofitable, and though he never formally denied the existence of an all-powerful and creative God, he did not assert it, much as if the matter were irrelevant. He did not seek to interfere with current beliefs in the Hindu gods and the whole body of familiar superstition, but concentrated instead on propagating a morality, not unlike the Stoicism of classical Greece and Rome, which encouraged emotional detachment and promoted a Middle Path between sensuality and asceticism. He instructed his disciples to aim at purity in thought, word and deed, observing ten vows: not to kill or injure living beings; not to steal; to remain celibate; not to lie; to abstain from intoxicants; not to eat after noon; to abstain from dancing and singing and entertainments; to abstain from the use of garlands, scents and ornaments; not to sleep on a raised bed; and not to receive money or valuables. What he offered, therefore, was a reformation of Hinduism rather than a different faith, and he did not make the reformation difficult. Of the ten vows, only the first five were binding on laymen, and the third of these was modified to permit lawful marriage. By taking them, both men and women could travel far along the path of holiness. Complete satisfaction, however, could only be obtained through the acceptance of all ten vows and membership of the *Sangha* or order of ordained monks. It was this order, indeed, which developed into a rich, powerful and tightly knit organization, and after the death of Buddha raised him to divinity, planting his cult throughout Asia and cultivating another religion.

Neither Jainism nor Buddhism became the prevailing faith of India's millions at any time, though under royal patronage one or the other was made the state religion of certain kingdoms. Brahminical or traditional Hinduism continued to claim mass allegiance, conceding a change here or a change there but preserving the core of its authority intact. What did develop within Hinduism, in reaction against the atheistic tendencies of the Buddhists and Jains, was *bhakti* or faith in and devotion to a personal God. The two great Hindu epic poems, the *Mahābhārata* and the *Rāmāyana*, both reveal the strong influence of *bhakti*, with the heroic legends edited by Brahmins so as to transform the epics into scriptures and make the heroes, Krishna and Rāma, incarnations of God in the form of Vishnu.

The *Rāmāyana*, composed roughly between 400 B.C. and A.D. 200, attributed to one author, named Vālmīki, and containing some 48,000 lines, tells the story of Prince Rāma, the son of King Daśaratha and his first wife Queen Kausalyā, who is driven into exile by the jealousy of the second queen, Kaikeyī, anxious to secure the throne for her own son, Bhārata. The adventures of Rāma and his loyal wife Sītā, the assistance given to the prince by Hanuman, king of the monkeys, the vindication of Sītā, unjustly accused of having been unchaste, the return of Rāma to share the kingdom with Bhārata, are – with numerous other incidents in the poem – as familiar and meaningful to Hindus all over India today as the parables of Christ must have been to the Puritans of seventeenth-century England. Rāma is reverenced as the ideal man, and Sītā as the ideal woman and wife; but Rāma is, in addition, as the incarnation of Vishnu, worshipped by millions, who have his name in the cry 'Rām, Rām' frequently on their lips.

Both the *Mahābhārata*, with its religious climax in the *Bhagavadgītā*, and the *Rāmāyana* provide object lessons in the need for every man and woman to follow their individual and caste *dharmas*. Sītā herself acquires *siddhi* or extraordinary powers through following her *dharma* as a wife. When Rāma voices his doubts about her chastity, she declares: 'If I have not sinned against my husband by word, deed or thought, may mother earth take me in.' And the earth opens to take her, so establishing her innocence. The *Mahābhārata* in one passage gives the colours of the four *varnas* or orders, with an accompanying moral and economic explanation for the origin of different castes.

> The lord then formed truth, righteousness, austere fervour, and the eternal Veda, virtuous practice, and purity for the attainment of heaven. He also formed the gods, demons and men, Brahmins, Kṣatriyas, Vaiśyas, and Śūdras, as well as all other classes of beings. The colour of the Brahmins was white; that of the Kṣatriyas red; that of the Vaiśyas yellow, and that of the Śūdras black ... Those Brahmins, who were fond of sensual pleasure, fiery, irascible, prone to violence, who had forsaken their duty, and were red-limbed, fell into the condition of Kṣatriyas. Those Brahmins, who derived their livelihood from kine, who were yellow, who subsisted by agriculture, and who neglected to practise their duties, entered into the state of Vaiśyas. Those Brahmins, who were addicted to mischief and falsehood, who were covetous, who

lived by all kinds of work, who were black and had fallen from purity, sank into the condition of Śūdras. Being separated from each other by these works, the Brahmins became divided into different castes ... He who is pure, consecrated by the natal and other ceremonies, who has completely studied the Veda, lives in the practice of the six ceremonies, performs perfectly the rites of purification, who eats the remains of oblations, is attached to his religious teacher, is constant in religious observances, and devoted to truth – is called a Brahmin. He in whom are seen truth, liberality, inoffensiveness, harmlessness, modesty, compassion, and austere fervour – is declared to be a Brahmin. He who practises the duty arising out of the kingly office, who is addicted to the study of the Veda, and who delights in giving and receiving – is called a Kṣatriya. He who readily occupies himself with cattle, who is devoted to agriculture and acquisition, who is pure, and is perfect in the study of the Veda – is denominated a Vaiśya. He who is habitually addicted to all kinds of food, performs all kinds of work, who is unclean, who has abandoned the Veda, and does not practise pure observances – is traditionally called a Śūdra. And this which I have stated is the mark of a Śūdra, and it is not found in a Brahmin: such a Śūdra will remain a Śūdra, while the Brahmin who so acts will be no Brahmin.[1]

Such texts fortified the colour-consciousness which accompanied the Aryan conquest and which survives in India today with hardly less vigour than it must have possessed over three thousand years ago. The lighter-skinned conquerors preserved, by scrupulous marriage, their light skins as symbolic of their moral superiority no less than their political and economic supremacy, and though there are dark Hindus today who are Brahmins, and light-skinned Śūdras or even untouchables, caste-stratification in modern India generally follows a colour pattern.

The rationalization of caste in the *Mahābhārata*, though historically false in the main, was not altogether so. Caste was – as it still is – hereditary, and members of a particular caste

---

[1] J. Muir, *Original Sanskrit Texts* (Trubner & Co., London, 1872), vol. i, pp. 139–42.

could as much escape it, short of all the horrors of excommunica-
tion, as they could escape their skins. But a whole caste might
itself fall in the accepted scale, from Kṣatriya to Vaiśya or even
Śūdra, by the adoption of degrading habits or despised occupations, while. twice-born castes might even become untouchable
– expelled from the Hindu communion altogether – by the
assumption of a polluting occupation like the skinning of dead
animals or sweeping. On the other hand, especially in the middle
regions of the structure, movement upwards was also possible,
with a lower caste able to raise its status by becoming vegetarian
and teetotal, pursuing a more admired occupation, and borrow-
ing as many Brahminical customs and rites as possible. Such
caste mobility has never been easy – there have always been
other castes, jealous of their relative status, to make it difficult
– but it has been possible and has recently gained some impetus
from the power bestowed on numbers by the ballot box. Politically and economically influential castes regularize their
advancement ritually. Doubtless few, if any, untouchables have
ever become Brahmins, and few Brahmins have descended to
untouchability, but Kṣatriya castes have not rarely fallen to
Vaiśya status and Vaiśya castes risen to a Kṣatriya one in consequence of concerted carelessness or effort. Rather more
frequently, castes have risen or fallen within the hierarchy of a
particular *varna* according to the diligence with which they
have observed the accepted standards of right conduct.

The Mauryan Empire

The first recorded contact between European and Hindu
civilization came with the invasion of India by Alexander the
Great in 326 B.C., an event of surpassing interest to Greek
authors of the time but one which made so slight an impression
on the Indians themselves that no distinct reference to it can be
found anywhere in ancient Indian literature. Aristoboulos,
a companion of Alexander's, noticed several strange customs
and was carefully reported by Strabo.[1]

He says that he had heard from some persons of wives

---

[1] Book 16, chapter 1, section 62, translated by McCrindle in *Ancient
India as described in Classical Literature* (Constable, 1901), p. 69.

burning themselves along with their deceased husbands and doing so gladly; and that those women who refused to burn themselves were held in disgrace. The same things have been stated by other writers.

The practice of widow-burning or *sati* was accordingly well established in India over two thousand years before a British Governor-General, Lord William Bentinck, outlawed it by Regulation XVII of 1829. The belief that the *dharma* of a wife was to serve her husband and that with his death her own life became not only irrelevant but wrong, the target of general execration, must have led innumerable women through the centuries to willing suicide on the funeral pyres of their husbands; but any natural reluctance would have been forcibly and speedily overcome by relatives and neighbours. As late as the decade 1817–26, the recorded number of *sati* cases in Bengal alone varied between 500 and 850 a year, with the victims rarely volunteers. And though the practice has been almost entirely suppressed in today's secular India, reports still appear in the press from time to time of widows forced on to the funeral pyres of their husbands by superstitious villagers. Considering the remoteness of most Indian villages from the newspaper offices of Delhi and Bombay, rather more cases may be supposed to occur than ever reach the headlines.

Alexander's inquisitive officers remarked the existence of caste and the veneration paid to the river Ganges, as well as the power of the Brahmins, whose authority was widely recognized and who almost everywhere held office as councillors of the rajas. The Brahmins were reported to eat meat, but not that of animals associated with man in his labours, and it is clear that the sanctity of all horned cattle was firmly established as part of the priestly code. No paramount power appears to have existed for all but the last few years of the fourth century, and in the Punjab and Sind, the two areas visited by Alexander, there were numerous independent states, some ruled by rajas and others, republican in character, by aristocratic oligarchies. Then, around 322 B.C., Chandragupta Maurya, aided by his Brahmin counsellor Vishnugupta – commonly known by his surname Kautilya – organized a successful revolution at Pātaliputra, on the site of the modern Patna in Bihar, and having killed the ruling Nanda family, extended his authority until, by the end of his reign in 298 B.C., he controlled all India north of the river Narbada and Afghanistan as well. In or about 302 B.C. Seleukos, heir after a struggle to the Asian empire of Alexander, sent as his envoy to the court of Chandragupta an officer named Megasthenes, who devoted his spare time to writing an account of Indian life and institutions, and this account, reinforced by other literary evidence like the *Artha-sāstra* – a cynical manual of government attributed by tradition to Kautilya himself – provides a detailed picture of the highly efficient and elaborate autocracy that was the Mauryan empire.

An enormous standing army, paid directly by the Crown, maintained authority and extended conquest, while a graded civil service, with well defined duties, staffed the various departments of administration. The court, situated in the splendid capital, was served with considerable ostentation, and the sovereign himself was surrounded by a multitude of attendants in a coruscation of purple and gold. Accomplished courtesans – under strict official control and paying licence fees to the treasury if they practised their profession – attended him when he sat on his throne or rode in his litter and presented him with perfumes, garlands and dress. The royal will was not limited by any law, and the only real frontier to despotism was the fear of rebellion or assassination. Chandragupta was not bound to consult anyone, but in practice he depended upon his ministers, most if not all of whom were Brahmins. Megasthenes reports that the armed forces were controlled by a special and elaborately constituted War Office, with a commission of thirty members divided into six *panchāyats* or boards, each of five members, to administer the Admiralty; Transport, Commissariat, and Army Service; Infantry; Cavalry; War-chariots; and Elephants. Viceroys assisted in governing the vast empire, and special officers supervised departments in charge of markets, rivers, canal irrigation, public works and various fiscal affairs, while there were superintendents for such occupations as hunting, wood-cutting, smithery, carpentry and mining. For the imperial capital itself, administration was the responsibility of another thirty-member commission, with control over public welfare and works, the maintenance of harbours, markets and temples, and the regulation of prices. This commission, too, was divided into six boards of five members each: one board in charge of industrial arts; another, entrusted with the care of all foreigners; a third, responsible for keeping a register of all births and deaths, so as to facilitate taxation; a fourth, to control retail trade and barter, with supervision of weights and measures and the stamping of all produce sold to prevent sales-tax evasion; a fifth, to control manufactures and their sale after proper stamping; and a sixth, to collect the tithe on the price of all goods sold. The author of the *Arthaśāstra*, writing with detailed knowledge of Mauryan administration, describes a municipal organization of great thoroughness, with officials required to conduct a permanent census and 'know not only the caste, *gotra* [caste subdivision], name and occupation of both men and women in the households of [each official's] block, but also to ascertain their income and expenditure'.

Property and the royal revenues were protected by a ruthless enforcement of fiscal regulations and severe penalties for crime. Homicide, theft of articles or money above a certain – by no means considerable – value, housebreaking, damage to royal property, injury to an artisan in the royal employment, and evasion of the municipal sales-tax were all, amongst many other crimes, capital offences, and torture to extract confessions from the accused was ordinary practice. Indeed, the superintendent of a jail who inflicted torture unjustly risked merely a modest fine, and even if he beat a prisoner to death, he faced a large fine rather than physical punishment. Death itself was meted out to the convicted in various forms, with or without torture, according to the character of the offence, and even where it could be escaped, mutilation often provided the alternative. The caste and rank of the accused were, of course, taken into account, and the authorities were instructed to note 'equitable distinctions among offenders, whether belonging to the royal family or to the common people'. Brahmins, for instance, were not to be tortured, but might be branded, exiled or sent to the mines for life. Yet, despite the formidable array of punishments facing offenders, corruption in the civil service seems to have been widespread, and rewards were offered to informers who could prove their charges. A secret service supported the whole structure of government, with spies and detectives employed in a variety of disguises. Special information officers at the headquarters of provincial administrations sent secret reports to the central government, and licensed prostitutes added to their income and security by supplying the espionage bureau with intelligence.

Land belonged to the ruler, and rent in the form of taxes and special levies took so much of the produce that the actual cultivator was seldom left with more than enough for bare subsistence. The government's share was theoretically limited – the author of the *Arthaśāstra* considered one quarter to be equitable – but in practice the state seized as much as it could, exacting additional assets when circumstances required, so that the peasant might judge himself fortunate if he could manage to feed himself and his family while still keeping sufficient over for seed. Nothing remained for the payment of rent to a landlord, and so no one intervened between the state and the interminable poverty of the peasant. Such may very well have been the position twenty centuries before, when the Harappā empire was at its height, and such would be the position for many centuries more. There was unquestionably much of Harappā civilization in the authoritarian centralized government and complex city culture of the Mauryan monarchs. The new empire, with its uniquitous bureaucracy and mercantile organization, its pattern of ritual and ceremony, must have taken not a little from the traditions of the old. For Chandragupta himself was no invader, sweeping down upon India from the north-west at the head of various tribes. He was an Indian, heir both to Harappā and to its Aryan conquerors. And there was in his rule, as in the rule of those who would come after him, the memory and spirit of oldest India.

The masses of India, then as now, sought refuge from the cruelties of their condition in concern with the lives that would follow their lives, in conciliation of those with power to raise or further debase them, in all the equivocal comforts of ritual and faith. And equivocal the comforts certainly were. For Hinduism promised no popular Islamic paradise of women and feasting, no Christian company of refulgent saints. It was as though the oppression of Indian life had sent its shoots beyond the grave. Man was enslaved by his actions, which followed him 'as the calf follows its mother'. He was, unless liberated by the surrender of all desire, condemned to be reborn, and since most human actions seemed to be maleficent, rebirth was more likely to provide a lower condition than a higher one. Nor were the ever-present possibilities of interference by gods and spirits in human affairs generally consoling. Divinity could be malignant as well as benign, and careful propitiation more urgent than a request for favours. The gods were jealous of their dignity, and if the little red goddess of smallpox suffered neglect, a sudden epidemic might be needed to provide her shrines with adequate attention. It was no less necessary to prevent divine intervention than to invite it.

Many of the deities worshipped by the villagers were local in character and operation, and these *grāmadevatā* ungrudgingly co-existed with a multitude of demons and ghosts and even streams and trees of magic properties. They might never in village estimation approach equality with the great gods of the Hindu pantheon, but the great gods, after all, were likely to have their heads full of great concerns, and the *grāmadevatā* presented more immediate menaces as well as offering a readier help in distress. In the more exalted regions, a Trinity or *Trimūrti* took shape, of Brahma – the masculine correlative of *Brahman* – the principle of creation in the universe; Vishnu, the principle of preservation; and Śiva, the principle of destruction, the great dissolver, death. Brahma, having performed his essential function in creating the universe, re- tired into the background, and there were few temples ever erected for his worship, few sects ever formed in his name. Vishnu and Śiva, however, soon numbered their adherents in millions.

Vishnu, the paramount deity of northern India, developed out of a not particularly prominent Vedic sun god of the same name and became the closest approximation to Christ in the Hindu pantheon. It is Vishnu who returns periodically to earth in the shape of man – as Krishna, or Rāma in epic legend – to save mankind from sudden peril; Vishnu, combining the attributes of god and hero, who gave most nourishment to the *bhakti* movement of personal devotion. In his worship is re- flected the lighter side of Hinduism, the hope of intercession, an affirmation of the benign. Very different is Siva, the dominant deity of southern India but adored in various guises throughout the country, who affirms the dark and the fearful, the struggle against evil, and the presence of pain, violence and death. His is the dance, so frequently represented in bronze, that proclaims the end of the world; his is the renunciation, as Śiva the Prince of the *Yogis*. Yet destruction is the counterpart of creation, even – as in Śiva's cosmic dance – the necessary prelude, and Śiva is, too, the principle of energy, worshipped widely as the *lingam*, or phallic symbol. Of all Indian gods, or manifestations of god, it is he who most closely belongs to the beginnings of India, to the age before the Aryans when the Mother-Goddess, both cruel and compassionate, taking and giving, ruled over the altars of Harappā. And it is he, in his double role of destroyer and creator, who most closely belongs to the India of the present, to the many births and early deaths, the sudden flourishing and sudden fall.

From the Guptas to the Moguls

Buffered by caste and fortified by belief in the moral basis of their condition, the many millions of India survived the intermittent empires, with the heavy exactions that they brought, and the disorders of their decline, with armies contending for power and for pillage. The Mauryas fell and, some five hundred years after, the Guptas arose, to resurrect the imperial court, provide leisure and patronage for art and learning, and annex provinces for busy bureaucrats. The land taxes were again diligently collected – for a vast civil service must be paid – but order induced a relative prosperity, and the criminal code was milder than the Mauryan had been. Fa-hien, a Chinese pilgrim to the birthplace of Buddhism, stayed in India from A.D. 401 to 410, during the reign of Chandragupta II, and recounted with joy the piety of the people. 'Throughout the country, no one kills any living thing, or drinks wine, or eats onions or garlic ... they do not keep pigs or fowls; there are no dealings in cattle, no butchers' shops or distilleries in their market-place.'[1] The caste system was strongly established, and the Chandālas or outcastes were required to live apart and when entering a town or bazaar to strike a piece of wood as a warning of their approach, so that others might not be polluted by contact with them. Fa-hien's testimony is doubtless too sweeping – who can

[1] *Oxford History of India*, third edition, p. 171.

believe that no one but the outcastes ate onions or drank wine? –
and must be taken as applying mainly to the practising Buddhists.
But clearly the sentiment of *ahimsā*, or respect for all life, had
popularly progressed since the days of Mauryan rule, when
even the Buddhist Emperor Aśoka had not forbidden his subjects
to slaughter animals; while asceticism had spread since the time
when the *Arthaśāstra* could not only treat the liquor trade as a
legitimate source of revenue, but even direct taverns to make
themselves attractive to customers. Buddhism itself was already
declining, though Fa-hien apparently did not notice the signs
of Hindu renaissance as Brahminical influence mounted with
the spread of Sanskrit; the Gupta coinage bore Sanskrit legends
and the Gupta court presided over a rich reflowering of Sanskrit
literature. Yet, ironically, with the very growth in the authority
of the Brahmins, the cultural army of Aryan dominance, old
India was re-establishing its sway. The respect for animal life
and especially cattle, the asceticism of diet, the occupational
rigidities of caste, were less a manifestation of Buddhist or Jain
influences than the spirit of Harappā, which the Brahmins had
adopted as their own.

The Gupta empire collapsed at the end of the fifth century
under the assault of nomads from central Asia – called Hūnas
or Huns by the Indians themselves – and another age of contest
and disorder followed, to be but briefly interrupted by the reign
of a powerful monarch, Harsha, from A.D. 606 to 647. From the
last of the Guptas to the closing years of the twelfth century and
the Muslim conquest, the unity of northern Indian history
vanishes. Yet the Huns.who came to rule, like the Aryans before
them, were absorbed by the traditional culture of the conquered,
and when Hinduism reappeared for record in the glare of
imperial authority, it was in all significant respects the Hinduism
of the Gupta – and previous – ages.

While northern India combined and disintegrated under
intermittent empires and invasion, the Deccan or middle India
and the Dravidian south endured similar fluctuations of order
and chaos. The kingdoms of the Deccan plateau, at the waist
of the country, generally resisted both northern and southern
expansionism – though strong emperors, like Aśoka in the
north, extended their influence throughout the Deccan – and
acted instead as a cultural passage-way between north and

south. In the south itself the Tamil states, probable cultural heirs of pre-Aryan India, waxed rich on ocean commerce with West and East alike. The area was trading with Egypt a thousand years before the birth of Christ, and extensively with the Roman empire during the first and second centuries of the Christian era. Pearls from the fisheries of the Tāmraparnī, beryls from mines in present-day Mysore and Madras, gems from Ceylon, pepper and other spices from the Malabar coast were shipped to Rome in return for pottery and coinage, while the fleets of the Chola kingdom on the coast of Madras took cotton cloth eastwards as far as the Malay Archipelago. Boundaries changed ceaselessly, but there were three principal powers: the Chola; the Pāndya, centred on the Madura and Tinnevelly districts of modern Madras; and the Chera, embracing present-day Kerala. Strong in their commerce and possessing regions of extraordinary agricultural richness like the Kaveri delta – southern India's rice bowl – and the rain-soaked western coast, the kingdoms fought each other and the island of Ceylon, with occasional ventures northwards into the Deccan. The language of the south, Tamil – with a dialect along the western coast that would eventually develop into Malayalam – produced a flourishing literature, both secular and religious, and this, like the language itself, had Dravidian, not Aryan, roots.

While northern India passed through its medieval night, the Deccan sustained a series of powerful empires, of which the most prominent, the Chālukya dynasties – the first lasting from the middle of the sixth century to the middle of the eighth, the second from late in the tenth to the middle of the twelfth – with the base of their power in modern Maharashtra, fought off attack from north and south alike. Though tolerant of all religions, as the Guptas and the Mauryas had been in the north, the early Chālukya kings were, like most Indian rulers, Brahminical Hindus, and under their reign the influence of Buddhism steadily declined. Maharashtra, however, was not alone in generating empire. The Telugu-speaking area of what is now Andhra Pradesh threw up a dynasty of kings – the Rāshtra-kūtas – who for a time during the ninth century were celebrated far beyond the borders of India, so that Sulaimān, an Arab merchant of the period, could compare them to the Caliphs of Baghdad and the Emperors of China and Constantinople. The

Kannada-speaking area of the Deccan, the present Indian state of Mysore, was ruled by the temple-building kings of the Hoysala dynasty during the twelfth and thirteenth centuries, while Ganga kings reigned in the region of modern Orissa for a thousand years, from the sixth to the sixteenth centuries.

Such history is by no means merely academic, the material of scholars and the occasion for university degrees. The present-day linguistic states of India, in the process of a cultural revolution that democracy and mass education have vastly advanced, find the nourishment for their regional loyalties in their languages, vernacular literature, and the individual splendours of their past. Each state has its own golden age, generally monumented in paper or stone, and if the record is invariably glamourized by legend and popular belief, the pride that it produces is all the greater. The people of Orissa are all the more aware of their identity within the Indian whole for the long succession of Ganga kings, and the people of Andhra Pradesh are all the more defiant of northern Indian dominance for the grandeur of the Rāshtrakūta dynasty and their own association with the culture of the Dravidian south.

In the south itself, while northern India lay distractedly in wait for the Muslim conquest, empires rose and fell upon each other. For some two hundred years, from the middle of the sixth to the middle of the eighth century, the Pallavas – a peninsular tribe or clan – dominated the far south, with the princes of the ancient royal families more or less subordinate to them. For a mysterious interlude, the three southern kingdoms of the Pāndyas, Cholas and Cheras ceased to preside over Dravidian history, and the Pallava kings – most of them Brahminical Hindus – sent their power into the Deccan, where briefly in the middle of the seventh century, after seizing the Chālukya capital, they were the dominant force on the plateau as well. In Kānchī (Conjeeveram) they had a city spaciously planned and rich in temples, while at Mahābalipuran, on the sea-shore, they built the beautiful Rathas or 'Seven Pagodas', temples carved out of enormous boulders. At the close of the ninth century an alliance of Cholas and Pāndyas broke the power of the Pallavas for ever, and the peninsula fell to a Chola power which, under Rājarāja the Great (A.D. 985–1005), stretched far into the Deccan and

encompassed Ceylon, and under his son, Rājendra Choladeva I
(1005–35), extended to parts of Malaya and Sumatra.

The Chola kings were, seemingly without exception, wor-
shippers of Śiva, but in general pursued the common Hindu
practice of religious tolerance. They maintained a strong fleet,
constructed vast public works, including dams, with forced
labour, and continued the temple-building tradition of their
Pallava predecessors. Of most interest, however, was their
highly systematized administration, with apparent roots in the
far past, of which the basic unit was a union of villages (kūrram),
enjoying local self-government through an assembly (mahā-
sabhā) elected annually by lot and subject to the ultimate control
of the royal officers (adhikārin). Such evidence as exists for the
Gandhian belief in traditional village democracy belongs to
Chola times, but it is reasonable to wonder how far, in practice,
the assemblies were free of imperial control and how far the
election of members was itself a truly popular procedure.
Certainly, the states claimed a sixth of all produce as land
revenue, and in addition levied a multitude of petty imposts
which brought the tax to something like a third on fertile land.
In any event, the Chola dynasty died out early in the fourteenth
century, and the whole Chola system of village administration
with it.

Muslim power entered India in earnest during the last
quarter of the twelfth century, controlled much of the country
through the Sultanate of Delhi by 1340, lost ground for some
two hundred years, and then, with the accession of Akbar in
1556, began an expansion which took Islam for a short while
at the end of the seventeenth century into the far south. Out of
Ghur, in present-day Afghanistan, the Muslim forces with their
swift and well-armed cavalry swept down upon India, defeating
the vast Hindu armies whose efficiency was eroded by caste and
multiple command, and whose mobility was limited by elephants. All northern India to the gates of Delhi, then Delhi
itself, the areas of present-day Rajasthan and Gujarat in the
west, Bihar and Bengal in the east, and eventually much of the
Deccan fell to the invaders, who mercilessly advanced not only
their authority but also their faith, reducing temples to rubble,
putting hundreds of thousands to the sword, and forcibly
converting the survivors. But the sultans themselves were not

safe from the violence they brought, and many succumbed to assassination by rivals, favourites and impatient heirs. One of the last of the powerful sultans, Fīrūz Shāh, who ruled from 1351 to 1388, added bribery to force in a new policy of conversion that showed massive results. In his own words – for he wrote a tract on his good deeds as he personally evaluated them –

> I forbade the infliction of any severe punishment on the Hindus in general, but I destroyed their idol temples and instead thereof raised mosques ... I encouraged my infidel subjects to embrace the religion of the prophet, and I proclaimed that every one who repeated the creed and became a Musalmān should be exempt from the *jizya* or poll-tax. Information of this came to the ears of the people at large, and great numbers of Hindus presented themselves and were admitted to the honour of Islam.

About 1340, some years before Fīrūz Shāh himself reached the throne, the power of the Delhi sultanate had begun to crumble, with successful rebellions by provincial governors and the establishment of independent sultanates. Fīrūz Shāh arrested the process, but his death was followed by anarchy, and in 1398 Amīr Tīmūr of Samarqand, the great Tamburlaine of Christopher Marlowe, invaded India, sacked Delhi itself, and carried away with him all but the name of the Delhi sultanate. Muslim rule survived in a scattered form throughout north and central India, but the united empire would not return for some two hundred years.

Unlike the conquerors who had preceded them, the Muslims retained their identity; their own revealed religion and the contempt which they felt for any other secured them from absorption by the Hindu masses they ruled. On the other hand, Hinduism, within the citadel of caste, did not succumb to the assault of the new religion; many Hindus were converted by force or the promise of profit, but the gates themselves were never surrendered. Even by the time of partition in the middle of the twentieth century, after a Muslim presence of nearly eight hundred years and a Muslim rule covering more than half that period, Islam could not claim more than a quarter of India's millions. Where a fusion did take place was in language and art. The Muslim administration was forced to employ a host of unconverted Hindus in minor official posts, and such contact led to the evolution of a common language, Urdu, with a mainly Persian vocabulary and a Hindi grammatical structure. Equally, the architectural styles introduced to India by the sultans, many of whom were irrepressible builders, were based on the models of Mecca and other Muslim cities, but were considerably modified by Hindu influences, since Indian craftsmen had to be employed on the construction of the buildings themselves.

The disintegration of the Delhi sultanate was not watched helplessly by Hindu India. The crumbling of Muslim power in the Deccan was the signal for a Hindu resurgence that, begun with the foundation of Vijayanagar in 1336, built a Hindu empire throughout central and southern India. Travellers in the fifteenth and sixteenth centuries testified to the power and wealth of the new rulers, their royal army of a million fighting troops at times of emergency, and their capital at Vijayanagar with its more than half a million citizens, its magnificent temples, lavish court and busy bazaars. The rulers themselves were in the main devout Hindus, and though they, together with most of their subjects, appear to have eaten meat and drunk wine, they pampered the vegetarian and ascetic Brahmins who held posts of high administrative influence. Yet, Muslim or Hindu, the separation of court from people remained vast. The kings of Vijayanagar were no less ruthless in their exactions than their Muslim enemies. Nuniz, a Portuguese, who visited the empire in 1535, stated that the peasants paid 'nine-tenths to their lord', and though the precise figure may be dismissed as improbable, it indicates that the land and other taxes which kept the court in such luxury were inordinately harsh. The criminal code was severe, directed at protecting the property of the rich – Nuniz reported that a thief had a foot and a hand cut off for minor crimes, and was hanged with a hook under his chin for major ones – while the more savage aspects of religious tradition were scrupulously observed. Nicolo Conti, an Italian who had visited Vijayanagar in 1420 during the reign of Davarāya II, recorded that the king possessed some 12,000 wives, of whom between two and three thousand would be required to burn themselves on his funeral pyre when he died.

At last, in 1565, with the Hindu empire much weakened by usurpations and internal conflict, an alliance of Muslim rulers in the Deccan defeated an enormous Hindu army and sacked the city of Vijayanagar, massacring many of its inhabitants and carrying off its treasures. Muslim power would henceforward be paramount in India until the coming of the British two centuries later. Yet the last of the great Hindu empires would not be altogether lost in history. The power of Vijayanagar secured the resilience of Hinduism throughout India, and produced a literary florescence that not only revitalized Sanskritic culture but enormously enriched the vernacular of the empire, Telugu. Some five hundred years later, soon after the achievement of Indian independence, it would be popular agitation in the Telugu-speaking area of Madras for a separate state that would lead to the establishment of Andhra Pradesh and, a few years afterwards, to the whole reorganization of Indian states on linguistic lines.

The sixteenth century marked much more than the end of the Vijayanagar empire: it ushered in the rule of the Moguls and the great age of Islam in India. Out of the north-west, along the beaten path of conquest through the centuries, Babur, King of Kabul, swept down on India in 1525, and in the following year, at the battle of Panipat, defeated the Afghan forces of Sultan Ibrahim. For the rest of the century, whole armies clashed across the north, pillage and famine rotted the peasantry, until with the reduction of Asirgarh in 1601, the emperor Akbar, Babur's grandson, extended his sway throughout the whole of upper India, from Gujarat in the west to Bengal and Orissa in the east. The real founder of the Mogul empire, Akbar (1556–1605) completely overhauled the traditional administration of power, creating departments with written regulations, so that officials were no longer subject to royal caprice, and changing the land revenue assessment, so that holdings were taxed according to the quality of soil. Above all the revenue was collected by salaried officials direct from the cultivator – the '*ryotwar* settlement' – not from *jāgīrdārs*, or intermediaries assigned revenue districts which they could exploit for themselves. The change, of course, merely cut a straight channel from cultivator to court; Akbar took the equivalent of one-third of the gross produce instead of the one-sixth prescribed by the Hindu scriptures, and though other levies were abolished, the peasantry could hardly have felt its burden any lighter. It was Akbar, however, who broke with the tradition of his Muslim predecessors – and all but a few of his successors – in promoting religious tolerance. Even when still a practising Muslim, he married Hindu princesses, accepting their relatives as his own; abolished pilgrim levies, and employed Hindus in responsible administrative posts. Then, in 1579, he issued an Infallibility Decree, by which he planned that Muslims and Hindus should together worship one god and treat the emperor as the authorized exponent of the one god's will. His attempt to create a new religion for the whole empire failed completely, but he invited Hindus of all sects, with Parsees and Christians – the Portuguese had established themselves on the west coast at the beginning of the sixteenth century and conquered Goa in 1510 – to his court, practising his policy of universal toleration towards all but the Muslims themselves, who were subjected to sporadic, if minor, persecution. His son Jahangir (1605–27) continued his policies, including the patronage of literature and the school of Indo-Persian painting which so flourished under the Moguls, but with his death the Muslim empire returned to its first principles.

Shahjahan (1627–58), after the violence and strife that generally attended Mogul successions – he ordered the execution of all his male collateral relatives and had two serious rebellions to crush – secured the throne and during his long reign brought the empire to its climax. He subdued by relentless warfare the Deccan and parts of the south to his control, and by the promise of his power preserved his whole realm from invasion. His court, with the celebrated peacock throne of jewels that he had made, displayed an unprecedented splendour, and his patronage of art brought Mogul architecture – in buildings like the Taj at Agra – painting and literature to one of the high points of Islamic achievement. Yet behind the screen of imperial glitter, he pursued a policy of unremitting repression and intolerance. He persecuted the Christians – not entirely without provocation, for the Portuguese themselves engaged in forcible conversion – and the Hindus, many of whose temples he reduced to ruins. His administration was so predatory that peasants abandoned their land rather than try and meet the exactions upon it. Bernier, who visited the empire at the close of

Shahjahan's reign, wrote that the despotism of local governors was

> often so excessive as to deprive the peasant and artisan of the necessaries of life, and leave them to die of misery and exhaustion – a tyranny owing to which those wretched people either have no children at all, or have them only to endure the agonies of starvation, and to die at a tender age – a tyranny, in fine, that drives the cultivator of the soil from his wretched home to some neighbouring state, in hopes of finding milder treatment, or to the army, where he becomes the servant of some trooper. As the ground is seldom tilled otherwise than by compulsion, and as no person is found willing and able to repair the ditches and canals for the conveyance of water, it happens that the whole country is badly cultivated, and a great part rendered unproductive from the want of irrigation. The houses, too, are left in a dilapidated condition, there being few people who will either build new ones, or repair those which are tumbling down.[1]

Even in the high summer of its riches and strength, the Mogul empire was rotting from within, and it was a suitable irony that Shahjahan himself should have granted, early in 1639, the site of Madras to an English factor, so initiating the British penetration and conquest of India. For another half-century after Shahjahan's death, under the long rule of his son Aurangzeb (1658–1707), the empire would be preserved, but its power was increasingly no more than an appearance. Continual warfare and administrative corruption, with the ceaseless exactions required to meet the cost of the splendid court and the army, frayed away the whole financial fabric of the empire. Luxury corroded the nobles and their military command, while the succession struggles destroyed the authority of the throne itself. Above all, the Hindu support of the empire which the tolerance of Akbar had won and the good sense of Jahangir had kept was speedily lost by the persecutions of Shahjahan and the even more fanatical Aurangzeb. At the beginning of the eighteenth

---

[1] François Bernier, *Travels in the Mughul Empire*, translated and edited by Constable and V. A. Smith (Oxford University Press, 1914), p. 226.

century, the Mogul empire seemed as strong as ever; long before the end it had collapsed in all but name.

The British succeeded in capturing India, however, not merely because the country was torn and exhausted, nor because they had leaders of distinction, disciplined troops and administrators, vast financial resources and supremacy at sea. They succeeded because their own vital interests did not clash with those of the Indians themselves, both Hindu and Muslim. The British did not introduce a nationalism of their own to supplant an existing nationalism; the Indians had no political ideal, only a passionate allegiance to certain social and religious principles, while the British, interested paramountly in trade and in political control only as an instrument for securing it, left religion and social organization generally alone. The Portuguese failed in India because they launched a religious assault upon both Muslims and Hindus; the Muslims failed when their rule ceased to be religiously tolerant of Hindus. To Muslims and Hindus alike, rule by the British, however odd their customs and remote their culture, was preferable to rule by the other.

It was war between Britain and France in 1742, and the resultant clash between French and British trading interests in India, that led to the establishment of Britain's Indian empire. While the French Compagnie des Indes Orientales was trading profitably from Pondicherry on the east coast, Malabar on the west, and Bengal in the north, the British East India Company was prospering from its three independent Presidencies of Bombay, Fort St George in Madras and Fort William in Bengal by trade in indigo (Gujarat and Bengal), saltpetre (Bengal and Bihar), spices (Malabar) and cotton goods of all kinds. In consequence of Britain's supremacy at sea and Robert Clive's military flair, the French forces were, after some fluctuation in fortunes, decisively defeated, and by 1761 French power in India was at an end. Nor had the war with France led only to the occupation of French positions in India. At the Battle of Plassey in 1757, British forces under Clive had routed the army of the Nawab, or provincial governor, of Bengal – whose allegiance to the Mogul throne had become merely nominal – and a new Nawab, owing his power to the Company, had been made the emperor's deputy in Bengal and Bihar. The Company continued to trade by imperial permission, its privileges and prestige much enhanced, but it had in fact, if not in name, become the paramount power in northern as well as southern India.

The period that followed was one of unbridled profiteering by officials of the Company, who found themselves no longer merely merchants, but the real governors of Bengal. They received – and extracted where necessary – 'presents' from the Muslim rich, if not in payment for favours already done, then in the hope of benefits to come; and they engaged unscrupulously in local trade, enjoying virtually limitless credit facilities and exercising wide intimidation. Parliamentary reports revealed that between 1757 and 1766 over £2 million had been given as presents to the Company servants and some £3,750,000 paid 'in compensation for losses incurred'. This was the age of the Nabobs, the men who went to India in junior positions and returned to Britain after a few years with enormous wealth, which they then expended on buying land, seats in parliament, and eventually titles. As Clive himself declared – and since he amassed a fortune himself, who should have known better? – 'I will only say that such a scene of anarchy, confusion, bribery, corruption and extortion was never seen or heard of in any country but Bengal, nor such and so many fortunes acquired in so unjust and rapacious a manner.' It was Clive himself who, having initiated the era of corruption, was the first to try and end it during his administration as Governor and Commander-in-Chief of Bengal (1765–7), by limiting the size of presents that officials could legally receive and regulating private trade. But 'though he reduced bribery and extortion he did not eliminate them, and it was not until the administration of Lord Cornwallis over twenty years later that the servants of the Company were disciplined at last.

Only one power in India blocked total British supremacy: the Hindu kingdom of the Marathas in the west. Sivājī, a robber chieftain born in 1627, had rebelled against Muslim authority in the Deccan and by guerilla warfare brought a considerable territory in what is now Maharashtra under his control, defeating or evading the imperial armies sent to subdue him. In 1667 he had even been granted the title of raja by Aurangzeb, but in 1674 had declared himself an independent king and set out on an expedition of southern conquest which, as a result of his ability in playing off the Muslim rulers against each other, had been spectacularly successful and cut short only by his death in 1680. A devout Hindu, he had devoted himself and his power to the defence of Brahmins, cows and caste, and he had given Hinduism itself its first militant political expression since the collapse of the Vijayanagar empire. Indeed his power had rested more on the devotion of himself and his followers to Hinduism than on his efficient army and effective – if singular – civil administration. In the territory he controlled directly – the *swarajya* or homeland – he had taken two-fifths of the crop as the land revenue of the state, but elsewhere had simply plundered or conducted a vast protection racket, by which he extracted as a pledge against pillage a quarter of the official land revenue assessment. Despite the religious character of his administration, therefore, with a Brahmin usually at the helm as *peshwa* or prime minister, Sivājī had founded a simple robber state.

After the death of Sivājī himself, the Maratha kingdom had survived to continue sapping the power of the Moguls; Maratha forces had conquered Gujarat and Malwa in modern Rajasthan and even, in 1737, appeared on the outskirts of Delhi. Power had moved from the raja to the *peshwa*, and a succession of notable *peshwas* had transformed the kingdom into an empire. By 1758, the Marahas had made themselves masters of the Punjab, and their authority, at its fullest extent, stretched from the Himalayas in the north to parts of the southern peninsula, with those territories not their own paying them tribute. Only the British, with their bases in the south and north-east, promised anything like effective rivalry for the control of India.

It was the unity of British power and the fragmentation of the Maratha that gave victory to the British. The Marathas knew how to conquer but not how to govern; the pillage which had brought them their initial successes became an addiction, and outside the *swarajya* they plundered Hindus as ruthlessly as Muslims, so that their claims to be serving the cause of Hinduism had rather less effect among the people of Rajasthan and Bengal than the peasants of Maharashtra itself. Moreover, the passing of power from the royal house of Sivājī to the *peshwas*, with the vast increase in territory under Maratha control, led to a dissipation of authority and prestige. With the battle of Panipat in 1761, in which the Maratha army was decisively defeated by Afghan forces, there was a swift decline in Maratha cohesion, and the northern generals became in effect independent chiefs, recognizing the *peshwa*'s nominal leadership of a Maratha confederacy.

In 1772 Warren Hastings was made Governor of Bengal and soon afterwards appointed to the new post of Governor-General, with authority over the other two presidencies at Madras and Bombay, as part of a parliamentary initiative aimed at regulating the conduct of the East India Company. The British parliament, roused by the scandal of the 'Nabob' fortunes and the absurdity of a commercial company's control over an empire, was beginning to intervene directly in Indian affairs. Hastings himself, though he had proved to be an able administrator who took somewhat less personal advantage of his position than had been the Company custom, was impeached in 1787, in a move that asserted the moral responsibility of parliament for the welfare of India; after six years of trial he was acquitted on all counts, but his impeachment had in itself served a purpose, by making clear that the acts of Company servants, however highly placed, were to be scrutinized, and any misdemeanours, if proved, appropriately punished. In 1784 parliament passed Pitt's India Act, by which the Company possessions fell under the joint government of Company and Crown. A Board of Control, consisting of six unpaid privy councillors, was appointed to 'superintend, direct and control all acts, operations and concerns' relating to the civil, military or financial government of the British territories in India, and the Governor-General, though still appointed by the Company directors, was made subject to recall by the Crown. The Governor-General's own powers were increased – his councillors were reduced in number to three, of whom one had to be the commander-in-chief of the armed forces, and he was, by subsequent amendment, enabled both to override his Council and to fill the post of Governor-General and commander-in-chief simultaneously – while the control of Calcutta over the subordinate presidencies was tightened. Then, in 1813, parliament shattered the Company's monopoly of Indian trade, so permitting the subsequent growth of commerce and industry in India, and in 1833 the

Company vanished altogether as a commercial agency in the
Indian territories, becoming the mere political agent of the
Crown. From 1853, six of the Company's twenty-four directors
were nominated by the Crown, and five years later, after the
outbreak of the Indian mutiny, parliament took the final step
and deprived the Company of any share at all in the government
of India.

The new importance attached to India by parliament with
the passing of the 1784 India Act, and the power exercised by
the new Board of Control, were reflected in the appointment of
so distinguished a public figure as Lord Cornwallis to succeed
Hastings as Governor-General. Cornwallis (1786–93) began by
cleansing the Company itself. He introduced generous fixed
salaries for Company servants and strictly enforced the prohibition against private trade, sending any offenders home. But his
attitude to the Indians themselves was draconian – 'Every native
of Hindustan, I verily believe, is corrupt,' he wrote – and he not
only refrained from appointing them to responsible posts, but
removed them wherever possible. By the Charter Act of 1793
posts worth more than £500 a year were limited to members of
the covenanted service, for which Indians were not eligible,
and members of the traditional administrative Indian class,
Hindu and Muslim alike, found themselves excluded from
public life in the Company's realm. The results were inevitable:
the myth developed that ability in public affairs had never
existed in India, and the gulf between governor and governed –
always wide in India – became racial as well as economic and
cultural.

It was over the ageless issue of land revenue, on which every
government in India ultimately depended, that Cornwallis
made his next important move. The system found in Bengal by
the British was *zamindari*, by which *zamindars* or landholders,
with hereditary rights, collected from the cultivators a fixed
share of their produce – usually a third – and retained a tenth
of this as their own remuneration, remitting the rest to the state.
Responsible for public order as well, they thus constituted an
official aristocracy of rent-collecting magistrates, whose hereditary complexion had evolved an understood relationship with
the peasantry. Cornwallis organized the Permanent Settlement,
by which a final financial assessment was made and the *zamin-*

dars, regarded as landowners on the British pattern, were required to pay nine-tenths of the assessed revenue to government collectors. The assessment was, however, too high for the existing state of cultivation; many *zamindars* could not meet their obligations and were replaced by men of means from Calcutta; the traditional tie between *zamindar* and peasant was in many instances cut; and a new class – enriched at peasant expense with the gradual increase in cultivation – developed, bound by interest to British power. The *zamindars* were, however, stripped of their policing and magisterial functions as well as their control over revenue; officials of the Company controlled the revenue districts as collectors, with magisterial powers, while district police maintained order and courts, circuit and provincial, with a Supreme Court for appeals, separated the judicial and administrative classes. The Cornwallis Code, as it came to be called, did much to establish stability in the countryside under British control and, by its division of revenue-collection and justice, gave India a new pattern of government. But the reduction of the *zamindars* to rent-collectors and the peasants to mere tenants, with the withering of all traditional relationship between the two, made the classes dangerously alien and hostile to each other.

The India Act of 1784 had declared that 'schemes of conquest and extension of dominion in India' were 'repugnant to the wish, honour and policy of this nation'; but jurisdiction all over India was so vague, successions so disputed, and the appetite for expansion – if only, as in the Maratha confederacy, to deflect internal dissensions – so fierce, that British power had to extend itself if it was to be secure. Already under the administration of Hastings, British authority in the north-east had moved westwards into part of what is now Uttar Pradesh to protect the flank of the Company against Maratha raids; under Cornwallis, it found itself at war with the Muslim kingdom of Mysore to preserve the Madras presidency and ended by annexing half the Mysore territories. Then, under the Marquess Wellesley (1798–1804), with the excuse of the Napoleonic wars, the British pursued a policy of expansion. Mysore forces were decisively defeated in 1799, and British hegemony in the south was finally established; Wellesley restored the Hindu royal family to the captive Mysore throne, and by subsidiary treaty

– a technique of ensuring supremacy that would be the model for British India's relationship with the princely states – retained for the Governor-General power to interfere in the internal administration of the state and even take over its management altogether in the interests of good government. The Company then annexed Kanara in the west, so encircling Mysore with British territory and, taking advantage of a disputed succession in the Maratha principality of Tanjore, absorbed that too. At last, choosing a moment when Maratha power appeared at its most distracted, Wellesley went to war, and though he did not succeed in crushing all the Maratha chieftains, emerged with supremacy in the Deccan, the annexation of Cuttack in the east (so joining Bengal to Madras in a continuous stretch of British territory), and the absorption of much territory in northern India, including Agra and Delhi. The British empire was assuming its final shape, and those Indians who considered the new *raj* must many of them have shrugged their shoulders and prepared themselves for the inevitable issue – rule by yet another alien people through the years of indisputable power to the slow decline and the sudden collapse.

After a period of stock-taking, it was the Governor-Generalship of Lord Hastings (1813–22) which consolidated conquest. Almost at the outset of the new administration, British India was for the first time faced by the kind of contingency that had tumbled so many empires in the past: an expansionary power in the north. Suddenly the Gurkhas of Nepal invaded the Indian plains, and British troops were defeated with heavy loss. By 1816, however, Company troops were marching on Khatmandu and the Gurkhas sued for peace. The British annexed the hill states, among them Simla, to which the *raj* would every year retreat from the summer, and the respect with which British and Gurkhas henceforward regarded each other's military prowess led to the formation of the celebrated Gurkha contingents in Britain's Indian army. Lord Hastings turned southwards, and by 1818 the Rajput states in the west had been subordinated by treaty and the Maratha Confederacy shattered, with all its chiefs defeated or submissive. The *peshwa*'s dominions – the Maratha homeland – were absorbed by the presidency of Bombay, the capital city of which, with the aid of Parsee and Gujarati merchants, soon became a flourishing commercial centre and the largest seaport in the country. The only open frontier remaining was the Punjab, where the Sikh kingdom was friendly, and elsewhere the surviving Indian states were islanded by British territory. India was more united under single rule than it had been under the Moguls, and Hastings set about dispelling the anarchy from which Britain herself had so profited. In 1818 he initiated the repair of the Mogul canals, whose waters had not flowed since the middle of the eighteenth century, and commenced the restoration of roads. He patronized the establishment of schools and enhanced the status of junior Indian judicial officers. Conquest was giving place at last to government.

This work of repair – and it was not entirely benevolent, for how else might the swollen Indian empire be made profitable? – was continued under the administration of Lord William Bentinck (1828–35), who initiated a whole series of reforms. He displaced Persian as the language of the judiciary by the vernacular in the lower courts and English in the higher ones, and increased the powers and salaries of the Indian judges. He stimulated the economy with the encouragement he gave to iron and coal production, tea and coffee cultivation, and irrigation schemes. But above all he laid down two principles of British government: interference with local custom where it seemed to contradict accepted morality, and emphasis on Western education. He outlawed the practice of *sati*, the burning of widows on the funeral pyres of their husbands, and he decreed that education should devote itself to Western knowledge, with English as the medium of instruction.

British expansionism on the sub-continent was almost, but not altogether, at an end. The waters of the Indus washed at the military and commercial imagination, and in 1843, after a series of discreditable manoeuvres and the blatant violation of their word, the British under Sir Charles Napier annexed Sind. 'We have no right to seize Sind,' Napier had written in his diary, 'yet we shall do so and a very advantageous, useful, humane piece of rascality it will be.' Not the least of the long-term consequences was the addition of a large Muslim population to British India; little more than one hundred years later, Sind would constitute the core of West Pakistan.

Only the kingdom of the Sikhs in the Punjab remained

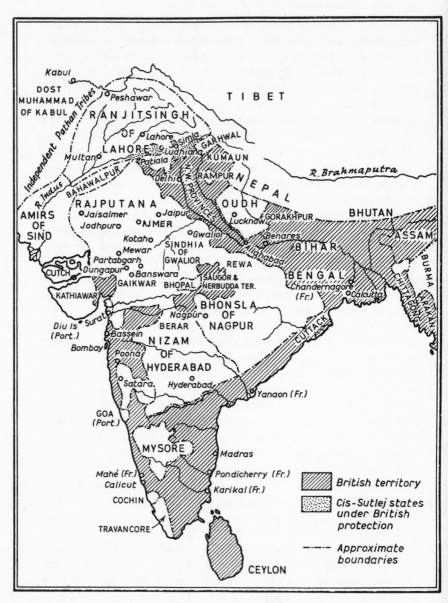

Map 5 INDIA IN 1836

(based on the map 'India, 1836' (from the *Oxford History of India*, third edition, p. 602) after *An Historical Atlas of the Indian Peninsula* by C. C. Davies, Oxford University Press, Bombay)

unsubordinated. The Sikhs or disciples began as pious Hindus following the first *guru* or prophet Nanak (1469–1539), who had taught the unity of God as a counter to religious extremism by Hindu and Muslim, and had condemned all distinctions of caste. Akbar had found such teaching to his taste and in 1557 had granted the Sikhs land at Amritsar, which became the site of their Golden Temple and the headquarters of the sect. Under Akbar's Mogul successors, however, the Sikhs had been mercilessly persecuted, and gradually they had retreated into the hills of the Punjab to transform themselves into a military brotherhood. Govind Singh (1675–1708), the tenth and last *guru*, had laid the basis for their military power by forming them into an order of the Khālsa or Pure, who were to be baptized by drinking consecrated water stirred by a sword or dagger and eating together a consecrated meal, rites especially designed to break caste laws. In addition, all Sikhs were to abjure tobacco, and wear the five Ks – *kesh* (long hair), *kangha* (a comb), *kuchha* (shorts), *kara* (a steel or iron bangle), and *kirpan* (a small steel dagger). With Govind Singh's death, the disciples had lingered leaderless in the hills, but their common consecration, custom and dress had unified them, while making them visibly different from anyone else. Gradually they had grown in numbers and in strength with the collapse of organized power in northern India, spreading over the Punjab and forming embryo states. The political unity had then come with Ranjit Singh (1780–1839), who had forged the twelve loose tribes or *misls* together and built a compact kingdom that stretched northwards to Ladakh and possessed the only strong army in India outside of the Company. His control had been complete, but it had been personal, dependent on his shrewdness and imagination, and on his death the kingdom rapidly deteriorated, with succession struggles and a strong discontented army, which had either to be disbanded or turned to war. The Sikh army crossed the Sutlej in December 1845, and in 1849 the Punjab was annexed to British India. The British were now masters of the sub-continent from the Indus in the east to the Bay of Bengal in the west, from the Himalayas in the north to the southernmost point of the peninsula.

The empire was complete, but the work of establishing order throughout it and promoting a general prosperity had barely begun. The *zamindari* system of revenue settlement pursued by Cornwallis in the north had led to the development of huge landed estates, and though the government made efforts to protect tenants from exploitation, these were never altogether successful, and the number of landless peasants, forced to work as hired labourers, constantly grew. Warned accordingly, the administration promoted a different system – the *ryotwari* – in the south and the west, by which a temporary revenue settlement, generally covering thirty years and fixed at half the estimated value of the crop after the deduction of cultivating costs, was made direct with the *ryot* or cultivator. This system removed the *zamindar* middleman between government and cultivator, and by offering the cultivator himself security of tenure and a fixed tax for a fixed period, encouraged him to improve his holding and increase his productivity. With the establishment of order all over the country and the profitable production promoted by the revenue settlements, the population increased at an unprecedented rate; the 100 million in the second half of the sixteenth century, which had risen only to 130 million[1] in 1800, became 206 million at the first census of 1872.

India's one important traditional industry was cotton goods, and to this British rule delivered an early blow: Britain exported her own cheap machine-made textiles to India, and the European market for Indian goods shrank with the protracted Napoleonic wars. By the middle of the nineteenth century, little more than village homespun was being produced in the country, and cotton fibre was being exported to Britain in bulk. Commercial activity, however, fast increased, with trade, both internal and foreign, stimulated by the security of British administration and the enlarged relationship with the West. At last the ascendancy of free-trade opinion in Britain broke the Company's commercial monopoly in 1813, and encouraged administrative action to further Indian industry in the cause of economic freedom. The key to real economic progress, of course, was the development of communications, and Lord William Bentinck, who had introduced tea and encouraged coffee cultivation, had initiated as well a road-building programme and the use of steam navigation on rivers. But it was the administration of Lord Dalhousie (1848–56) which finally

[1] Estimates made in the *Oxford History of India*, p. 641.

solved the transport problem with the introduction of the railway. By the outbreak of the Mutiny in 1857, some two hundred miles of track had been constructed, and since these proved to be of military as well as commercial value, railway development was subsequently rapid. Fuel could at last be brought to the centres of production, and the products of such centres distributed widely and cheaply; it was no accident that the mining of coal and iron, and the development of the jute, cotton, tea and coffee industries progressed so slowly before 1850 and so swiftly afterwards. And the railways had other consequences too: they reduced the threat of famine by making possible the provision of bulk supplies to stricken areas, and they popularized the joint-stock system of financing trade and industry. Above all, they gave to the people of India a new mobility, which did much to establish an all-Indian awareness and promote the nationalist struggle against alien rule.

Britain was making India over in her image of what a modern and civilized state ought to be, interfering with customary law where it offended the moral traditions of the West, establishing a network of English schools and colleges, both through misssionary effort and government grants – the first three universities were opened in 1857 – and annexing princely states for misgovernment or disputed succession. The displaced old *zamindari* class and the dethroned princely families were disaffected, but unable to arrest British power on their own; it was the discontent of the orthodox Hindu and Muslim alike – who watched with growing alarm the attempts to westernize Indian culture, the feverish activity of the Christian missions, innovations like the railways and the telegraph, and the shrinking area of participation by Indians in public affairs – that threatened rebellion. In the event it was the soldiers who took the lead. By far the bulk of the Company forces were Indian, and the Bengal army, the core of the whole, contained many high-caste Hindus. Reports that cartridges for the new Enfield rifle had been smeared with the fat of cows and pigs outraged the feelings of both Hindus, to whom the cow was sacred, and Muslims, to whom the pig was unclean, and military unrest increased. On May 10th, 1857, some troops at Meerat refused the cartridges, were placed in irons and released by three mutinying regiments. Delhi fell to mutineers on the following day, and the uprising spread across the north, from the borders of Rajasthan to the neighbourhood of Patna in Bihar.

By the middle of 1858 the mutiny had been crushed, because the peasants and the commercial class throughout the country, enjoying some stability at last, had more to lose by the success of rebellion than by its failure. Yet the consequences were considerable. Acts of gratuitous cruelty had been committed by both sides, and they left a legacy of fear and distrust behind them. The Government of India Act in 1858 deprived the Company of all participation in Indian government and established at the summit of administration a Secretary of State for India advised by a Council of India and directly responsible to the British Cabinet, while within India itself the Governor-General became in addition the Viceroy, a personal representative of the Crown. His Executive Council was reorganized in 1861 to include a fifth member, and a portfolio system was introduced, with members placed in charge of specific departments; the Legislative Council of 1853, a mock parliament of two judges and four provincial representatives, was remodelled into a group of six to twelve members, nominated by the Governor-General for two years, and at least one half of these were to be non-officials.

In 1859 the Bengal Rent Act, applying to the whole north-west as well as Bengal, was passed to protect cultivators from extortion by the *zamindars*; all cultivators who could prove possession of their holdings for more than twelve years were given occupancy rights, and a ceiling was placed on rents. The discontented princes were offered a new policy, which rewarded the loyal with gifts of money and land and treated them as subordinate partners rather than dependants awaiting death. All states became subject to royal paramountcy, as in the Mogul empire, but as such were to be cherished unless they provoked intervention by poor government. The army was reorganized, and the ratio of Europeans to Indians set at fifty-fifty in Bengal and two to one in the other presidencies. Only the new class of Westernized Indians, in whose hands the future would lie, was left uncajoled by any closer association with government.

The governors were more conciliatory to the governed, but the gulf between the two had widened with the mutiny. Lord Dalhousie had proposed the appointment of an Indian to the new Legislative Council; in 1880, some twenty-five years later,

Lord Northbrook complained that hardly anyone in India could bring himself to believe any Indian to be capable of responsibility. In 1873 it had been enacted that a European could be tried only by a European magistrate or sessions judge, and when Lord Ripon, a Gladstone appointment as Viceroy (1880–84), attempted in the Ilbert Bill to have Europeans tried by Indian sessions judges he raised such a storm in the European community that he felt himself forced to grant Europeans the right to claim a jury, half of whose members would be European.

The period following the Mutiny was one of considerable economic expansion, stimulated by the massive railway programme. In 1853 the first successful cotton mill had been opened in Bombay, and by 1914 India was fourth among the world's cotton-manufacturing countries. The first jute-spinning machine had been installed in 1855, and the industry rapidly grew in Bengal with the help of Indian coal deposits developed by the new East Indian Railway. Coal itself became a major industry, producing 500,000 tons in 1868, over 1,000,000 in 1880, over 6,000,000 in 1900, over 12,000,000 in 1912, and over 21,000,000 tons in 1917. India accordingly made itself almost self-supporting in one of the chief prerequisites for heavy industry. Together with coal came the iron and steel industry. The Parsee Tatas founded the Tata Iron and Steel Company in Bihar in 1907, and the plant eventually became the largest single steel works in the world, producing a million tons a year and helping to make India sixth among the world's steel-producing countries. Inevitably, around these two major industries a number of other industrial activities developed, and India soon possessed thriving chemical, shellac, cement, paper and sugar-refining plants. The development of the tea industry meanwhile was phenomenal: until 1850 Britain imported all her tea from China; in 1869 she took 10 million pounds from India and 100 million from China; in 1900 she took 24 million from China and 137 million pounds from India. The major capital investment for all this came, of course, from Britain, but an increasing proportion after 1900 emerged from the prospering Indian commercial class, especially for the cotton, iron and steel industries. The population, which had totalled 206 million in 1872, rose to 294 million in 1901, and 318 million in 1921.

The Mutiny had an effect on social policy as well, and the emphasis moved from moral to material interventions – massive irrigation schemes, like the canal system in the Punjab, made huge stretches of waste land richly productive – with the avoidance of any overt attempt to change the Indian social structure. The educational system continued its expansion, but with concentration on high schools and colleges rather than primary vernacular education, and the standards were not high, so that British India produced no impressive intellectual élite. Such changes as were attempted in Indian society were pursued only by general consent. In 1872 half the municipal council of Bombay was elected by ratepayers for the first time, and in 1878 half the council of Calcutta. Then Lord Ripon in the 'eighties, 'as a measure of political and popular education', established a network of district boards in the rural areas and municipal committees in the towns, with half or more of the members elected, enjoying powers over health, sanitation, public works education, and certain levies.

The administration itself, however, changed very slowly. In 1853 a Charter Act had thrown open the covenanted service to competitive examinations, but since these were held in Britain, few Indians could sit for them. Subsequent reforms, with the division of the civil service into imperial, provincial and subordinate sections, did little significantly to increase Indian participation in government, and it was only in the shockwave of the First World War that effective action was at last undertaken. Of all Westernizing influences, it was perhaps the press that was to prove the most revolutionary. From the foundation of the first newspaper in India, the *Bengal Gazette*, in 1780, the press had been forced to wage sporadic war against authority for freedom of speech, but by 1882 even the restrictions on the vernacular press had been repealed. Gradually the success of English newspapers stimulated the development of a vernacular press as well as English-language newspapers owned by Indians, and when nationalist resistance to British rule developed, it was these which embarrassed authority by their criticism and encouraged disaffection by their reports of struggle and repression.

The orthodox hostility to British power and its cultural innovation had led into the cul-de-sac of the Mutiny; a more enduring reaction was that of the Indians who realized that religion in its existing state could not withstand alien encroachment and so sought to strengthen their heritage by purifying it in the very sources of their faith. In 1828 a Bengali intellectual and publicist, Ram Mohan Roy, had founded the *Brahmo Samaj*, a reformist Hindu group which, proclaiming its authority in the high reasoning of the *Upanishads*, denounced such corruptions of Hinduism as idolatry, polygamy and female infanticide. The group was intellectual rather than popular in its appeal, but though it was small its influence was considerable, especially among the Westernized middle class. Of more popular significance was the *Arya Samaj*, founded in 1875 by Swami Dayananda from Gujarat (1824–83), who equally denounced idolatry, polygamy and caste, and relying on the four *Vedas*, preached a return to the simplicity of Vedic ritual and manners. The movement had considerable appeal in the north, especially in the Punjab, and, attacking both Muslim and Christian activity, did much to stimulate a new Hindu awareness. Finally, the followers of Ramkrishna Parahamsa (1834–86), a *bhakti* who spent most of his life at a temple near Calcutta in devotion to God and self-surrender, helped to restore Hinduism's confidence in itself. Led by Swami Vivekananda (1862–1902), who himself lectured widely in the West and did much to raise there the status of Hinduism as a world religion, the disciples added social service to devotion, and the Ramakrishna mission movement practised good works while preaching the basic unity of all religions.

It was nationalism, however, not religious revival or reform, which was eventually to unite the new Westernized classes with a significant portion of the peasantry in common resistance and aspiration. As the security of British rule had encouraged the development of merchants and industrialists, so the character of British administration had created an abundance of new professions with social status and influence. The new colleges and schools required teachers; the new legal system, lawyers; the new medicine, doctors; the new emphasis on material progress, the technicians to help run the public services. The old upper class, too proud or orthodox, had held aloof from subordinate posts in administration; the new middle class, commercial and professional, expanded to fill them. Moreover, the new middle class was united beyond regional differences by a common language, knowledge and set of values; the new press helped its ideas to circulate and the new communications allowed its members to travel easily and make contact with one another. It was this new class, stimulated by the liberal political precepts of the nineteenth century, that sought a political expression; yet it was to the old upper class, rigid and withdrawn, that the British administration looked fruitlessly but repeatedly for collaboration.

The Ilbert Bill controversy of 1883–4, with its manifestation of racial hostility and distrust, excited members of the new middle class to action, and in December 1885 the first meeting of the Indian National Congress took place in Bombay. Only seventy members, who had elected themselves by paying a small fee, were present, and they were mainly lawyers, journalists and teachers, representatives of the professional class which British rule itself had brought into being. The new body was moderate and Westernized in attitude and was welcomed by liberal Englishmen – three Englishmen would serve as Presidents between 1885 and 1900 – as well as, more reticently, by the administration, which responded by allowing elections, masked as recommendations for nomination, to the Legislative Council under the Indian Councils Act of 1892. Congressmen filed through this narrow passage at once, and an extension of the Council's powers to include consideration of the budget permitted them to discuss general policy as well as particular proposals. One of them, G. K. Gokhale from Bombay, early made his mark, and his annual budget speech at Calcutta ranked with the annual address of the Congress President as a highlight of nationalist activity.

From its second session, containing some four hundred and fifty members chosen by public meetings and organizations, Congress itself progressed rapidly, forming local branches, establishing an allegiance much larger than its membership, developing the annual conference and presidential election, the working and general committees, the whole procedure of debate and resolution, into instruments of political struggle. Only the Muslims as a community held back from any participation, in the belief that democratic government would inevitably be Hindu government. Yet the ideological unity of Congress was precarious, and a clash soon developed between the 'moderates' like G. K. Gokhale, with their Westernized approach, and the 'extremists' like Bal Gangadhar Tilak, the editor of a Marathi newspaper in Bombay, who sought inspiration in the career of Sivājī and hinted at the efficacy of violence.

The empire which had formally been proclaimed in 1876 found its appropriate Viceroy in Lord Curzon (1899–1905). An efficient if imperious administrator, he decreed many measures of land reform which reduced revenue assessments, preserved cultivators from eviction for debt, and established co-operative credit societies with the aim of liberating the peasant from the grip of the moneylender. He stimulated the development of scientific agriculture by creating a special agricultural department with laboratories, experimental farms, and a research institute, and stimulated industrialization by creating a new department of commerce and industry, to be headed by a sixth member of his Council. Alone with Warren Hastings among British administrators, he concerned himself with art and architecture, patronizing the Asiatic Society of Bengal which Hastings had founded, founding himself the Imperial Library, and, above all, creating a department of archaeology to undertake excavation and preserve India's fast-decaying antiquities. But Curzon was an inflexible paternalist both in aim and in manner, and before his departure he had hopelessly antagonized the nationalist opinion he despised. 'My own belief is that the Congress is tottering to its fall,' he wrote in 1900,[1] 'and one of my great ambitions while in India is to assist it to a peaceful demise.' Ironically, if not unexpectedly, Curzon accomplished the opposite, and left Congress a great deal stronger than he had found it. He appointed a commission to consider higher education and characteristically did not include a single Indian among its members. Then in 1904 he produced his Universities Act, which set out to raise standards by stimulating scholarship through post-graduate schools, introducing a residential system, increasing the nominated element in the governing bodies of the universities, and controlling the recognition and conduct of affiliated colleges. The nationalists saw the measure as an attempt to erode their influence and reduce education to a servant of the *raj*, and they attacked it bitterly; but their protests were ignored. Then, in 1905, with

[1] Quoted in the *Oxford History of India*, third edition, p. 759.

the declared objective of facilitating administration and furthering the development of the backward regions, Curzon partitioned Bengal into two new provinces: West Bengal, advanced
and predominantly Hindu, with 45 million people, and East
Bengal united with Assam, poor and badly serviced, predominantly Muslim, with some 31 million people and its
capital at Dacca. Bengali sentiment, much stronger than the
government had believed it to be, was outraged, while nationalists all over the country suspected that the partition scheme
which so neatly divided Hindu from Muslim was aimed at
meeting the demands for political advance with the distractions
of communalism. As Curzon disregarded all protest, public
agitation became clamorous, with frequent mass meetings, the
boycott of foreign cloth, and in the background, the stirrings of
terrorism. The partition of Bengal was revoked in 1911, but
by then much of the middle class had been permanently alien-
ated and distrust in British professions of eventual self-government for India was widespread.

The world outside of India was changing also. The victory
of Japan in the Russo-Japanese war of 1904–5 delivered a serious
blow to Western prestige. If Japan could become a great power
on its own, what – but for the British grip – was holding back
India? Soon the First World War would show the West itself
as fiercely divided, with Britain, once thought to be invincible,
suffering defeats and struggling with all its resources for victory.
In Britain meanwhile the general election of 1906 marked a
radical revival which encouraged Indian nationalism; and in
1908 Congress for the first time formulated its political goal as
the achievement of self-governing colonial status on the Cana-
dian model. With the First World War this was to become
dominion status in its modern sense, and by 1929 complete
independence.

Soon after the departure of Curzon, a terrorist movement
appeared in Bengal, in the Punjab and Bombay, and several
political murders took place. The administration passed two
measures visiting harsh punishments on anyone found guilty of
inciting to murder or illegally manufacturing explosives, and
Tilak himself was imprisoned for six years on a charge of incite-
ment. Terrorism received no mass support and gradually faded,
but it was a symptom of political impatience and an indication

of the danger in further delaying political development. In 1909 the government responded with the Morley–Minto reforms (John Morley was Secretary of State for India, and Lord Minto was the Viceroy), which increased Indian participation in various administrative councils. The Imperial Legislative Council was expanded to sixty members, of whom twenty-eight were to be nominated officials and five nominated non-officials, while twenty-seven non-officials were to be elected indirectly by the provincial legislatures; and in the provincial legislatures themselves, non-official majorities were introduced, though election was indirect, from municipal and district boards, chambers of commerce and universities, landholders and special interests like the jute- and tea-growers. The powers of council members were also increased, to enable the asking of supplementary questions and the tabling of resolutions, and though the government could not be defeated or censured, information could now be extracted from official reticence and opinions at least promoted through resolutions. The reforms lowered the political temperature in the country, but not for long. They made no allowance for popular representation and did not depart from the principle of executive irresponsibility; the official majority in the central council, though small, was preserved, and the powers enjoyed by governors in the provinces made little of the unofficial majority in the legislative bodies. The measures lagged behind the real requirement of the times and failed to provide that act of political imagination which would have set India on a clear course to democratic self-government. Above all, by granting communal representation to the Muslims – six special Muslim constituencies of landholders were created for the Imperial Legislative Council, and others in provincial legislatures – the reforms encouraged communal identification and planted the seed of Pakistan.

At the 1907 meeting of Congress in Surat the dissension between the 'moderates' and 'extremists' had come to a head, and though 'moderates' like Gokhale had secured their supremacy, helped by the imprisonment of Tilak in the following year, the inadequacy of the Morley–Minto reforms nourished nationalist discontent and promoted demands for sharper struggle. The administration of Lord Hardinge (1910–16) began well with the promotion of the reforms, the Government's retreat from

Bengali partition, and, in 1911, the move of the administrative capital, to popular acclaim, from Calcutta to Delhi. With the outbreak of the First World War in August 1914, there was a general rallying by the middle class to Britain, who was expected to emerge victorious within six months. There was an abatement of political agitation, a force of 800,000 combatants was recruited, and £100 million was given outright, with £20–30 million annually, by India to Britain for the prosecution of the war. But the war dragged on, British prestige was irreparably damaged, the Muslim community – generally orthodox and recognizing the Turkish Sultan as *Khalifa* – was antagonized by the campaign against Turkey, economic strains led to a considerable rise in food prices, and recruiting agents in the Punjab and western India began employing compulsion to meet the constant demand for manpower. When the war did end in British victory, this was overshadowed by the influenza epidemic which claimed five million lives in India; by severe economic dislocations; and by the difficulties experienced by thousands of demobilized soldiers returning to a disorganized countryside.

In 1915 Gokhale died, and in 1916 Tilak, who had been released from prison two years before, re-entered the political arena. With his skill and vision much sharpened, he joined forces with Mrs Annie Besant (who had founded the Home Rule League in 1915), achieved Muslim League support for his programme by the Lucknow Pact – an agreement of Congress and the League on separate communal electorates – and captured Congress itself at its Lucknow session. The once dominant 'moderates' were decisively beaten and soon left Congress altogether, to become the Liberals, a group of political elders with no mass support, who attempted, with occasional success, to mediate between government and Congress at times of crisis. To the new alliance of Hindu and Muslim only a dynamic leadership needed to be added – Tilak was dying by 1918 – and this came in the person of a lawyer from Gujarat, Mohandas Karamchand Gandhi.

Gandhi, who would soon be dubbed the Mahatma or 'Great Soul' by the Indian masses, had studied in London and then settled in South Africa, where he had led the Indian community with courage and skill in a movement of civil disobedience against racial discrimination. The technique of struggle which he had developed, calling it *satyagraha* or 'soul force', was passive resistance as a form of morality, aimed at purifying the practitioner himself and exercising in consequence a spiritual influence over his opponent. Amongst other people, such a technique, promoted not as strategy but as a principle and associated for Gandhi himself with various injunctions on diet and dress, may well have been considered crankish and futile; but amongst Indians it combined a method of resistance with perhaps the most powerful of Hindu precepts and traditions: *ahimsā*, or respect for all life, and its corollary non-violence. Gandhi succeeded in recruiting substantial mass support for the Congress struggle not only because he represented, by the austerity of his life and devotion to God, another in India's line of spiritual leaders, a man of goodness rather than of riches or power, but also because the way of struggle he had chosen was one sanctified by centuries of popular belief and practice. To the Indian peasant who never ate meat, vegetarianism was not an eccentricity, but a moral principle, and *satyagraha* no more than *ahimsā* projected into politics. Gandhi, who returned to India in 1915 with a wide reputation for the work he had done in South Africa, would not take long to emerge as the new national leader, to promote a policy of extremism in resisting British rule while keeping the resistance non-violent.

On August 20th, 1917, the coalition government in Britain, through Edwin Montagu, Secretary of State for India, declared:

> The policy of H.M. government, with which the Government of India are in complete accord, is that of the increasing association of Indians in every branch of the administration, and the gradual development of self-governing institutions, with a view to the progressive realisation of responsible government in India as an integral part of the Empire.

Britain was talking of eventual responsible government while Congress was demanding immediate home rule. Moreover, once the British had decided on a further measure of constitutional advance, they took over two years to provide it, and meanwhile did their best, by a policy of gratuitous repression, to ensure that any response to their concession was hostile or, at the very least, reluctant. Early in 1919, against the vote of every non-official Indian in the Imperial Legislative Council, the protests of Congress and the pleas of Gandhi himself, the government forced into law the two Rowlatt Bills, allowing judges to try specified types of political case without juries and giving provincial governments the power of internment. In fact the new laws were unnecessary – the powers bestowed by them were never used – but the administration had resolved to crush resistance to its authority, and ended, of course, by nourishing it. Gandhi organized successful *hartals* – the suspension of all business, with prayer and fasting – in protest at the laws, and these led to riots in Delhi, Ahmedabad, Lahore and Amritsar. In Amritsar on April 13th troops under General Dyer fired on a prohibited meeting, killing – by official estimates – 379 people and wounding over 1,200. Martial law was proclaimed in the Punjab, and punitive measures like public floggings and even, in one place, enforced crawling by all Indians set nationalist opinion aflame throughout the country.

It was in such an atmosphere that the Montagu–Chelmsford reforms (Lord Chelmsford served as Viceroy from 1916 to 1921) were promoted. The Imperial Legislative Council was replaced by a Legislative Assembly, with a majority of elected members, and a Council of State containing an unofficial majority, while the Executive Council was enlarged and Indians included for the first time among its members. The provinces, under a policy of devolution, were empowered to raise their own revenue through specific levies and legislate on certain subjects, while the new principle of 'dyarchy' divided the provincial administration into 'Transferred Subjects', like local self-government, education, public works and agriculture, controlled by ministers responsible to the provincial councils, and 'Reserved Subjects' like land revenue, justice, labour and irrigation, controlled by councillors responsible to the governor alone. A new electoral system, with general qualifications based on property and tax payments, enfranchised some five million voters for the provincial councils, nearly one million for the Legislative Assembly, and 17,000 for the Council of State, while special constituencies represented special interests like great landholders and industry, and communal representation, confirmed for the Muslims, was extended to the Sikhs in the Punjab, the Indian Christians in Madras, and Anglo-Indians and Europeans in specified provinces.

The display of conciliation was clearer than the content; the executive remained irresponsible, and the Viceroy and governors were empowered to pass Bills and authorize expenditure over Legislative opposition if such measures were 'certified' as necessary for the safety and peace of India; certain types of expenditure, like that of defence at the centre, were not subject at all to vote by the legislatures; and in the provinces the governors were empowered to administer the 'Transferred Subjects' in the absence of ministers. In August 1920 Congress rejected the reforms and, under the leadership of Gandhi, launched a campaign of boycott entailing resignation from office, refusal to participate in the coming elections, and withdrawal from government schools and colleges. If the resignations and withdrawals that followed were few, the boycott of the elections was a limited success; only a third of the middle- and upper-class electorate, expectedly more moderate than a mass electorate would have been, went to the polls, while the Liberals who manned the new ministries lacked any popular support and worked in the knowledge of the hostility felt by most of their countrymen. The administration repealed the Rowlatt Acts, introduced measures to improve labour conditions, started with the Indianization of the officer class in the army, secured Indian membership of the new League of Nations, and championed the cause of Indians overseas; but its doubling of the salt tax – by the new process of 'certification' – in order to balance the budget, and the persisting opposition of Congress to the reforms, left it as isolated from popular support as ever. Yet, despite the developing mass nature of the Congress struggle, enforced by orthodox Muslim participation through the *Khilafat* movement, government survived, crushing sporadic riots and biding its time till nationalist enthusiasm would have exhausted itself. In the months of December 1921 and January 1922 some thirty thousand people were arrested, including a distinguished lawyer from Allahabad, Motilal Nehru, and his young son Jawaharlal. Then, early in February 1922, Gandhi suddenly suspended the resistance campaign on the grounds that its whole non-violent nature had been denied when villagers at Chauri Chaura had set fire to a police station and burned the policemen inside.

102797 EMORY AND HENRY LIBRARY

A few weeks later Gandhi himself was arrested and sentenced
to a long term of imprisonment. The Congress leadership was
resentful at what it considered an unnecessary surrender but,
as Jawaharlal Nehru was later to recognize, there was political
astuteness behind Gandhi's decisions of principle.

Gandhiji has often acted almost by instinct; by long and
close association with the masses he appears to have developed, as great leaders often do, a new sense which tells
him how the mass feels, what it does and what it can do.
He reacts to this instinctive feeling and fashions his action
accordingly, and later, for the benefit of his surprised and
resentful colleagues, tries to clothe his decision with reasons.
This covering is often very inadequate, as it seemed after
Chauri Chaura. At that time our movement, in spite of its
apparent power and the widespread enthusiasm, was going
to pieces. All organization and discipline was disappearing;
almost all our good men were in prison, and the masses had
so far received little training to carry on by themselves...
There is little doubt that if the movement had continued
there would have been growing sporadic violence in many
places. This would have been crushed by Government in a
bloody manner and a reign of terror established which
would have thoroughly demoralised the people.[1]

C. R. Das, the Bengali leader, and Motilal Nehru led the
opposition in Congress to Gandhi's policy of boycotting the
legislatures, and they decided in 1923 to fight the new elections
as the Swaraj Party, so as to subvert the Montagu–Chelmsford
reforms from within. While Gandhi after his release retired
from the stage, therefore, concentrating on his campaign for
the advance of the 'untouchables' or *Harijans* and waiting for
Congress to accept his views again, the Swarajists entered constitutional politics, securing enough seats in Bengal and Bombay
to prevent the formation of ministries and, with 45 out of the
106 elected seats in the Legislative Assembly, able to present a
powerful opposition at the centre. But constitutional obstruction
seemed to lead nowhere – C. R. Das, the chief apostle of such

[1] *Jawaharlal Nehru: An Autobiography* (Bodley Head, London, and the
John Day Company Inc., New York, 1936; reprinted 1958), pp. 85–6.

strategy, died in 1925 – and the Swarajists moved towards Gandhi and direct action again.

The British government resolved once more upon concilia-tion, and once more provoked more hostility than good will; in November 1927 it established the Simon Commission to con-sider constitutional change and did not appoint a single Indian to membership. The Madras meeting of Congress in 1927–8 declared independence to be the goal of Indian development, and an All-Parties Conference during 1928 produced a scheme of self-government known as the Nehru Report – after Motilal Nehru, its architect – which antagonized the Muslim leader-ship by rejecting the principle of separate electorates, but revealed a growing Hindu unity of opposition. By the end of 1928 Gandhi's leadership had been recognized again, and Con-gress prepared itself for a struggle behind the demand for a round-table conference as a prelude to the grant of dominion status. In the autumn of 1929 the new Labour government in Britain declared that dominion status was the goal of British policy and that a round-table conference would be called to consider constitutional advance; but it refused to promise that such a conference would grant dominion status at once, and Gandhi launched a campaign of civil disobedience. In a move of sharp political insight that prodded mass sympathy all over India, he walked with chosen followers from his *ashram* to the sea and there, on April 6th, 1930, in defiance of the unpopular salt tax, made salt in the sunshine. Within six months, some 60,000 people had been arrested, including all the leaders of Congress, for having broken the law; women, for the first time, participated widely in a political campaign, with significant results for their status in nationalist India; a boycott of British goods proved effective; and outbreaks of violence, including a serious rising in the Frontier Province, made further difficulties for the administration without unduly embarrassing the civil disobedience movement.

The Simon Commission's report did little to still the storm, since it proposed self-government for the provinces alone and suggested, in what seemed like a plan for indefinite postpone-ment, that responsible government at the centre should wait upon a federation joined by the princes. Having persuaded the 'moderate' parties that the government would not be bound by

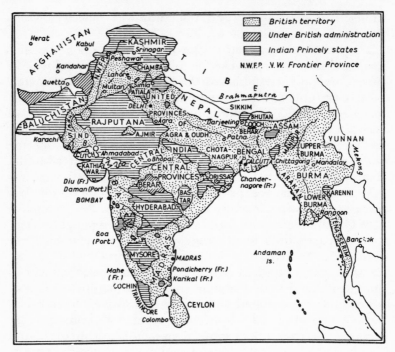

Map 6 INDIA UNDER BRITISH RULE IN THE TWENTIETH CENTURY
(based on the map 'India in the twentieth century', from the *Oxford History of India*, third edition, p. 899)

the recommendations in the Simon Report, Lord Irwin, the Viceroy (1926–31), got them to attend a round-table conference, and this concluded on January 19th, 1931, with a statement from the British prime minister, Ramsay MacDonald, that 'with the legislature constituted on a federal basis', the government 'would be prepared to recognize the principle of the responsibility of the executive to the legislature'. Gandhi and other Congress leaders were immediately released and Irwin began talks with Gandhi that ended in the celebrated Gandhi–Irwin truce, under which the campaign of civil disobedience came to an end, all political prisoners but those convicted of crimes of violence were released, and Congress agreed to be represented – by Gandhi alone, Congress subsequently decided – at a second round-table conference. Gandhi himself had been convinced of the Viceroy's good will and was prepared to put his conviction to the test.

Before the conference met, however, communal rioting at Cawnpore had embittered the Muslims, the execution of Bhagat Singh for terrorism in the Punjab had inflamed a substantial body of Congress opinion, and in Britain itself the financial crisis had led to the fall of the Labour government and its replacement by a Conservative-dominated 'national' administration. Congress and authority were moving further apart at the same time as they were preparing to consider moving closer together.

'We were not joining the Round Table Conference to talk interminably about the petty details of a constitution,' Jawaharlal Nehru was subsequently to write. 'We were not interested in those details at that stage, and they could only be considered when some agreement on fundamental matters had been arrived at with the British Government. The real question was how much power was to be transferred to a democratic India. Any solicitor almost could do the drafting and the settlement of details afterwards ... The British Government had, however, no intention of falling in with our wishes in the matter. Their policy was to postpone the consideration of fundamental questions and to make the Conference exhaust itself, more or less, on minor and immaterial matters. Even when major matters were considered, the Government held its hand, refused to commit itself, and promised to express its opinion after mature consideration later on. Their trump card was, of course, the communal issue and they played it for all it was worth. It dominated the Conference.' [1]

Certainly, the British government – as it would do so often in the future, when dealing with nationalist struggles in Africa – disguised its unwillingness to grant effective self-government in a careful playing for time, a concocting of provisos and safeguards. The Indian participants, some of them representing particular interests like industry and the large landowners, with not a few representing only themselves, failed to agree on a formula for communal representation in the legislatures, and the British were compelled to make their own award. Gandhi's presence at the Conference had stimulated mass interest in its

[1] *Jawaharlal Nehru: An Autobiography*, pp. 291-2.

proceedings, and its failure accordingly caused all the greater disillusionment and dismay. The British government resolved upon repression, arrested the leaders of Congress including Gandhi, and proscribed Congress itself, while terrorism reappeared in Bengal, a 'no rent' campaign by the peasants in the United Provinces commenced, and civil disobedience revived. In April 1932 almost 35,000 people went to jail for breaking the law; but the administration did not crack. By July the number of new political prisoners had fallen to less than 4,700, and the civil disobedience campaign trickled to an end, leaving the country exhausted and sullen.

Meanwhile the large Muslim minority – in 1941 it numbered some 92 million people or 24 per cent of India's total population – was being drawn by its leadership ever further from the nationalism of Congress and ever nearer to the policy of separatism that would end with the partition of the country and the establishment of Pakistan in 1947. The natural leaders of the community, the princes, landowners and intellectuals, had stood aloof from Congress in its early days and, having watched it become in consequence dominantly Hindu, had taken fright at its developing influence. It was this fright that had led to the founding of the All-India Muslim League in 1906 and stimulated a Muslim deputation, with the Aga Khan at its head, to approach Lord Minto and demand separate Muslim electorates if any form of representative government was introduced, on the grounds that the Muslims were generally poorer than the Hindus and would therefore be swamped in any franchise system qualified by income. The outbreak of the First World War and the hostilities between Britain and Turkey had then submerged fear of Hindu rule in pan-Islamic sentiment, and for a short time the two communities had joined in a common resistance to British rule. But the culmination of this partnership, the campaign of non-cooperation led by Gandhi in 1920-2, had been the prelude to its dissolution. The success of Kemal Atatürk in promoting a resurgent and secular Turkey, with the deposition of the Sultan in 1923 and the abolition of the *Khilafat* itself in 1924, had swept all conservative Muslim support from the alliance with Congress – the British had again become the safeguard against Hindu domination rather than the enemy of Islam – and only the Westernized Muslims, reinforced in their secular approach by Ataturk himself, had remained attached or at least friendly to Congress.

Of these last, unquestionably the most distinguished was Mohammad Ali Jinnah from Bombay. He had been largely responsible for bringing Congress and the Muslim League closer together, and had himself been a member of Congress till the celebrated Calcutta meeting of 1920, which had initiated the era of Gandhi's leadership with its appeal to the Hindu masses, its stress on the wearing of *khadi*, its increasing use of Hindi at Congress meetings, its employment of *satyagraha* as sanctioned by Hindu doctrine and tradition. For the truth is, ironically, and tragically, that it was Gandhi, the passionate apostle of Indian unity, who did most, by the very character of his leadership, to divide the Indians; who, by giving the Congress struggle a peculiarly Hindu cast, antagonized the Muslims at the same time as he attracted the Hindus. Jinnah's break with Congress was at first far from complete. As leader of the Independent Party in the Legislative Assembly, with thirty seats at his command, he held the balance of power and frequently allied himself with the Congress Swarajists to secure a government defeat. Not irrelevantly, Gandhi himself was in political retirement at the time, and the Swarajist leaders, C. R. Das and Motilal Nehru, gave Congress a more secular appearance. But as constitutional reforms brought the possibility of self-rule nearer, as Gandhi once more took control of Congress, and Muslim fears, heightened by communal clashes, promoted the search for Muslim unity, Jinnah moved further away from Congress. Had Britain acted with speed and imagination to grant India a democratic government, Hindu and Muslim might well have found in practice the national unity that evaded them in principle. But with each new discussion of communal safeguards, each new delay in political concessions, communal identification and communal suspicions increased. In 1934 Jinnah, who had retired from active politics three years before, emerged to lead a reorganized and much stronger Muslim League. The virtually united Muslim community – only a few nationalist Muslims, of much individual distinction but little influence, remained in Congress – pressed for communal representation in government service as well as the electoral system, and sought a federal constitution with a weak centre and autonomy in the Muslim-dominated areas. In 1930 the Muslim leader Sir Muhammad Iqbal had suggested the union of the Frontier Province, Baluchistan, Sind and Kashmir into a Muslim state within an Indian federation, and in 1933 Choudhri Rahmat Ali had developed this idea at Cambridge with a proposal for the establishment of Pakistan – P for the Punjab, A for the Afghans in the Frontier Province, K for Kashmir, S for Sind, and the whole word meaning 'Land of the Pure'. Under the leadership of Jinnah, this demand would become the declared aim of the League in 1940 and be realized with the partition of India in 1947.

Britain's communal award of August 4th, 1932, was followed by the Poona Pact of September 24th that year, which secured general as well as special representation for the depressed or 'scheduled' classes under threat of a fast to death by Gandhi. Then at last, on August 4th, 1935, the Government of India Act, embodying the new set of constitutional reforms, with all their careful provisos and safeguards, became law. The new constitution was federal, with three detailed lists of legislative powers – federal, provincial and concurrent – and a federal court for interpretation and the settlement of disputes; but the new central executive depended upon accession by the princely states, and until then, the old central government was to continue operating. The immediately important innovation was the introduction of responsible government in the provinces, with the disappearance of dyarchy and the arrival of ministerial administration appointed by the governor but responsible to a popularly elected assembly. Governors, unless their reserved powers were invaded, were required to act on the advice of the provincial premiers, and even at the centre, where dyarchy now appeared, ministers dependent upon popular support controlled all except defence and foreign affairs, for which the Governor-General appointed counsellors. The new popular assemblies in the provinces were backed by new electorates, based on a small property qualification but now expanded to include some thirty million voters, including women, or nearly a sixth of the country's adult population; and Muslims in all the provinces, Sikhs in the Punjab, Christians mainly in Madras, and Europeans mainly in Bengal received special representation.

The reforms marked a clear advance towards self-government, but were still very far from granting dominion status. The Viceroy remained a combination of prime minister and head of state, and one responsible not to the Indian people but to the British Cabinet; at the centre he controlled the reserved departments, could certify legislation in the form of 'Governor-General's Acts', and could issue ordinances with the force of law for six months at a time. Even in the provinces the governors had powers to discharge their 'special responsibilities' like the protection of minorities, and in the event of an administrative breakdown might exercise legislative authority themselves. The British still controlled the Imperial Civil Service and the police force, members of which could be directed but not dismissed, and who therefore retained a clear degree of independence. Finally, federal legislation, once the federal legislature was brought into being by princely co-operation, would be subject to 'refusal of assent or reservation by the Governor-General, acting under the control of the Secretary of State'.

The requisite proportion of princely states never in fact acceded, the projected federal legislature was never formed, and government at the centre continued under the control of an irresponsible executive, while the provisions for communal representation reinforced Muslim separatism. The constitution in practice, therefore, formalized division in India without promoting any real opportunity for the settlement of differences.

What the reforms did achieve was a dampening of Congress resistance. They offered a possibility of peaceful progress to independence and assisted Gandhi in preserving his non-violent policy. Tension would fluctuate in the next twelve years and Congress resort to unconstitutional pressures, but revolution would never become a serious prospect.

The Muslim League was critical of the Act, but agreed to give it a trial, and though Congress condemned the Act altogether, it allowed itself to be persuaded into working the provincial reforms. Elections to the Central Assembly in 1935 took place on a restricted franchise but none the less gave Congress 44 seats of the 104 elective ones, to reveal the movement's dominance of the Hindu community. The provincial elections of February 1937, on the new wide franchise, produced even more marked a success: Congress secured clear majorities in five of the

eleven provinces and in addition was able to form a ministry in
Bombay with the help of supporters, while its Pathan allies
in the North-West Frontier Province were swept into power.
Only Bengal, where a Muslim coalition ministry took office,
and the Punjab, where the inter-communal Unionist Party of
rural interests secured a majority, disappointed the Congress
leadership.

Until the outbreak of the Second World War the Congress
ministries worked smoothly, but Congress itself did not disband
its national organization nor cease its campaign against the
irresponsible central executive. In fact, the principal Congress
leaders did not take provincial office and exercised the stric-
test discipline over those of their colleagues who did through
the Congress Working Committee, which determined the
patterns of policy and supervised the functioning of the provincial ministries. Under Gandhi himself, who held no official
position in Congress but continued to dominate it, four other
men, of different opinions and appeal, enjoyed considerable
influence – Jawaharlal Nehru, a democratic socialist and
agnostic, whose background, education and manner made him
the natural leader of the Westernized nationalists, whose participation in the no-rent campaign of the early 'thirties had
turned him into the hero of the landless peasantry in the United
Provinces, and whose close relationship to Gandhi seemed to
promise him the secular succession in an independent India;
Rajendra Prasad, who represented the conservative nationalism
and orthodoxy of the Hindu heartland; Sārdar Vallabhbhai
Patel, spokesman of the Indian business classes and the natural
leader, with his powerful personality and administrative gifts,
of the Congress right wing; and the Bengali, Subash Chandra
Bose, who spoke for the militant left. At the end of 1937 Bose
succeeded Nehru as Congress President, but in 1939 he broke
with Gandhi, resigned from Congress to form the Forward
Bloc, adopted a policy of violent resistance to the British, and
left India during the Second World War to broadcast from
Germany and organize the Indian National Army out of
Indian prisoners of war in Japan. Rajendra Prasad would be-
come the first President of independent India; Nehru, Prime
Minister for some fifteen years; and Patel, the Minister of Home
Affairs, who would supervise in a few short years after indepen-

dence, with ruthless efficiency, the integration of the princely states.

The Congress Working Committee regarded and conducted itself as a kind of nationalist Shadow Cabinet, while Congress as a movement claimed to represent all the Indian people, whatever their religious affiliations. No separate Muslim representation in the legislatures was therefore necessary, the Congress leadership declared, and no coalition between Congress and the Muslim League could properly be entertained. Jinnah, however, saw Congress as a Hindu, not a national, organization, and the Muslim League as its Muslim equivalent. He had campaigned during the elections of 1937 for independent co-operation with Congress in Hindu-dominated provinces through coalition government. 'There is really no substantial difference between the League and Congress,' he had proclaimed. 'We shall always be glad to co-operate with Congress in their constructive programme.' Perhaps, if Congress had taken him at his word, some bridge, however rickety, might have been built between the two communities and the partition of India been avoided. In the event, however, the hostility of Congress to any coalition with the League, its policy of speaking for all Indian nationalism, antagonized the Muslim leaders even further and confirmed them in their suspicion that Congress rule would mean Hindu dominance. Jinnah turned his attention to arousing the Muslim masses, and after the Congress ministries resigned in October 1939, he proclaimed 'a day of deliverance and thanksgiving as a mark of relief'.

When the Second World War broke out in September 1939, the Congress leadership was uncertain and divided over its proper response.

War and India. What were we to do? For years past we had thought about this and proclaimed our policy. Yet in spite of all this, the British Government declared India to be a belligerent country without any reference to our people, to the Central Assembly, or to the Provincial Governments. That was a slight hard to get over, for it signified that imperialism functioned as before. The Congress Working Committee issued a long statement in the middle of September 1939, in which our past and present policy was defined and the

British Government was invited to explain their war aims, more particularly in regard to British Imperialism. We had frequently condemned Fascism and Nazism but we were more intimately concerned with the imperialism that dominated over us. Was this imperialism to go? Did they recognize the independence of India and her right to frame her own constitution through a Constituent Assembly? What immediate steps would be taken to introduce popular control of the Central Government? ... The British Government's answer was clear. It left no doubt that they were not prepared to clarify their war aims or to hand over control of the Government to the people's representatives. The old order continued, and was to continue, and British interests in India could not be left unprotected. The Congress Ministries in the Provinces thereupon resigned as they were not prepared to co-operate on these terms in the prosecution of the war. The Constitution was suspended and autocratic rule was re-established.[1]

For a while after the fall of France, Congress hostility to Britain was muted, and few if any of the Congress Working Committee members supported Gandhi in his pacifist stand. Men of Nehru's background and beliefs especially were anxious to assist in the fight against fascism but not unreasonably wished first to be assured that in doing so they would not be strengthening a Britain they would later have to fight themselves. If India were granted independence, then Indians would gladly rally to Britain's side; as enemies of Britain still in the struggle for independence, they could hardly transform themselves into passionate allies. The British War Cabinet replied with the 'August offer', which promised that the post-war constitution would be devised by an Indian constituent assembly; but there was no indication of how such an assembly would be composed, and whether any new constitution would be more than just another qualified advance towards independence. Britain had not collapsed to German power, and there seemed a decreasing danger that she would do so; was she not just playing for time till she was strong enough again to maintain her Indian empire intact against popular pressures? Congress demanded an

[1] *Jawaharlal Nehru: An Autobiography*, pp. 608–9.

immediate settlement on the basis of independence between
'India as represented by Congress, and England'.[1] Britain rejected the demand, and the Muslim League, recently furnished
with its Pakistan ideal, insisted that any national government
should be controlled equally by Congress and the League.
Congress returned to the direction of Gandhi, who preached
pacificism and conducted civil disobedience in support of his
right to do so; but the campaign never reached the heights of its
predecessors, and after its climb in May 1941 to the imprisonment of some 14,000 Congressmen, slid to a stop.

Meanwhile the entry of Japan into the war, with its threat
to India itself, had produced new pressures for a settlement,
and these pressures were reinforced by President Roosevelt.
On March 11th, 1942, the British Prime Minister announced the
dispatch of Sir Stafford Cripps, a Cabinet Minister, to India
with a new offer, promising an Indian dominion, with the right
to secede from the Commonwealth, as soon as possible after the
war, and proposing as a means to this end a constituent assembly,
elected by the provincial legislatures in the shape of an electoral
college, which would negotiate a treaty with the British government. The only rider was the right of any province to reject the
constitution and 'retain its present constitutional position,
provision being made for its subsequent accession if it so
desires'.

Nehru was sympathetic to the proposal but Gandhi was not,
and many of the Congress leaders in between, like Maulana
Azad, the Muslim President of Congress at the time, insisted on
an immediate earnest in the establishment of Cabinet rule.

I had not objected to Cripps's basic principle that independence would be recognized after the war. I felt, however,
that unless *de facto* power and responsibility were given to
the [Executive] Council during the war, the change would
not be significant. During my first interview with him,
Cripps had given me an assurance on the point and said that
the Council would act like a Cabinet. In the course of discussion, it became clear that this was a poetic exaggeration.

An even greater snag was the option given to the Provinces
to stay outside the Union ... Cripps tried to persuade me that

[1] Gandhi, reported in the *News Chronicle*, August 14th, 1940.

the Indian political problem could not be solved till the communal problem was settled. This could be done in one of two ways. One was to settle it forthwith. The other was to defer a decision till after the war, when power would be in Indian hands. Cripps said that in his opinion it would be wrong to raise the issue at present ... I told Cripps that the right given to the Provinces to opt out meant opening the door to separation.[1]

The Congress leaders rejected the Cripps plan and fell in behind Gandhi, who declared that the British presence in India was a provocation to the Japanese and demanded that the British withdraw at once or face new civil disobedience. 'There is no question of one more chance,' he proclaimed. 'After all, this is open rebellion.' On August 7th, the All-India Congress Committee gave its approval to his 'Quit India' campaign, and the Viceroy acted at once. The whole Working Committee, with Gandhi himself, was arrested and interned at Poona. A short but sharp outbreak of violence followed; police stations and government buildings were set on fire, railway lines disrupted, and British officials assaulted and killed; by the end, some nine hundred lives had been lost and more than a million pounds' worth of damage had been done. But yet again the firmness of the government survived all threats to it. And meanwhile, with the Congress leadership in jail, the Muslim League increased its hold over the Muslim masses and strengthened its bargaining position.

War at first brought commercial and industrial prosperity to India, which was the supply base for the Middle East. New steel plants were constructed, the production of cement and textiles enormously increased, the country's deposits of bauxite were developed to create a new aluminium industry, and the mica industry was urgently expanded. The peace-time army of 175,000 was increased till more than 2,000,000 men were under arms, while the whole force was mechanized and the necessary technicians trained; the navy was improved into a substantial and efficient force, able to play an important part in the Burma campaign; and an air force of effective fighting power was

[1] Maulana Abul Kalam Azad, *India Wins Freedom* (Orient Longmans, 1959), pp. 57–8.

created. The war with Japan, however, placed severe strains on the economy, now geared to the whole war effort and not merely to the campaigns in the Middle East. The transport system was inadequate to meet all demands upon it, and the large sums of money spent by Britain and America in military preparations caused a rise in prices from which the country had so far been in the main exempt. Food shortages developed, hoarding sharpened the crisis, and by the summer of 1943 Bengal was in the grip of famine. The British army undertook relief administration, and rationing was introduced in the larger towns, but hundreds of thousands starved to death. By the end of the war, the economic gilt had worn thin and patchy. Moreover, the large increase in the Indian armed forces, so needful during the war, represented a threat in a peace-time of renewed Congress struggle. The loyalty of the new troops could clearly not be assured, as the naval mutiny of 1946 would show.

A new Viceroy, Lord Wavell (1943–7), set out to reconcile Hindu and Muslim opinion in a national administration to help conclude the war with Japan and then organize the Cripps-promised Constituent Assembly; but negotiations faltered and fell apart over the allotment of seats in the Executive Council and the refusal of Congress to accept the League as the sole representative of India's Muslims. Wavell called a general election for the winter of 1945–6 to test the extent of League support, and it became clear that the League dominated the Muslims as completely as Congress dominated the Hindus. In the pivotal province of the Punjab, the Unionist Party was all but eliminated, and could survive in office only with open Congress support.

On July 26th, 1945, the Labour Party had decisively won the British elections, and Clement Attlee, who had been a member of the Simon Commission, replaced Churchill as prime minister. The new British government now intervened and dispatched to India in April 1946 a Cabinet mission led by Lord Pethick-Lawrence, Secretary of State for India, with Sir Stafford Cripps and A. V. Alexander. In May the mission published its report, to propose a federal union of the provinces – the princely states were to be included after negotiation – with powers over foreign affairs, defence and communications.

Individual provinces could form subordinate unions of their own, and these would determine the extent of the powers they would exercise outside those in federal hands. To bring this about, a constituent assembly, representing all parties, would be convened, and meanwhile a national government would be established to secure the transition. To proposals for partition, the mission was strongly opposed. The Pakistan demanded by the Muslim League would contain a non-Muslim minority of 37 per cent in the west and 48 per cent in the east, leaving 20 million Muslims in Hindu India, while a smaller Pakistan (the one which exists today) was regarded by the League itself as 'quite impracticable'. In any event, a smaller Pakistan would require the partitioning of Assam, Bengal and the Punjab, a measure which, in the judgment of the mission, 'would be contrary to the wishes of a very large percentage of these provinces'.

Both Congress and the League accepted the proposals of the mission as a basis for settlement, but rancour soon revived over a press conference given by Nehru, as President of Congress, in Bombay on July 10th, at which he declared, in reply to a question, that Congress would enter a constituent assembly 'completely unfettered by agreements and free to meet all situations as they arise'. Congress had agreed only to participate in the constituent assembly and considered itself free to change or modify the Cabinet mission plan as it thought best. The statement was unwise and certainly inaccurate, since Congress had in fact accepted the plan as a whole and was accordingly bound by all its provisions; but Nehru's longing for a strongly centralized and secular government, with his belief in the basic weakness of the League and its leadership, had led him to a premature revelation of his objective – to expel British power and then enforce national unity by popular demand. Jinnah immediately declared that Congress intended to change the mission plan through its majority in the constituent assembly; at the end of July the Muslim League formally rejected the plan and resolved to use direct action for the achievement of Pakistan. The Congress Working Committee met and reaffirmed acceptance of the mission plan in its entirety – a clear contradiction of Nehru's statement without actually saying so – but the League was now adamant.

'If the Muslim League accepted our Resolution', Azad was later to write, 'it could return to the early position without any loss of prestige. Mr Jinnah did not however accept the position and held that Jawaharlal's statement represented the real mind of Congress. He argued that if Congress could change so many times, while the British were still in the country and power had not come to its hands, what assurance could the minorities have that once the British left, Congress would not again change and go back to the position taken up in Jawaharlal's statement?'[1]

On August 12th the Viceroy invited Nehru to form a government, and though Nehru went to see Jinnah and offered him a choice of places in the Executive Council, Jinnah would have nothing to do with the implementation of the mission plan. Instead he declared August 16th 'Direct Action Day'. A four-day riot followed in Calcutta, claiming – in the estimate of Lord Pethick-Lawrence – 'some five thousand dead and fifteen thousand wounded'. Retaliation against Muslims by Hindus swept Bihar, and violence spread to East Bengal and the United Provinces. Without the intervention of Gandhi, who visited areas of communal distraction and protected Muslims against Hindu attack, the wave of arson and murder might have swept further than it did; as it was, all hope of a peaceful settlement between Muslim and Hindu now vanished, and partition became inevitable. In October the League joined the Executive Council; but it soon became evident that Jinnah's representatives had come to sabotage and not to strengthen the government. With possession of the Finance portfolio – held by Liaqat Ali Khan – which Congress had offered as a gesture of conciliation without sufficiently considering the consequences, they were able to intervene in the conduct of every department and dictate overall policy. Jinnah's tactics were masterly: his representatives should obstruct all government, so that the leadership of Congress itself would be frustrated into choosing partition as the only way of ever achieving effective power. Rapidly the patience of the Congress leaders wore thin. In December the constituent assembly met, but the League boycotted its sessions; Nehru found himself in constant danger from League supporters when he visited the North-West Frontier Province in the same month; early in 1947 the Congress-

[1] *India Wins Freedom*, pp. 157–8.

backed minority government of the Punjab fell and the province had to be governed by emergency powers to prevent
civil war.

The British government decided to intervene and summoned
Nehru, Sardar Baldev Singh, a Sikh leader, and Jinnah, now
called *Quaid-i-Azam* or 'great leader' by his followers, to London;
but the discussions proved futile. Attlee attempted shock tactics
and announced in the House of Commons on February 20th
that Britain would leave India 'by a date not later than June
1948'. Lord Mountbatten would succeed Lord Wavell as
Viceroy, and was charged with the task of supervising an
ordered transfer of power. But not even the prospect of a
political vacuum could draw the raging communities together,
and Mountbatten arrived in India to find, in his own words,
a 'terrible pendulum of massacres swinging wider and wider'.
He himself believed that the proper solution lay in a united
India, but the Muslim League insisted upon Pakistan, and
though Congress was not prepared to cede large non-Muslim
areas to a Muslim state, it increasingly saw partition as the only
alternative to prolonged civil war, and in May itself proposed
the division of the Punjab to avoid further loss of human life.
Mountbatten told Jinnah that Congress had provisionally
agreed to partition.

> ... he was overjoyed. When I said that it logically followed
> that this would involve partition of the Punjab and Bengal
> he was horrified. He produced the strongest arguments why
> these provinces should not be partitioned. He said they had
> national characteristics and that partition would be dis-
> astrous. I agreed, but I said how much more must I now feel
> that the same considerations applied to the partitioning of
> the whole of India. He did not like that, and started explain-
> ing why India had to be partitioned, and so we went round
> and round the mulberry bush until finally he realized that
> either he could have a United India with an unpartitioned
> Punjab and Bengal or a divided India with a partitioned
> Punjab and Bengal, and he finally accepted the latter
> solution.[1]

[1] Address to the Royal Empire Society in London, October 6th, 1948.

On June 3rd Mountbatten announced that the British government had accepted the principle of partition and had resolved to withdraw its authority from India on August 14th, some ten weeks away. The provinces of the Punjab and Bengal would be partitioned provided that their Legislative Assemblies, voting if necessary by communities, asked for this, and boundary commissions would determine the dividing lines. British treaties with the princely states, and so British paramountcy, would come to an end, and though the states would then in theory be independent, they could hardly survive in that condition for long and were strongly advised by Britain to associate themselves with one or other of the two new dominions.

In an atmosphere of mounting emergency, the Legislative Assemblies of Bengal and the Punjab voted for partition, the boundary commissions made their awards, and the two nations prepared themselves for power. As the calendar leaves left before the declaration of independence were one by one torn off and crumpled, tension rose in the partitioned areas. The Indian Army was split, with one-quarter going to Pakistan and three-quarters to India; services and finances, assets and liabilities, were proportionately divided. On August 15th, 1947, India and Pakistan came into existence as independent states within the Commonwealth; Mountbatten became Governor-General of India at the request of Congress, with Nehru as prime minister; Jinnah himself became Governor-General of Pakistan, and chose as the prime minister his trusted lieutenant, Liaqat Ali Khan. Gandhi could not reconcile himself to what he had called the 'vivisection' of India, and he refused to attend the independence celebrations in Delhi; instead he went to Bengal, in preparation for the communal violence that he knew would come. In the new India, forty million Muslims waited, stunned and now feeling themselves defenceless, while in the new Pakistan the Sikh and Hindu minorities prepared to stay or suddenly to leave. Partition had separated the communities tidily on paper; in towns and villages the untidy left-overs survived. Someone somewhere lifted a knife or lit a match, and in the weeks that followed a fury of murder and burning, rape and pillage swept across the partitioned provinces. On September 20th Gandhi told a prayer meeting that a convoy fifty-seven miles long was journeying towards India from West Punjab.

'It makes my brain reel to think that can be. Such a thing is unparalleled in the history of the world, and it makes me, as it should make you, hang my head in shame.' Seemingly endless lines of refugees crept painfully from Pakistan to India, from India to Pakistan. Some say ten million, some say fifteen million people abandoned their homes in the two states, leaving un-numbered thousands of dead behind them. Without the inter-vention of Gandhi, who stilled the rage in Calcutta by beginning a fast to death, humanity in Bengal may have been ripped apart even more terribly than it was. And on the afternoon of January 30th, 1948, Gandhi was assassinated in Delhi by a high-caste Hindu journalist, inflamed by reports of Muslim atrocities against Hindus.

CHAPTER THREE

THE CHARACTER OF CUSTOM

I T seems to me undeniable that a people has its individual character, its peculiar capacity for trust or suspicion, kindness or cruelty, energy or lassitude. There are, of course, innumerable exceptions, but on the whole the Ghanaian is a different sort of person from the Frenchman, the German from the Pakistani, the Indian from the Nigerian or Swede. A bus strike in London is quite different from a bus strike in Rome, and a farmer in France treats his animals differently from the way that a farmer in Bengal or Gujarat does.

This is not, of course, because the Indian is generally shorter and darker than the Frenchman – though there are still men and women sufficiently primitive to think so – or because the Roman has naturally stronger sexual urges than the Londoner (a proposition that is popular but, on such evidence as exists, scarcely tenable). The Indian is a different sort of person from the Frenchman because his history has been different, his culture is different, his political and economic experience has been different, his relationships to his family, his neighbours, his people and his world are different. If his character is peculiar, it is because his customs are peculiar, the consequence of different events, sanctions and ideas. He behaves in a particular way because he is expected -- and educated – by his context to behave in such a way. It is not his blood or the shape of his skull, but his society, that makes him broadly different. And because he is part of society, however paltry a part, he in turn confirms the broad difference of his society by accepting and transmitting it.

This is not to suggest that given an identical environment, all human beings would be carbon copies of a single script, typed by an average hand. The creative imagination would not become as common as fingers, and tempers would never become equally even. But the broad 'racial' and 'popular' differences of conduct and attitude, now so apparently immutable, would soon enough diminish and eventually disappear. Jews today remain Jews wherever they live to the degree that they accept traditional Jewish sanctions and standards of behaviour. But German Jews who adopt German standards and English Jews who adopt English standards are more unlike each other than they are alike. The Eichmann trial stunned the younger Israelis because the evidence revealed how millions of European Jews had gone unprotestingly into the concentration camps and gas chambers. Why had they not resisted, fought those who came to arrest them, at least rushed their guards at the entrance to the gas chambers, so that they could die at some cost to their killers? Instead, outside of the Warsaw ghetto, the Jewish experience of Nazism in Europe had been one of fundamental acceptance, a fatalistic capacity for suffering that centuries of persecution had shaped. The Israelis sixteen years ago, menaced by Arab armies, had acted very differently, and the Israelis today believe that they would have acted just as differently had they been menaced by Nazism in Europe. They cannot know, however, because they are no longer Jews, they are Israelis. Their character is different because their circumstances are different, because their relationship to the land, to themselves and to their neighbours is different, because Jewish customs and Israeli customs are not the same.

All this has been said before, but needs saying again here, for the character of India today significantly results from the peculiar character of its people, and to see the problems of Indian development as solely economic and political, and not as social and psychological also, is to mistake the shape for the body. However dependent social and psychological attitudes and behaviour may be on economic and political conditions, they possess a creative faculty in their very dependence, like one half of a mating. They can help to change, or they can help to freeze, their economic and political context.

One of the most important studies of India to emerge from the years of independence is *Blossoms in the Dust* by Kusum Nair, an Indian sociologist who travelled through rural India for one year from August 1958, visiting villages in different states to measure 'the impact of deliberate development on the individual men and women who make up India's millions'. Her discoveries were little short of terrifying.

In the *Harijan* colony of the village of Kabistalam [in Madras], they are all landless but like everyone else in this district are engaged in rice culture. In fact they are the primary producers, being the ultimate 'hired' who actually work in the fields – gaunt faces, thin black bodies, all shirtless, their children with matted hair, in scanty rags or completely naked; in the background, mud walls under straw roofs and dark interiors with little in them beside a few pieces of unglazed pottery. Could they conceivably find life so comfortable that they do not want more?

'If the government were to offer to give you as much land as you want, absolutely free of any charge, how much would you ask for?' I ask them. I repeat and clearly explain the magnanimous offer.

'You would like to have land of your own, wouldn't you?'

'Yes.' Many heads nod.

'Then how much?'

Samu is the first to speak. He is an old man. He has never possessed any land. There are five members in his family. But he wants only one and one-third acres. He is precise. Even from that, he says after some mental calculation, he would be prepared to share 50 per cent of the produce with the *mirasdar* (landlord). Rangarajan is middle-aged, tall and slim. He also has five in his family to feed, and two acres would suffice. Manickam, with six in the family, already has three acres on lease. If he could, he would like to add to it two more acres. Srinivasan looks an artist. He wears a beard and shoulder-length hair. No, he is a mere labourer, has four in the family, wants just two acres and is prepared to share the produce on a 50/50 basis. Vidival is a young man, clean-shaven, one eye defective. I look to him more hopefully. But no, he also wants only two acres on a 60/40 basis. Govindan is already the proud cultivator of ·03 acre which he has on lease. He has six in the family, wants only two acres and will be prepared to give 40 per cent of the produce to the landlord. Ammavin also is a young man, clean-shaven and wearing a

comparatively white *dhoti*. He has six in the family. With
obvious hesitation he makes bold to ask for three acres, the
produce of which he is prepared to share on a 60/40 basis.
And finally, it is the same story with another young hopeful – Velayuthan. There are nine in the family, and at
present they are cultivating ·3 acre. Yet he asks for only
three acres on a 60/40 basis.

'Are you sure you would not like to have more?' I ask
again incredulously.

Yes, they are sure, quite sure.[1]

I have seen slums in South Africa that looked like a disease
of the earth, with the rusted tin and boxwood shanties rotting
where they stood. But they have seemed, somehow, all the same,
human habitations, with children making the movements and
noises of children, with an essentially human resistance in the
flash of a newly washed white sheet seen through a doorway or
the violence of a woman's stride across the street. In India I
saw slums that were like some disease of humanity itself, with
men and women and children in the still shapes of their septic
acceptance.

In the busy city of Bombay, there is a place called Abhyudaya
Nagar, the Township of Prosperity, where a clump of four- and
five-storey blocks of flats, built once – I was told – to assist in
slum clearance, now shelters the less affluent, or more thrifty,
members of the middle class. Around its edges there clings –
no, not clings, for clinging is a vivid movement – sprawls a
slum in which ten or fifteen thousand people – nobody knows
how many – marvellously survive. When I visited it, on a dry
winter day of December, small signposts of flies stood buzzing
over the piles of human waste and garbage everywhere around,
while in between the rotting shanties were streams of open
sewage, and a smell of decay, sweet and pungent, overwhelmed
the air. In the centre of the slum there had recently been a deep
pool of refuse, but a man had fallen into it and drowned, and
the authorities had stirred at last to fill it with sand and level
the ground. Now a huge mound of refuse had taken its place,
swelling as one watched it. When the monsoon rains swept
Bombay, I was told and could easily believe it, the slum became

[1] *Blossoms in the Dust*, pp. 30–31.

a knee-deep bog of filth, with the flies like a dark fog hovering over it. No one, sanity would suppose, could live here from choice. Yet the inhabitants, my trade-unionist guides informed me, were paying up to 1,000 rupees – (over £75), a small fortune to the poverty of India's poor – for occupation rights, and 8 to 10 rupees (almost 15s.) a month in rent for a shack. Perhaps my guides exaggerated; perhaps they meant half, or even a quarter, of what they said. All the same, it seemed to me, no more corrosive commentary on the conditions of Bombay's over four hundred thousand pavement-dwellers could be imagined than that this vast cesspool should be relatively desirable, a costly escape.

I don't know what I expected from the people of the place – I started searching for reactions only when I found none – anger, I suppose, and a scarcely concealed hatred, a frenzied gaiety perhaps, with a hint of violence and cruelty. What I never expected, from my African experience, was the indifference, the stridently silent lassitude of body and mind. There seemed to be no movement in the place apart from that which I and my companions made; we might have been walking through a series of photographs. I remember especially one gaunt old woman, who was leaning against the doorway of her shack, and whose huge eyes did not flicker as we wandered past, hardly a yard from her face. These were people who seemed to have given up living while they were still alive. I used to think that hatred was degrading. But there is no degradation like indifference. Hatred is human. Indifference is the final denial of humanity.

Stories of encounters with Indian fatalism are inescapable. During my own stay in India I must have heard a dozen times or more of car accidents, where the man – sometimes drunk, sometimes not – lying in the middle of the road had swayed to his feet and, when questioned or abused, shrugged his shoulders or simply wandered off to the pavement to lie down again. One such casualty had given a sort of brusque Hindi paraphrase of Hamlet's perception: 'If it be now, 'tis not to come; if it be not to come, it will be now; if it be not now, yet it will come: the readiness is all.' The British newspaper correspondent who had been driving the car had found this composed comment even more unnerving than the accident itself. A short while later he had met the same composure, though this time unspoken. He had gone shopping with his two young sons and passed a figure squatting in an alley with all but the two sunken black eyes concealed in rags. The younger of the boys had darted up to the shape, peered into the wrapped-up face, and suddenly shouted 'Boo!' The wide-open eyes had stared back unblinking, and the boy had fled back to his father. When I heard the story on a hot winter afternoon, with the crows raucously wheeling over the lawn in front of the correspondent's modern home, I shuddered with an ageless terror in the presence of the strange. 'In Africa,' I said with a nervous laugh, 'the figure would have leapt up and shouted "Boo!" back. Then your son would have had reason enough to run.' But I knew that I, like the boy, would then have been much less afraid.

Indian fatalism, whether the root or the foliage of Hinduism, is plainly an essential part of the growth. The scriptural injunctions to pursue the *dharma* of one's caste and condition uncomplainingly, to cultivate the capacity to act without desire, the interpretation of life as a necessary trial with the verdict contained in a subsequent incarnation, all make of indifference the ultimate Hindu virtue. The whole system of caste nourishes resignation. A western psychologist, with unusual experience of Indian society, has described the inducements to conformity:

> Acceptance of one's place in the caste system was unquestioning. It was a part of the order of nature. As a consequence of this, there was little room for ambition. A Rajput might be (and generally was) proud of the reputation of his clan; but only rarely could he hope to add to it with a conspicuous feat of valour. A Bania might hope to amass a fortune and to have his death celebrated with prodigiously meritorious feasts, but he would always remain a merchant: whereas a Brahmin was born already a god, and his only ambition was to attain Release. The new non-hereditary occupations cut across these old forms, but in the village at least each person has the assurance of knowing that if he refuses to compete, preferring to conform to his traditional caste role, he will be able to perform a task which is not exacting and can rely on the approval

and ultimately the support of his fellows, even though his material rewards may be pitifully small. The old system puts a premium on conformity at the expense of personal initiative: the individual achieves integration and stability in his life habits by adhering to the pattern of his enveloping society, rather than by asserting his own personality.[1]

A walk through a typical Indian bazaar is a journey among the myriad stratifications of caste. A row of cobblers gives sudden place to a row of cloth-merchants, which then stops short before a row of jewellers, and though each cobbler looks quite different from each cloth-merchant and jeweller, the cobblers themselves, like the cloth-merchants and jewellers, look startlingly the same. It is as though there was only one cobbler, one jeweller, one cloth-merchant, multiplied by mirrors. The bazaar is not an assembly of individuals pursuing different trades, it is an assembly of different trades pursued by people. The only personality seems to be a collective one; the only distinction, generic. A man is not merely identified with a particular occupation; he becomes that occupation animate. His peculiar god or peculiar manifestation of God is not his choice but the choice of his occupation. He does not behave as his private personality suggests – what private personality he possesses, it is his duty to suppress – but as his caste and his occupation – still, for most Indians, identical – dictate.

Of course this is not invariable; the slow secularization of independent India has done a little to loosen the hold of caste on character. But it is general enough to make any real social progress conditional upon a psychological as well as an economic revolution. Banias may flinch from eating meat or fish. The more tender-hearted, or devout, may even strain their water in case they should swallow living organisms too tiny to notice. But the generic function of the Bania is to make money – he ritualistically worships wealth – and few self-respecting Banias would recoil from lending money at six per cent a month, whatever the eventual effect on the lives of the borrowers. Lorry-driving in India is a preserve of the Sikhs and the Hindu martial castes, and the great trunk road to the west for some

[1] G. Morris Carstairs, *The Twice Born* (Hogarth Press, London, 1961), p. 146.

two hundred miles from Calcutta is littered with the casualties of battle. To someone who has not travelled along that road, the driving of lorries for long distances, day after day, may seem a dreary enough occupation. To someone who has, lorry-driving is rather like the tournaments of medieval Europe must have been, with ceremonious rivalry, challenges, clash, and frequently mortal collision. The drivers – the impression is unavoidable – drive dangerously because dangerous driving is expected of them. They dress, talk, drink and walk with a swagger and a provocation; every encounter is a contest. And the style, even grace, the sense of fun with which the clashes are conducted should not disguise the waste of life and equipment involved.

Far more wasteful and far less picturesque is the caste conformity of the rural proletariat. It is not merely that the landless submit to their condition; they believe that it is right for them to do so.

'But then,' asks Kallatatiah with puckered eyebrows, 'how can we get other people's lands? If we are destined to be landless we must remain so.' Elderly, turbaned, dark, with a white mousey moustache, Kallatatiah himself has no land. Still, he says, 'I don't want any land reforms.' He is cultivating two acres on oral lease now. That does not suffice, and he has to supplement his income by working as a casual labourer on other people's farms ... Venkanna used to be a tenant on ten acres. An elderly man, this year he could not get a single acre on lease. He complains that no tenants are left. 'We are unable to get any land even on oral contract.' Now he is struggling to live by his coolie labour and on loans. On the question of land reform, however, he says: 'They say some word has come that the tiller of the soil will become its owner. But I don't like such a law because it enables distribution of other people's property. I don't like it on principle. I feel it would be morally wrong' ... Krishnaswamy of Someswaram, however, puts an effective and final seal on the issue. He is a young man and owns 30 cents (·3 acres) of land. Besides, he works as a coolie to support his mother and two children; he lost his wife. Yes, he has heard of the ceiling proposal (setting an upper limit on individual land-holdings) but holds that: 'Even if it comes I am not in favour of the principle of someone taking someone else's land and giving it to others.' When I suggest that compensation will be paid to the landlord, he concedes reluctantly: 'Well, if compensation is paid I would agree to take, but only with the consent of the landlord. I myself would want only one acre. Its produce will be enough for my needs. But if the land is taken away compulsorily and given to the poor, I am not for it. But then,' he dismisses the prospect calmly with a shrug of the shoulder and without a trace of doubt or anguish in his voice, 'no such law can come into force for the simple reason that no one will give up his land.'[1]

Here is no militant peasantry, bitter and hostile to hereditary landlords, driven by centuries of need into rural rebellion. These are landless labourers, with a standard of living indistinguishable from mere survival, resigned to their condition because they see it as a reflection of a moral far more than of a legal arrangement. And in any conflict between law and morality, it is law that will inevitably (and, in the nature of things, should), they feel, succumb. Men of their condition have never had land, and it is their *dharma* to accept this, just as it is the *dharma* of those in the land-owning castes to own land and struggle successfully against having to surrender it. In such a moral context, the landowner who evades the state ceiling on individual ownership by distributing his holding among members of his family encounters little popular resentment or censure. He, too, is doing as he should, and it is the state which earns the opprobrium of having challenged unsuccessfully the traditional sanctions. Such a society generates no mass revolution of rising expectations, and plans for any sustained economic advance must stumble constantly against popular indifference. Kusum Nair's conclusions emerge naturally from the unending present of Indian stagnation.

Planning in India is framed on the assumption – which in view of the extreme poverty of the people would seem logical – that the desire for higher levels of living is inherent

[1] *Blossoms in the Dust*, pp. 66–8.

and more or less universal among the masses being planned for. According to this assumption, every prevailing standard of life becomes minimal as a base for further progress.

From what I have seen and experienced, however, it would seem that a great majority of the rural communities do not share in this concept of an ever-rising standard of living. The upper level they are prepared to strive for is limited and it is the floor generally that is bottomless. This does not mean that the desired standard is always fixed at the subsistence level. It varies with different communities. In some groups it is very much higher than in others, and it may be considerably more than the minimum necessary to breed and survive. But whatever the level, it tends to be static, with a ceiling rather than a floor, and it is socially determined. Generally, the lower the level, the more static the aspirations tend to be.[1]

Sweeping is one of the most degrading of all Indian occupations, and the sweeper one of the most degraded – in appearance, habits and existence – of the Indian poor. Yet upon him the very survival of Indian society in its traditional form depends. In street and park, even in bus and train, Indians abandon their litter, sometimes scrupulously relieve themselves, in the knowledge that a special outcaste population exists to make the places more or less clean again. And if the sweepers do not visit one place for some time, it does not really matter. Sooner or later someone or other will come with his bunch of thin sticks and sweep the filth away. The individual's sole concern is to save himself from personal pollution by avoiding all contact with his own or anyone else's excreta as far as possible, even if – the contradiction is unconsidered – in doing so he makes it difficult for anyone else. It is care and not carelessness that produces the disgust of Indian ponds and pavements.

In Udaipur there is a modern cinema, garish with new paint, the street wall of which is used as a public urinal; the sandy pavement below is blotched with stains, and a sour stench seems to stretch and grab at you like a predatory beggar. I did a timid little detour on my way back from the bazaar, having leapt ludicrously from one dry patch to another on my first encounter.

[1] *Blossoms in the Dust*, pp. 192–3.

Fascinated, from the safety of the street, I watched the passers-by on the pavement; they seemed to notice nothing under their feet. I don't think that they saw the stains at all.

Bordering the town of Panjim on the west coast is a delicately curving beach, with blue water and palm trees crowded on the bank beyond. In the early morning dozens of crouching figures dot the sand, leaving little piles behind them when they move into the water to wash. A large notice, forbidding the use of the beach as a lavatory, stands solitary guard. By midday, if the morning tide has been low, the beach-front is to be avoided. 'Why', I asked a young Indian helplessly, 'don't they do it in the water, where it won't stand and stink in the sun?' 'Ah, but then,' he said, 'the water might wash it back at them.'

In every city I visited, I met African students bitter and bewildered at the strange world of Indian sanitation. They lived, almost all of them, in hostels, and were united in their dismay at the perpetual spitting. 'Haii!' said one young man from a village in northern Uganda, shaking his head. 'At home, especially when everyone is eating, no one spits on the ground, where one walks. Perhaps an old man, who coughs, will get up and spit into the fire, but no one else. Here they spit all the time. And when we complain, they say we are savages, just out of the trees.'

I am not obsessed with the handkerchief as a symbol of progress. I have no doubt that it is possible to blow one's nose on one's fingers in a highly civilized society and use a handker-chief attentively to mask the smells of a Buchenwald barbarism. That one should walk down a Bombay street in fear of bom-bardment from other people's noses and throats is in itself merely disconcerting, and costly if one troubles about the state of one's clothes. What must be of far more moment is that those who spit and blow their noses in easy disregard of destination are conscious not of a society to which they belong and whose needs they must respect, but only of themselves. No nation can plan coherent progress if it is divided into countless self-regarding, nationally indifferent units.

In the eastern state of Orissa, along the great trunk road that joins Madras to Calcutta, nightfall brings thousands of men and women, with their little brass jars of water, to the space between the tarmac and the fields. Having relieved and cleansed themselves, they return to their homes, and in the early morning walk bare-foot to their fields over the careful evacuations of the night before. This would matter much less if hookworm, carried from infected to healthy through human excrement, were not so debilitating a disease. As it is, however, a large if never counted number of peasants in Orissa have been reduced to physical husks by hookworm. I discussed the problem with a senior economist at the Indian Statistical Institute in Calcutta. He regarded me coldly and interrupted my descriptions. 'The English don't bath,' he said. I confessed to my ignorance of English bathing habits, but suggested that dirt in England was individual and not communal. 'Well, you see,' he replied, 'it is all a difference of custom.' I lost my temper and raged at him: 'Hookworm is not a difference of custom. And you as an economist should know that better than I. How can you plan for higher agricultural yields without planning for health?' He stared at me and whispered with elaborate politeness: 'Ah yes, that is a problem, of course.' I apologized – I still don't know for what – and, whispering as well, changed the subject.

'The Indians', Professor D. R. Gadgil, Director of the Gokhale Institute of Politics and Economics at Poona, complained, 'have no sense of neighbourhood. The individual thinks of himself as a member of a caste rather than as a member of a community, and it is the caste system which accounts for the state of Indian sanitation. Only personal cleanliness needs to be observed, with careful – no, scrupulous – attention to the taboos against pollution. Each one, nursed by the caste complex, takes it for granted that someone somehow will get rid of the refuse afterwards. Perhaps one way of cleaning up India would be to outlaw the traditional sweeper altogether.'

The caste system disintegrates social responsibility, it does not diffuse it. It is true that caste occupations supplement each other in a traditional pattern, but the pattern is rigid and hierarchical, suitable to the preservation of discrepancy, not the excitement of progress, and conditioning loyalty to a series of fractions instead of the whole. The sweepers do not serve the community, they serve the separate castes, and their acceptance of their condition is not the acceptance of a social function but submission to a hereditary debasement. No one else will do their work for them, since that would entail descending to the same ritual debasement, and so, where the sweepers do not do their work adequately or exist in insufficient numbers, the dirt merely accumulates. Perhaps Professor Gadgil is right. Perhaps if the traditional sweeper were outlawed, India would experience a far more profound agitation than the struggle against, and departure of, alien rule. Indians of all castes would have to organize social sanitation in order to survive, and in doing so would produce a pervasive social recognition that India needs more than anything else if it is ever to emerge from the ages of want and neglect.

The sweepers, of course, are not alone in fulfilling a function of the caste system rather than of society. The Bania turned industrialist, the Brahmin civil servant or, for that matter, a low-caste Hindu elected Chief Minister, feels his responsibility to his family and – when it goes further – to his caste much more strongly than his responsibility to the society as a whole. A sense of social service is exceptional and based – in the context of India's repetitive centuries – on very small sanction.

It puzzled me for a time that so many Indian politicians, administrators and businessmen – the rulers of the new raj – could discuss the poverty of India without once referring to the Indian poor. At first I thought that they had merely depersonalized the poor for convenience; until now they could only communicate with statistics and converse in percentages. It was later, when having lunch with an industrialist, that I realized the rich did not see the poor at all. I had been talking of a large fetid slum three or four miles away from my host's office when he interrupted me in surprise: 'Is it still there? I thought it had been cleared months ago.' I am sure that the industrialist felt little cause to visit the slum, but it was central enough for him to have passed its outskirts in his car several times in the previous few months. He had simply not noticed it. Suddenly it seemed to me how like a white South African he was. For white South Africans are frequently startled and disbelieving when they are told of the squalor and sickness hardly a handful of miles away from their homes. They do not see the suffering in their own kitchens, since they do not really see the non-whites who work for them at all. They acknowledge the service to themselves but not the servants. And that is why they can so smoothly think and talk of their cities as white, though there may be twice as many non-whites in them as whites. Without such psychological camouflage, they would feel themselves besieged, and survival itself would become a tormenting question instead of an automatic assumption. In both South Africa and India unseeability, far more than untouchability, is a prerequisite for comfortable rule. Traditionally an outcaste in Kerala could not approach, without polluting, a Nayar closer than twenty paces, a Pattar Brahmin closer than forty, and a Namboodiri Brahmin closer than sixty. And in the past, when a Namboodiri Brahmin walked in the street, he was preceded by a Nayar runner who shouted 'Ha-ha' as a warning. In modern India the rich, as the whites in South Africa, seem to carry their runners in their heads, ready to draw a blind behind their eyes when the unseeable appear.

Of course, India and South Africa are vastly different societies, the second existing on the constant exercise of force, a deliberate oppression, the first on resignation, a common acceptance of discrepancy. There is in India little of that lunatic will to domination which so mutilates humanity in South Africa. Yet in one important particular, India and South Africa are the same; they are both multiple societies. Each is not one community but several, with South Africa divided by race and India by caste. Many other societies are divided, of course – but by class, with the division not so hereditary, so rigid as to make them multiple. They are, in essence, single societies containing different classes, and their ruling cultures stress the objective of single development. South Africa and India, on the other hand, consist of different communities, and the ruling culture of the state – imposed by a minority racial government in South Africa, and popularly upheld, despite government policy, in India – supposes a different development for each community to be both natural and proper. Even such single societies as promote a hereditary poor in practice denounce such promotion in principle and claim an individual basis for discrepancy. The cult of free enterprise is centred on the gospel of individual competition. In India and South Africa discrepancy in wealth and development has a communal basis, and communal competition is denounced – by law in South Africa, and in India by popular tradition and religious teaching.

Both societies have substantially increased their net national incomes in the past few years, South Africa by an annual average of 12 per cent in the period 1949–60 (from £830·4 million to £2,017·4 million), India by an annual average of 4·5 per cent in the period 1950–51 to 1960-61 (from 9,530 crores of rupees, or about £7,147·5 million, to an estimated 14,500 crores, or about £10,875 million). In both societies, the drop in the real value of money and the population increase have not consumed the additional income altogether, yet in both societies the bulk of the population is little better off, if better off at all, than before. The increase in wealth has gone in the main to the communally wealthy, while the communally poor – and so almost all, if not all, the individually poor – have remained as poor as ever. What sets India apart, even in this respect, from other multiple societies like South Africa is that such unequal development, the perpetuation of discrepancy, is generally condoned by the sufferers themselves.

It is not the caste system alone, with its sanction in traditional Hinduism, that nourishes submission in India's multiple society. Discrepancy is sexual as well as caste in character, and the Indian woman is commonly as resigned to her inferior condition as the landless peasant is to his. In *The Hindu Woman*,[1] Dr Margaret Cormack has examined the place and function in society which the Indian woman enjoys and accepts for herself. Drawing her material in the main from ten Indian women graduate students at Columbia University, all with educated, urban and affluent backgrounds, she concludes that Hindu women, 'though relatively secure psychologically', are submissive and 'do not fulfil their potentialities or fully develop their individual personalities'.

The family is patriarchal, with all its members economically dependent upon the father, who by tradition receives respect and obedience from his wife and children, displaying care rather than warmth in return, preserving distance and controlling conduct. From the first the girl child perceives the distinctions of sex. The son is more important than the daughter because *Punnamna naraka trayate tat putr* – 'The son is he who rescues a man from hell.' Only a man's own son can perform the funeral rites necessary for salvation. Moreover, as the girl

[1] Asia Publishing House, 1961.

soon enough discovers, the son is a potential wage-earner and support of his parents in their old age, an economic asset in his very sex, since his marriage brings a dowry into the home, while the daughter must remain an expense before and especially with marriage, since she must go with a dowry to her husband. And just as the son is religiously and economically more useful than the daughter, so the father, religiously and economically, takes precedence over the mother. As Dr Carstairs reports in *The Twice Born*:[1] 'A Hindu youth invariably addresses his father and elder brother as "Ap", which is the honorific, deferential mode of address, and he will use the polite form of an imperative, such as "berajie – pray be seated"; whereas in talking to his mother he will generally use the more familiar "Tum" and the brusquer expression "baitho – sit down".' Sons and daughters alike may be emotionally closer to their mother, who is permitted by custom to display her love towards them, but are left in little doubt of the father's supremacy. From tradition, from folk-lore, and from the scriptures they will learn the message of Miltonic Puritanism so close to Hindu teaching: 'He for God only, she for God in him'.[2] They will be informed, if they do not notice themselves, the quiet submissiveness enjoined upon the Hindu wife, her serving of her husband at meal-time before she herself may eat, and her periods of uncleanliness, while menstruating, when she must eat apart from her family, or immediately after childbirth, when traditionally she must stay outside the home.

Boys enjoy considerable freedom to play in the streets and fields, but girls, especially those from upper-caste or devout families, live more or less within the house and courtyard, playing with members of the family or with the children of approved neighbours. Sisters are taught to regard their brothers as protectors, and on *Rakshabandan*, or Brother's Day – *Raksha* means protection – the sister ties a red thread round the right wrist of her brother, wishing him a long life and binding him to protect her. From early childhood girls learn of their dependence, therefore, and their minds are directed towards marriage as the purpose of their lives. They play games about marriage and learn, from each other and their relatives, the intricate details of the ceremony. Indeed, most play for them

[1] P. 70.   [2] *Paradise Lost*, Bk. IV, line 299.

is a reproduction of real life, and much traditional culture is transmitted in this way. Their lives are, in the main, sheltered, and then suddenly there comes to all of them – very often unprepared for it – the first experience of menstruation. For many it has a traumatic effect. Dr Cormack quotes one of her informants.

> Indian girls become acutely aware of the limitations. For instance, that of not touching boys or men, of eating separately when menstruating, not even drinking water from the same place. It gives them a hostile, derogatory feeling. They are, in fact, treated just like the untouchables, and there is absolutely no sympathy involved in it. No one is sorry for girls.[1]

The comparison with untouchability may be a little forced, but there is no doubt that the periodic defilement which menstruation is commonly considered to be must fill many young girls with a sense of shame, bewilderment and inferiority, and since Hindu culture emphasizes patience and self-control, adolescence becomes a silent battle against rebellion, a private suffering and eventual submission.

 The submission is a proper preparation for marriage, which ties a woman traditionally for life, and traditionally by the choice of her parents, to a man. Not so long ago marriages were commonly arranged at birth, but in 1927 the Sarda Act made marriage below the age of fourteen a criminal offence, and the Nehru government raised the minimum age to fifteen for girls and eighteen for boys. Between the edicts of New Delhi and practice in village India, however, there is a world of difference. The 1951 census, for instance, revealed that perhaps as many as half the rural marriages in India had taken place in contravention of the Sarda Act. Besides, the minimum legal age applies to the marriage itself; betrothal can be arranged between babies. The incidence of present-day child-marriages is, of course, difficult to measure with anything approaching reasonable accuracy, since those who have arranged or contracted such marriages are unlikely to provide the information for official statistics. It is certainly lower in the towns than in the villages, and certainly lower in the more economically

[1] *The Hindu Woman.*

developed areas. When I asked the Vice-Principal of Andhra University whether any surveys on the subject had been conducted in the villages around, he smiled thinly. 'It's so common in Andhra, what would a survey achieve?' I told him of what I had seen along the road from Madras, a few girls, surely not yet adolescent, with their heads shaven as a sign of their widowhood. He shrugged his shoulders. 'Between the town and the village in India there are two thousand years.'

Perhaps, after all, most marriages in India today are contracted in adolescence. Certainly, all but a very few of them are parent-arranged. The Indian girl is not expected to fall in love and then marry; she is expected to marry and then fall in love if she can. But whether she falls in love or not, her marriage is permanent. Divorce, though now legal, remains for the overwhelming majority of Indians unthinkable. Nor are these attitudes restricted to the rural millions. Dr Cormack's Westernized graduate informants share a belief in marriage as a matter of parental choice and an indissoluble union. One quoted the doctrine of *sati*, or widow-burning, without disapproval, and another proclaimed: 'Husband and wife are a union of souls – a permanent union. Such a union can't be discontinued; it is eternal and will always take on rebirth as husband and wife.'[1] The only permissible relationship with men outside of the immediate family is marriage, and few parents would regard the possibilities of a casual friendship between a young man and a girl with anything but fear and hostility. The girl is therefore married in most instances not only to a relative stranger, chosen for her by her parents because of his family, caste, earning capacity and, frequently, his favourable horoscope, but enters marriage without the most innocent experience of other men. She is seldom instructed in sex, and yet by tradition the male is the passive and the female the active element. She is told to submit to whatever is required of her, and to make her submission satisfying to her husband.

It is not marriage, however, that fulfils a woman's purpose, but motherhood. The mother-goddess cults are everywhere vital in rural India – not to mention the crowded shrines in cities like Calcutta – some 3,500 years after the destruction of the mother-goddess Harappā civilization by the Aryan invaders,

[1] *The Hindu Woman*, pp. 90–1.

and the word *mata* (mother) has a significance far beyond the secular. As Dr Carstairs writes:

> It is invariably linked with the sacred cow, *gau-mata*; and it is as a symbol of motherhood, succouring, gentle and the antithesis of violence that the cow is liable to be worshipped with a show of feeling which leaves non-Hindus embarrassed and bewildered. *Mataji*, also, is the generic name for the Mother-goddesses, whose shrines are to be found in every village in Rajasthan.[1]

The plight of the childless woman is only less pitiful than the spinster or, even worse, the widow, and there can be few sights in India as moving as that of a tree bearing the offerings of the barren like a crop of prayers. The childless endure any humiliation or trial in pursuit of divine intervention. In one South Indian ceremony, held each year, the barren women, bathed by their families in the village tank, lie face downwards on the main village road, their arms extended above their heads, their hands together and holding plantains, coconut, and betel leaves. At last the priest, accompanied by shouting and drumming, and bearing a tall phallic symbol covered with marigolds on his head, walks along the road stepping on the backs of the prostrate women, who are then lifted up by their husbands and sometimes carried further down the road for a second 'step'.[2] On the other hand, the pregnant woman is regarded as auspicious and receives respect in public, while the woman who has produced a child, especially a son, acquires a new value both within the family and in Hindu society at large.

At every stage of her life, therefore, the Indian woman is dependent for her status and, commonly, her survival upon a man – her father, her husband, her child. With age and children she commands regard, and may order the lives of others, with the coming of daughters-in-law into the home. But whatever her age and fruitfulness, she is traditionally the adjunct of a man, and very seldom rebels against being so. Despite the careful instruction that they should use their own names, many thousands of Indian women are struck off the registers at election time for having used the names of their fathers or husbands. She is, as wife and mother, the servant of the family,

[1] *The Twice Born*, p. 65.   [2] *The Hindu Woman*, pp. 141-2.

but she is also its centre, for it is through her that the family is
perpetuated and in that lies the pride of her submission.
Doubtless, as Dr Cormack concludes in her survey,[1] there are
compensations for her inferiority. She has little initiative or
personal ambition, but then her role in society is carefully
prescribed by religion and culture, and her acceptance of this
role earns general approval. She does not have to search for
distinction, she submits to receiving it, for the only distinction
that society recognizes is her conformity to custom. She may
not enjoy individual success, but then she escapes, in the main,
individual blame. 'A woman, if faithful and dutiful, regardless
of difficulties or tragedies, will retain the approval of society –
an essential ingredient of her self-respect.' She learns that her
position in society is inferior to that of men, but in return she
is taught to expect protection, to be dependent and to be
cherished, and in general, therefore, she does not feel insecure.

There is no reason to suppose that the Indian woman is any
less contented with her condition than the American or Swedish
woman is with hers; indeed, if contentment is measurable at
all, the Indian woman would seem to be far more contented
than her Western counterparts. She is not tormented by individual responsibility or ambition; she does not compete with
men, economically or, in a private contest of power, emotionally.
She does not swallow pills to make her sleep and pills to keep
her awake; she does not desert her husband, and it is very
seldom that her husband deserts her. Almost always she holds
the home she has; she does not fear for her old age, because
her children, she knows, will not abandon her to the loneliness
of an institution. If anything, her security grows with her years.
Above all, she believes – as she is taught – that she is the
transmitter of tradition, the instrument by which Hindu culture
is preserved. A few unfortunates may never marry or, having
married, remain childless; but the chances are overwhelmingly
that the Indian woman will have a husband, without personally
having to manoeuvre for one, and acquire the near-sanctity of
motherhood. Then it is through her that the whole Hindu
pattern of virtue, of obedience and self-control and ritual
purity, of what foods to eat and when and with whom, of what
festivals to celebrate and why, will survive.

[1] *The Hindu Woman*, pp. 188–9.

One Hindu has put it succinctly enough: 'Hindu society is based on group morality, with the freedom of the individual subject to the interest of the group. The concept of duty is paramount ... It is logical that Hindu marriage should be indissoluble. It is logical that Hindu marriage should allow a second wife if the first is childless ... A Hindu woman is given the opportunity to realize rather than to express herself. She is given the opportunity to be a woman ... Woman represents the continuity of the racial life, an energy which cannot be divided or diverted without a corresponding loss of racial vitality; she can no more desire to be something other than herself than the Vaishya could wish to be known as a Kshattriya, or the Kshattriya as a Brahmin ...'[1]

The phraseology may sound sinisterly modern, but the sentiments are securely traditional. Womanhood is another *varna* or rank, like the Brahmin or the Śūdra, with specific privileges and obligations; containing a variety of caste functions and practices, it has an immutable overall character which sets it apart, making it yet another element in the multiple society. As other elements, it is traditionally required to be content with its condition, and like other elements, it does not advance or stand still as the whole society moves, for the whole society does not move; economic progress may be – and frequently is – limited to one element within the society, no less than social, political or intellectual progress. Wives, in other words, do not invariably, or even generally, accompany their husbands in any advance. I have met Indian intellectuals whose wives are hardly literate, and businessmen whose wives do not reflect, in their conduct or appearance, the prosperity of their husbands. A man may be rich or educated without extending his condition to his wife, may recognize the need for personal or caste advance without conceding any need for the advance of the women in his family, let alone of womanhood itself. Yet women constitute no smaller a part of the total population in India than in most other countries, and no real national progress is possible until they become economically, politically, and above all intellectually productive themselves.

Kerala is like no other state in the Indian Union. Armies of

[1] A. K. Coomaraswamy, *The Dance of Siva* (Sunwise Turn, New York, 1924).

school-children, with scrubbed faces and neat uniforms, carrying slates and small piles of books, march along the sides of the roads. In no other part of the country is there less squalor and more evident literacy. There are thirty-two daily newspapers, and many families take more than one a day. There are travelling dramatic companies producing contemporary plays before village audiences, while the coffee shops of Trivandrum and other towns are crowded with disputants discussing politics, the latest novels and the prospects for the rice or coconut crop. The singularity of Kerala is revealed by the 1961 census statistics. Though among the poorest states in the Union – it is the most densely populated, with 1,127 people per square mile, compared to the national average of 373 and the average in Uttar Pradesh, the most populous state, of 649 – it is, with Delhi (a state containing little more than the huge bureaucratic capital of the country), by far the most literate. A comparison between Kerala, thirteenth state in population ranking, with 3·35 per cent of the total, and Uttar Pradesh, with 16·81 per cent of the total, is illuminating.

Table 1

	Kerala	Uttar Pradesh
Population (to nearest 1,000)	16,903,000	73,746,000
Males	8,361,927	38,634,201
Literate males	4,596,265	10,546,795
Male literacy (rate per 1,000)	550	273
Females	8,541,788	35,112,200
Literate females	3,322,955	2,466,388
Female literacy (rate per 1,000)	389	70
Overall literacy (rate per 1,000)	468	176

The female literacy rate in Kerala is accordingly over five and a half times the rate in Uttar Pradesh, while its overall literacy is more than two and a half times as great. A comparison of female occupations in the two states is no less significant.

Table 2

	Kerala	Uttar Pradesh
No. of female workers	1,517,995	226,851
Cultivators	264,045	14,088
Agricultural labourers	446,000	4,299
Mining, quarrying, livestock, forestry, plantations, orchards, etc.	87,186	2,403

Table 2 (*continued*)

	Kerala	Uttar Pradesh
Household industry	272,331	66,730
Other manufacturing	113,004	11,725
Construction	2,407	1,774
Trade and commerce	16,101	19,520
Transport, storage, communications	5,574	1,455
Other services	311,347	104,857
Non-workers	5,752,411	4,020,188
Total of females in survey	7,270,406	4,247,039

In Kerala therefore, one out of every five women is a worker, while in Uttar Pradesh the rate is one out of twenty. Yet it is Uttar Pradesh that is typical of India as a whole, not only because it is by far the most populous state, but because it is the heartland of Hindu tradition, washed by the Ganges and containing the most sacred of all Hindu pilgrimage places, Benares. If India today is in substantial measure the product of Hindu culture, the peasant in Uttar Pradesh, with his proud piety and prejudices, his beliefs and his customs, is the typical Indian.

It is not easy to establish what accounts for the singularity of Kerala. The wide popular support enjoyed by the Communist Party – which governed the state from April 1957 to the end of July 1959, and which polled 44 per cent of the total vote in the state elections of 1960 – is not a cause, as some propagandists would have it, but a consequence. A poor, largely literate, intellectually alive society will search for revolutionary resolutions, where a poor and largely illiterate society, intellectually submerged by tradition, will submit – in lassitude, piety or despair – to its circumstances. Not surprisingly, the political and economic revolution promised by the 1957 Communist victory at the polls was preceded by what seemed to be an intellectual revolution – conducted by touring theatrical companies with revolutionary plays, by revolutionary newspaper comment and novels, by party workers who took their revolutionary message to every village in the state. The plays would have gone unattended, however, the newspaper comment and novels unread, the party workers unheard – had they existed at all – if the peasantry of Kerala had been listless and submissive. The real intellectual revolution had taken place long before, long before even the rise to leadership of talented Marxists within Congress during the struggle against British rule. This revolution had, in the first place, been an educational one. The Christian Churches, especially the Roman Catholics, had for centuries been active in the two princely states of Travancore and Cochin, with the Malabar district of the Madras Presidency, from the Malayalam-speaking areas of which the new state of Kerala was constituted in the linguistic reorganization of 1956. At the time of the contentious Education Act in 1957, which would lead to the supplanting of Communist government by President's rule some two years later, three and a half million were at school out of the state's nearly seventeen million people. There were some 10,000 schools, one for each square mile of inhabited territory, and of these as many as 1,000 were high schools. There were 80,000 matriculants each year, and between 7,000 and 8,000 graduates from the 50,000 university students. Barely 4,000 of the 10,000 schools in the state were government ones, however, and of the 6,000 private schools some 4,500 were Christian-controlled.[1] In an overpopulated agrarian economy, the educated unemployed provided a vast – and ever swelling – source of discontent.

Nor had the intellectual revolution been restricted to the classroom. Under pressure from religious reformists and with the co-operation of an enlightened Maharaja, all temples in Travancore had been opened, by the Temple Entry Proclamation of 1937, to all Hindus, even the 'untouchables', in the first major move of this kind anywhere in India. A whole series of progressive rulers had occupied the Travancore throne, not only nourishing religious change, but initiating political reform. The state had been the first in India to introduce a semblance of democratic government, and an Assembly had been nominated as early as the 1890s. This Assembly had then become increasingly popular in form over the years, with men and women enjoying equal status as members and voters, though full adult suffrage had been granted only on the eve of Indian independence, and fully responsible government had come only in 1948.

Political, social and religious changes had not, however, been

[1] Figures given by R. Sankar, Chief Minister of Kerala, in a personal interview at the beginning of January 1963.

matched by economic ones, and the intellectual revolution, stimulated and sustained by spreading education and political, social and religious progress, had increasingly demanded economic progress as well. Yet, despite certain reforms in land tenure, the feudal character of the economy had persisted, with the pressures of increasing population swelling the ranks of the landless. Inevitably there had been great and general expectations of economic change with the attainment of Indian independence and democratic rule, but the Congress administration had provided neither land reform nor industrialization. The Communist Party leaders in Kerala, who had shared the glamour of the Gandhi-led Congress struggle till 1945 and diligently laboured in the villages, spreading their influence especially through the *Kisan* (Peasant) Sabha (Union), accordingly encountered little resistance to their ideas among the alerted peasantry. When Thoppil Bhasi, a prominent Communist and the most popular playwright writing in Malayalam, took his play, *You Made Me a Communist*, on tour through Kerala, he found an attentive audience in the villages.

Yet the singularity of Kerala is not altogether explained by the activity of the Christian Churches, the Hindu religious reformers, or the series of enlightened Maharajas in Travancore. Not surprisingly, the Christians – mainly Roman Catholics – who constitute between 25 and 30 per cent of Kerala's population, are the staunchest supporters of Congress, though the Church is not happy with the party's policy of non-alignment in international affairs. The Muslims, constituting some 20 per cent of the population and politically powerful in the north of the state where they are concentrated, belong in general to the Muslim League, in electoral alliance on the state level with Congress. It is from the Hindus, therefore, constituting just over half the total population, that the Communist Party of India – the C.P.I. – in Kerala draws the bulk of its support.[1]

Yet elsewhere in India the Hindu peasantry has shown itself largely – in most of the states overwhelmingly – inattentive to the revolutionary call of the Communists. Only in Andhra (21·05 per cent) and West Bengal (29·38 per cent), the second because of its substantial industrialized population, did the

[1] Assessment made by C. Achuth Menon, Secretary of the Kerala C.P.I., in a personal interview at the beginning of January 1963.

C.P.I. poll more than 20 per cent of the valid votes cast in the 1962 general election, to become, as in Kerala, the leading opposition party.[1] In Madras, next door to Kerala, the C.P.I. polled 10·24 per cent of the votes, and the opposition to Congress centred around the right-wing southern separatist Dravida Munnetra Kazhagam or D.M.K., which secured 27 per cent. In Bihar, Gujarat, Rajasthan, and – with the support of the traditionalist Ganatantra Parishad – Orissa, the right-wing Swatantra Party, backed by princely families and a substantial section of the business community, emerged as the single strongest opposition party; in Madhya Pradesh and Uttar Pradesh, two states with a combined population of 106,000,000 or almost a quarter of the country's total, the right-wing Hindu traditionalist Jana Sangh constituted the chief rival to Congress; in Assam, and the Punjab (where the Akali Dal is agitating for a separate Sikh state), regional parties to the right of Congress assumed dominance of the opposition. Only in Maharashtra (5·36 per cent) and Mysore (14·49 per cent), where the Praja Socialist Party emerged as the principal opposition party in the state assemblies, and where Congress itself polled more than half the total popular vote – 52·9 per cent in Maharashtra and 54·82 per cent in Mysore – could organized opposition, however small, at least be termed left-wing, if not necessarily to the left of Congress in all major respects. In nine of the fourteen states, therefore, the main opposition to Congress is right-wing in character; in two of them it is ineffectually Praja-Socialist; and in three it is Communist. But only in Kerala does Congress, with 34·28 per cent of the votes, have less popular support than the largest single opposition party; only in Kerala, where the C.P.I. polled 35·46 per cent of the votes in the 1962 parliamentary elections, does an organized movement with revolutionary aims enjoy the support of more than a third of the total electorate.[2]

I was sitting at a café in Madras discussing the singularity

[1] Figures from the *Eastern Economist* of March 30th, 1962.
[2] In my interview with him, C. Achuth Menon claimed a popular Communist support of 500, if the votes cast in 1962 for Independents backed by the C.P.I. were included: 18 seats in the Lok Sabha were contested, and of these the Muslim League won 2, the Revolutionary Socialist Party 1, Congress 6, and the C.P.I. 6. The three Independents elected were – Mr Menon maintained – openly backed by the C.P.I.

of Kerala with a young musician, whose Tamil parents had gone to live in Kerala and brought him up there. 'It's the position of women,' he said decisively. 'In Kerala the women count. And when women have education, when they are respected not just as wives and mothers but as people, they are able to help educate their children, they bring them up to respect themselves and receive respect. Have you seen the women here? In Rajasthan and U.P.?' He grew scornful. 'They're treated like oxen, not like people. They have bangles and necklaces, but so have many oxen. To the men they are just the same. How can they teach their children to be clean, when they aren't clean themselves? How can they teach their children to want something better, when they are satisfied themselves with things as they are?' Perhaps he exaggerated with a private bitterness, but there was something of truth, certainly, in what he said. Nowhere in village India are there women like the women of Kerala, buying newspapers and books, discussing crops and schooling and politics, displaying an interest and aspiration that their counterparts in Rajasthan or Bihar would consider improper if not altogether impious. But then Kerala is singular within civilized India in possessing a substantial matrilineal community. The Nairs (or Nayars), a twice-born caste that constitutes some 15 per cent of the Hindu population in the state, was once a warrior community prac- tising polyandry and is still matrilineal, with kinship, descent, succession and inheritance following the female line. There are even Brahmins in the state whose succession is through the sister's son, a feature of the matrilineal order, and the ruling house of Travancore, Kṣatriya in status, practises inheritance through the female, with the maharajas specifically authorized to adopt their sisters' sons for the succession.

All this, of course, is not to say that matrilineal societies in India are necessarily progressive – there are tribal communities in parts of the country like Assam where matrilineal organiza- tion seems merely another aspect of the primitive and stagnant – much less that succession through the female line is essential to the spread of Communism among the Hindu peasantry. What it does suggest, if the interpretation of the Tamil musician may be generalized, is that rebellion against circumstance, the phenomenon in India of individual aspiration, ultimately depends upon the emancipation of women from the character of Hindu custom. In traditional Hindu society, where the woman is in practice degraded – whatever the rationalizations of dogma – submission to the ageless pattern of inequality, in status and standards, is conveyed along a belt of ignorance from mother to child. But where a different, conflicting custom operates, as in Kerala, even within Hindu society, to raise the condition and responsibilities of women, then discontent with the pattern of inequality, however sanctioned by centuries, must grow, and the demand for change, for betterment, assumes an articulate and organized form. The revolution of rising expectations must take place in the kitchen before it can reach the streets.

The relation of the sexes to each other, and the attitude of both to the act of sex itself, are aspects of the contradiction that exists at the core of traditional Hinduism. The function of a woman is to bear children, and motherhood is woman's one exalted state. Without sons, the father cannot usually attain salvation, and without children the family – and the whole body of Hindu tradition – will not survive. Yet the sexual act is physically and spiritually degenerating for the man, while much that is connected with her sexual functions is degrading for the woman. All the villagers in Rajasthan with whom Dr Carstairs discussed the subject subscribed to a belief in the virtue of celibacy, since the strength of a man resides in his semen (*viriya*) which is ultimately stored in his head and each drop of which takes forty days and forty drops of blood to form. 'Celibacy was the first requirement of true fitness, because every sexual orgasm meant the loss of a quantity of semen, laboriously formed. Here was another inescapable dilemma, because one's sons must be procreated, one's wife satisfied – hence the need to compromise, to restrict sex to a defined number of occasions.'[1] The ideal man, the *yogi* who can abjure sex altogether, is rewarded with magical powers, like the ability to become invisible or practise levitation, while the practical man who has sexual intercourse once or twice in his life will produce correspondingly robust children. Yet very few men are able so to control their desires, let alone observe the many other prohibitions – against eating the 'hot' foods (like vegetable oil, millet

[1] *The Twice Born*, p. 84.

flour and spices, the cheap staple diet of the poor), mixing and eating with those of inferior caste, acting disrespectfully to elders, giving way to anger or fear or excess worry – which drain the semen. Such conduct causes the semen to curdle and go bad, so that it cannot be retained and issues involuntarily from the body. This involuntary discharge (*jiryan*), real or imagined, is taken as a sign of physical and spiritual degeneration, and Dr Carstairs considers the widespread preoccupation with it to be 'the commonest expression of anxiety neurosis among the Hindu communities of Rajasthan, and perhaps elsewhere as well'.[1] The Hindu man, therefore, is in a constant state of struggle against his natural impulses, especially his sexual ones, and his whole function as husband and father conflicts with his view of the devoted and ideal Hindu.

Not surprisingly, it is the woman who is blamed for his temptation and fall. As the *Kama Sutra*, a Hindu classic in the art of love, makes clear, it is the woman who should rouse the man, and this is consistent with the traditional view in Hindu philosophy of the male as the passive, the female as the active element. 'You see, women never talk about sex problems, for they don't feel there could be any on the woman's part,' one of her informants told Dr Margaret Cormack.[2] 'A woman is expected always to give physical satisfaction to her husband. If the husband is satisfied, then the relationship is good.' Men maintain that women need sex far more than they themselves do, that it is women who take the initiative in suggesting intercourse.

The need to procreate a son and the need to satisfy one's wife were felt as two major impediments to leading a good life. Girdari Lal mentioned, as a rider to his description of the virtues of celibacy, that a well-instructed man will satisfy his wife twice in a night, when she shows that she desires it. Birmal reminded me that every woman needs sexual satisfaction at least once a month; if she is not given it within the ten days following her period, she is bound to go astray. Many people told me instances of the cunning with which adulterous women seduced their lovers. Promiscuity, it was generally agreed, is more women's fault than men's.[3]

[1] *The Twice Born*, p. 87.   [2] *The Hindu Woman*, p. 110.
[3] *The Twice Born*, p. 73.

Yet, despite such common interpretations of her nature, the woman is also required by the most rigid of all traditions to seem – and indeed be – shy, humble, modest, reticent, even timid and ignorant, always obedient and respectful. She is to be a slave in the kitchen and a tyrant in bed. As a woman she is disregarded, even despised; as a mother she is exalted and acclaimed; yet the very functioning of her capacity to change from the one to the other is suspect and feared. In menstruation and childbirth she is unclean, a source of pollution to others, and in the very act of conception she saps her husband's strength. Uncertain of her own purpose and character, she extends her uncertainty to her children, in a perpetuation of unresolved conflict. Through her son she achieves status and consideration, and through her son she seeks the emotional fulfilment that other women find in their husbands. Almost all students of the Hindu family report the extreme indulgence shown by the mother to her children, especially her sons, nursing them for two or even three years, feeding them whenever they are hungry or upset, sleeping next to them, fondling them, never scolding or slapping them. In the son's mind there is raised an image of limitless love and service, before the image cracks and shatters. At the same time as the child is weaned, he is supplanted at his mother's side by his father; he is old enough to notice how, in the presence of her parents-in-law, his mother grows distant and seemingly indifferent to him; gradually he learns that at certain times his mother becomes unclean, mysteriously bloodstained, and must be avoided. Soon enough he discovers the womanhood of his mother, her inferiority to men, while his father, always a distant figure, becomes an exalted one as well, the source of power. The child is subjected to instructions, threats, even occasionally anger and hurt, yet his mother does not intervene. And then, at last, he learns the function and the virtue of semen, with woman as its pillager, the pirate of his strength. Yet his first vision of motherhood never altogether leaves him, the pieces of the image remain, and a combination of mother and woman, the protective and predatory, becomes the object of his fear and devotion in the goddess cults. The mother-goddess, the Mataji, is frequently portrayed as beheading men and drinking their blood, her fury appeased by offerings and absolute submission alone. Her proper offering, significantly, is the symbolic castration of a male animal, and in the most widely revered of her forms, as Kali, she appears as the black she-demon, naked, four-armed, wearing a garland fashioned from the heads of giants and dancing on the breast of her prostrate consort, Mahakala, who is Lord Shiv.

Not unnaturally it is the mother whom the son seeks in marriage, and his inevitable discovery of the wife instead does much to promote that confusion, that sense of ever-present, pervasive deceit which he sees as *maya*, the earthly world of illusion. A perceptive Hindu woman has luminously described the ravages of this conflict.

> Little do even the most educated Indians – blinded by the glamour of mystical interpretation – dream that this shining exaltation of motherhood, this worship of woman-hood in the abstract, upon which they pride themselves inordinately, hides unplumbed subconscious depths of uncertainty, hatred, and fear. Little do they realize that this exaggerated worship of the 'mother' is the very cause of their deep-seated contempt for 'woman'; of their uncon-querable distrust of, yet hungry dependence upon them; of the frustration of their desire to find fulfilment in matehood because they seek in the wife a mother instead of a mate; of men's ultimate attempt to free themselves forever from all desires of the body.[1]

During my stay in Madras I talked with a young Tamil about Kamaraj, then Chief Minister of the state, whom I had just met and who had impressed me as a peasant leader of great simplicity, earnestness, strength and resource, a man who might yet, I thought, help to save Congress from itself. My Tamil friend was sceptical. 'Kamaraj has no support at all, he is only popular in the villages.' I looked at him with astonishment. 'But Madras is made up of villages,' I said. 'In the same breath you tell me that he is popular in the villages and that he has no support at all. What do you mean?' He waved a hand impatiently. 'Both things are true.' I was to encounter several instances of such casual self-contradiction during my

[1] Frieda M. Das, *Purdah, the Status of Indian Women* (Vanguard Press, New York, 1932).

visit to India and always, when I pointed out the conflict between two neighbouring statements, I was answered with the bland assertion that both statements were true. Dr Carstairs quotes numerous examples[1] from his contact with the villagers of Deoli in Rajasthan. One informant, Nar Singh, told him emphatically: 'I never see ghosts, I'm not that kind of man', and then went on to describe how he had seen a ghost in the jungle, quite recently, which had appeared first as a flame and later as a crying child. Another villager exclaimed on the subject of ghosts: 'I *never* see them – I remember seeing one once ...'; while a third reported: 'That Khub Chand was killed by sorcery, I'm sure of that – perhaps, though, he got a chill after being overheated.' Rao Sahib Rajendra Singh, ruler of the village, whose powers and privileges had been, with much of his income, removed by the Indian government in 1948, proclaimed: 'All my people love me ... some of them are opposed, just twenty or thirty of these Banias and Brahmins.' His personal attendant, Amar Singh, proved himself fiercely traditionalist and communally bigoted, but not altogether so in his paradoxical way: 'I hate all Mussulmans, they are not to be trusted ... that Muslim driver is my good friend.' Shankar Lal, a poor teacher, progressive in politics but conservative in religion, informed Dr Carstairs: 'There is a serious competitive exam ... it is nothing, it is farce only,' and described the Shaivite *lingam* or phallic emblem as 'invariably black, generally black; sometimes it is also white or yellow'.

The capacity of the Indian to admit apparently irreconcilable contradictions in himself accords with his vision of the world about him as itself everywhere contradictory and deceptive. The dilemma of sex, the conflicting images of mother and woman, the conflicting duties of husband and man, mirror the ultimate contradictions of the real world, the struggle between the allurements of the senses and the requirements of salvation. The normal man is incapable of satisfying all the demands of traditional morality; the rules are so rigid and numerous – on eating and drinking and washing and travelling and mixing with other people, on sex and the whole careful control of emotions – that he inevitably breaks them, and in breaking them confirms his view of his own imperfection. Of course he

[1] *The Twice Born*, pp. 52–3.

contradicts himself. How should he not when his life is an unending series of contradictions? How is he to resolve incompatibles, when incompatibles are inherent in living? Life itself assumes an increasingly false aspect under the assaults of experience, and his one comfort is in the acceptance of general illusion. Nowhere is this more manifest than in the Indian's use of language. I arrived in India soon after Chinese forces had swept through a substantial area of Indian territory, inflicting a succession of defeats – widely regarded as humiliations – upon the long-proud Indian army. Rich right-wing industrialists and poor Socialist intellectuals, with journalists and clerks and traders of all income and political complexion in between, joined voices in crying for the rapid liberation of Tibet. Yet those who shouted loudest were the first, under pressure of argument, to admit the impossibility of such a venture. One prominent Bombay businessman demanded massive rearmament and an increase in Indian military forces while opposing higher taxation and stricter government controls; indeed, he condemned taxation as far too high and government controls as far too strict already. In June 1962, at the Convention of the Gandhi Peace Foundation in New Delhi, those two ardent Gandhians, former leaders of Congress and now its most strident opponents, C. Rajagopalachari and J. B. Kripalani, endorsed a call for India's unilateral disarmament. Four months later both men were flaying the Nehru government for having failed to make adequate military preparations to meet the Chinese threat.[1] The political somersault is not of course an Indian phenomenon; but there can be few instances anywhere else in the contemporary world of so altogether obvious and obviously genuine a political about-face performed by responsible public figures.

At first study the Indians appear to use language as a flourish rather than as a vehicle, with the object of producing an effect rather than conveying a belief or statement of fact. And this impression is confirmed by the custom of religious chanting, when crowds will mutter 'Rām! Rām!' over and over again in a kind of verbal trance, by the daily repetition of sacred texts which very few understand, by the popularity of traditional songs in an archaic language which are sung

[1] *Blitz*, a weekly, December 8th, 1962.

with a display of emotion that competently disguises their unintelligibility. It is certain that some Indians frequently, and many sometimes, play on language as though it were a musical instrument, to make patterns of sound and establish a mood rather than a meaning. But the apparent inconsistencies in Indian speech and thought – constituting what outsiders often suppose to be considered hypocrisy – are no more than the reflections of a characteristic changeableness. The world itself is inconsistent, fickle, full of sudden changes, and the natural – indeed, moral – response is to report the contradictions, not resolve them. At one moment unilateral disarmament seems a proper principle to pursue; at another, massive militarization; and on each occasion, since all action is moral, the principle of the moment must be viewed – and commended – as a categorical imperative. Strange as it may seem, therefore, it is not really hypocritical for a state governor who has just spent a substantial amount of money on redecorating the official residence, to inveigh against extravagance during a national emergency. A few days before it was right to spend money on appearances; now it is not. The state of national emergency has not changed, but the governor's view of the world has suddenly shifted. The official who wears a Gandhi cap and practises simplicity may be nourishing his bank account with bribes; but if he recognizes the inconsistency, he sees no reason to abandon it. It is right to live simply, in the uniform of renunciation, and it is right to secure one's family for the future. Sometimes there are months between conflicting acts and principles; sometimes there are days; sometimes there is hardly a comma.

Vinoba Bhave is widely regarded in India and beyond as the spiritual heir of Gandhi; he journeys through the country persuading landowners and even whole villages to donate land for the landless (*bhoodan* – the gift of land), and calling upon villages to give themselves (*gramdan* – the gift of a village) to co-operative community service. In January 1963 he wrote an article for a Calcutta newspaper[1] on the border war with China and the power of non-violence. It provides a classic instance of the bland inconsistency, the unresolvable, undisguised contradiction.

[1] *Amrita Bazar Patrika*, January 26th, 1963.

We must understand that even if there is peace, our country cannot afford to rest for many years to come. It will be our duty to strengthen our country in every way and we must do all we can to achieve this end. A country does not become strong by only strengthening the army. If we try to develop our military strength, we must devote so much money and energy for the purpose that there will be no room left for the development of the peasants. In a poor country like India where there is little land and production and science is not developed, development of military strength will be a very heavy burden. It needs thousands of rupees to build one aircraft. When we consider all this, we realize that we shall act foolishly, if we try for military superiority only. And this, in effect, will mean exploitation of our country by our own country. It is difficult to say whether our poor country will survive under such circumstances.

When we consider the present situation we realize that India has not yet developed adequate strength to achieve all its ends through non-violence. I believe that non-violence has this power, but it is hidden and asleep today. The only reason for satisfaction is that it is not entirely lost; it is revealed only to a small extent and India has faith in it. An experiment was carried out under the leadership of Gandhi. Besides, this country has the spiritual strength of teachers from the time of Gautama Buddha onwards. Thus I say that the power of non-violence is not entirely lost. It will take time to awaken it fully. Only time will not be enough, but we shall have to work for it. And this work will take some time. In the meanwhile our country will also develop its military strength. This is a vicious circle, the more the military strength is developed the more will non-violence be squeezed out. We must work with such wisdom and skill that the power of non-violence may develop along with true heroism ... We should work in such a manner that our activities may either stop war or help in war efforts. I once said humorously that by walking I am doing both – supporting and opposing war effort. If you like, I am helping war effort in that I am freeing the railway and other conveyances for military movement. I

place no impediment and thus I am helping war effort. Or,
if you like, by not buying a ticket and refusing to use the
railway, I am not giving a single penny to war effort. Thus
I am opposing war effort.

Thus our efforts will help a nation that wishes to defend
itself with true heroism or a nation that wishes to rise above
by avoiding war ...

What ordinary Indian citizens – let alone members of the
Indian government who have to produce and pursue a coherent
policy – are to make of this, I myself fail altogether to see. Is
the Indian government to spend more money on military forces
or less? Are India's many millions to assist the war effort or
hamper it, or find some way of doing both at the same time so
as to do neither? Yet Vinoba Bhave is not a crank with a tiny
fringe following. He is widely regarded as the foremost living
heir to the tradition of India's 'good men', those who have
renounced personal comforts and aspirations to lead a life of
selflessness, service and spiritual purity, providing a source of
wisdom and guidance to others. In the conflicts of such a man
the conflicts of ordinary Indians are exalted.

The world, then, is illusory, confusing, full of conflicts and
contradictions. Yet this is not all. For frequently it reveals itself
as malignant, cruel and hostile to human happiness as well.
Everywhere evil spirits and jealous deities abound, requiring
propitiation, safe only when cajoled by prayers and presents or
misled by the appearance of misery. The small red goddess of
smallpox and the smaller red sister goddess of chickenpox dis-
pense sickness unless they are appeased. Pregnant women talk
little of their expected children, are careful not to make
excessive preparations, for fear of exciting the gaze of the evil
eye. Shastha Devi, a malevolent goddess, is propitiated by
mothers and their friends. And even when born alive, children
are not safe. Indian women do not praise their children in front
of other people and frequently blacken their eyes to make them
appear less attractive than they are. For who can say what
malicious deity or spirit may not be incited by the good looks,
talent or contentment of humans to destroy them? Many – if
not most – Indians regard illness as caused by the assaults of
deities, or by the invasion of evil spirits which must then be

summoned by priestly practitioners of the skill and exorcized with bribes or appropriate threats. Even the air is believed by some to carry a poisonous element or *garab* which enters the body and produces illness.

The world of deities and spirits is treacherous and frequently menacing, but so too is the world of human relationships. Studies of Indian village life record the deep distrust felt by villager for villager, the extraordinary abundance of quarrels between members of different castes, members of the same caste and even members of the same joint family.[1] There is a ubiquitous cynicism, which few visitors to India can have failed to encounter, not only towards authority, but towards the human condition itself. Everyone knows how people should – by tradition and scriptural injunction – behave, and everyone expects people to behave differently. This cynicism alone must argue against the extent of political and official corruption it claims. That there is widespread and growing corruption among Indian politicians and officials cannot be doubted; the evidence is more than adequate. But that corruption on the scale commonly supposed should exist cannot be believed; people would be so busy giving and receiving bribes that effective administration could not survive, and every office would turn into a bazaar. Indians in the main simply expect the worst of each other. During my own visit to India I was frequently warned to distrust the motives and judgments of everybody but my informant, to guard myself against the avarice or violence or dishonesty of Banias or Brahmins or Bengalis or Rajasthanis, the double-talk of that Minister or the insincerity of that trade unionist. Two senior members of the government told me enough about their colleagues in short interviews to make me wonder how they could sit with any confidence in their own safety at a single Cabinet meeting. The evidence of Dr Carstairs, with his native background and trained scientific method, is doubtless more authoritative.

For some weeks, I assumed that it was simply as a foreigner that I excited so much suspicion. Gradually, however, the evidence accumulated that my informants

[1] See especially *Caste and Communication in an Indian Village*, pp. 27, 32–3, 61, 73–4, 77–8, 114–21, 214–18.

were also distrustful of each other. Several of them warned me not to leave any belongings in my room, as the others would be sure to steal them. They insistently reminded me that the door leading to the flat roof of my office had no lock, and must be secured. It never was, and yet nothing was ever taken from the room. The instances continued to multiply ... A further indication of reluctance to trust one's neighbours, or even one's nearest kin, was given by frequent references to the practice of making a secret cache of one's gold and jewellery, or savings in coin. It was taken for granted that every man did this, keeping the secret even from his wife and family. After a man's death his relatives often probed the walls of his house, or excavated likely-looking corners of his courtyard, and sometimes they were rewarded by finding a pot full of valuables.[1]

The late Professor Majumdar[2] provides one easy enough explanation for this widespread suspicion of each other among Indians. Village elders under study by a research team from Lucknow University showed themselves, he reported, indifferent to the formation of their children's characters. Correct behaviour was only expected from girls who had reached their seventh or eighth year, and from boys over the age of nine or ten. Children of six and seven years from every caste were allowed to smoke *bidis* (leaf-wrapped cigarettes) unchecked, though the habit was recognized to be a bad one, and even when telling lies in the presence of their parents were generally unchided. Gambling and swearing were common, and the children displayed great acquisitiveness. If a toy were lost, the child who found it would seldom return it but pretend instead that it was his own. The desire to possess was so great that the children frequently stole, and if an article – even the copy file of a research worker – was left unguarded for a few moments, it disappeared. Parents knew all this and disapproved, but seldom took steps to prevent it. 'Brought up in this way,' Professor Majumdar concluded, 'the children grow up into men and women whose first thought is about themselves, and not of others.'

Such findings would seem to suggest that Indians are justified

---

[1] *The Twice Born*, pp. 42–3.
[2] *Caste and Communication in an Indian Village*, pp. 211–14.

in distrusting each other, that the indulgence displayed by Indian parents towards their children leads to rampant greed and dishonesty and so to countless occasions for conflict. The incidence of dishonesty, however, as the testimony of Dr Carstairs confirms, is nowhere so considerable as the popular measure of it, and Professor Majumdar, with his research assistants from Lucknow University, may well have suspected greater grounds for distrust than actually existed in the village under survey. Besides, the spoiling of children, even if a cause, is also the consequence of character.

The truth appears to be that the Indian character is coloured, through history, tradition and religious teaching, by a profound pessimism. And this is hardly surprising. For at least four thousand years India has suffered invasion, conquest, violence and disorder, hunger and disease with frequent famine and epidemic, poverty and insecurity of a kind barely credible to most modern European minds. Even today the figures for infant mortality and average life-expectancy are little short of terrifying. Some 142 out of every 1,000 males born alive, and 128 out of every 1,000 females, die before they reach their first year, while the life-expectancy for males is only 41·7 years, and for females 42·1. The rate of infant deaths is many times that in the rich white world and much higher even than the rate in most of black Africa. Small wonder, then, that mothers shrink from the evil eye and do not praise their children for fear of exciting attack by some jealous deity or spirit. With cholera and smallpox still numbering its victims in thousands each year, and hunger never far from the threat of famine, the world must seem a malignant place indeed.

The Hindus have often been compared to the Jews in their rigid attention to ritual and diet, their scrupulous, even fanatical observance of so many religious injunctions. The comparison is not forced, though the Hindu requirements for attaining spiritual purity are far more numerous and complex, with all the additional hazards of caste. It is difficult enough for a Jew to avoid sin; for a Hindu it must be virtually impossible. The similarities are those of mood rather than of manner, therefore, and as such they may reasonably be pursued a great deal further.

The character of the Jew in the Diaspora – it is significant

that diet and ritual are of shrinking account in Israel itself –
was in large measure shaped by centuries of persecution. The
law became a substitute for the land, a citadel of conduct which
protected and preserved religious and cultural identity. In the
world-wide enemy territory of the Gentiles, ritual was the only
armament against assault and eventual extinction. The eating
of pork was a sin not so much because Moses had forbidden it:
its peculiar horror was derived from its character as a distinction. Christian persecution was frequently aimed at forcing the
Jew to eat pork, and the refusal to do so was accordingly a
triumph of Jewish survival. The survival of Judaism, indeed,
was the paramount objective of the Jew in the Diaspora,
demanding if necessary – and few generations were free of the
threat – the physical sacrifice of self and family. Not strangely,
children – and especially boys, since men alone could say the
proper prayers for the dead or constitute the required numbers
for a religious service – were cherished as pledges of this survival
and so commonly indulged. But indulgence very seldom if ever
encompassed betrayal, and children who married out of the
faith or renounced Judaism were discarded as dead, their
parents saying the funeral prayers over them and sitting the
set period of mourning.

In the poor and constantly menaced Jewish communities of
Eastern Europe, fear of the evil eye was general, and a schizo-
phrenic universe of good and evil in constant conflict, with the
Devil and his minions giving battle to the one God and His
angels, replaced the jealous Jehovah-dominated universe of the
Old Testament. The world of magic and spirits drew close to,
even merged with, the real world, which was increasingly seen
as antagonistic and deceitful, with escape into the spiritual
world the reward of the pious and just. There were rabbis
reputed able to communicate with spirits and perform miracles,
and several false Messiahs arose to accumulate disciples and for
a short while delude many thousands with the promise of a
final release from suffering. Yet cynicism was never far from the
surface, and though Jews in the Diaspora were compelled to
trust and depend upon each other for their very survival,
surrounded as they were by the hostility of their neighbours,
they could laugh at their own trust and dependence. The
Jewish joke is peculiar for its irony – its mocking assertion of

faith in the piety and power of rabbis, the integrity of communal leaders, the benevolence of marriage brokers, the righteousness of Jews in their dealings with one another – for the Jews required a psychological safeguard against their overwhelming need of the fallible. They armed themselves with irony, as the Hindus armed themselves with a ubiquitous distrust, against the inevitability of disappointment.

The character of Jews in the Diaspora accordingly took shape from their constant need to defend themselves against their environment. Since the world outside the community was hostile and untrustworthy – what Gentile friendship would survive the frenzy of a pogrom? – the Jews turned inwards, to the firmer footholds of Jewry itself, the family, and, above all, the individual relationship with God. The individual relationship with God was primary, for what else was not subject to deception and death? Fellow Jews might betray or extort – for what could fear and greed not accomplish? – and a whole community be swept away in a sudden surge of persecution. Children might desert – for what was not possible in a world visited so often by the Devil and his messengers? – or be seized by the enemy. Only God and His commandments provided a certain refuge.

Against the violence of invasion, the extortion of despots and the fury of famine and disease the Hindus too defended themselves by turning inwards, to the fastnesses of caste, the joint family, and, above all, the individual relationship with God in His multiplicity of forms. The whole intricate caste system constituted a first line of defence, since its cellular structure was able to survive the amputation of vast areas by invasion or the establishment of centralized control by ravenous and even religiously hostile aliens. The single village, with its caste-diversified economy, could retreat into self-sufficient isolation, while the priests of the new order lost themselves in the enormous countryside and the tax-gatherers plundered what they could and departed. Far away from the capital of alien rule, the village pursued its own caste pattern of government, maintaining order and preserving traditions, exercizing its own disciplines and securing Hindu society from disruption. Each caste was a miniature community, the members of which helped each other at times of need and which could govern

itself through a special caste council or the respect commanded
by the elders. Together the castes composed an independent
and resilient village society with a careful division of labour
and authority. India, therefore, was not a single society but
thousands of separate, virtually self-contained societies, and
though conquest might unite them for a while in common
subjection, it was never able to merge them.

Such at least was the theory of caste, and in impressive
measure it was the practice. The centuries of Muslim rule may
have called or compelled millions to the ranks of the faithful,
but they failed to absorb or suppress the mass rural allegiance
to Hinduism. Buddhism, Christianity and, most of all, Islam
wore away the edges of Hindu society, but they never altered
its basic shape. Yet if Hinduism survived the centuries of
violence, as Judaism survived the persecutions of the Diaspora,
it did so at incalculable cost. The caste system was principally
a social protection, and the individual suffered despite it, and
not infrequently because of it, a seemingly endless series of
human and natural ravages. What the officers of conquest left
behind, famine and disease carried off. The village society
might be self-sufficient, but it was self-sufficient for most of the
time at the lowest possible level of existence, and when it moved,
it moved almost invariably downwards, to starvation and sometimes extinction. Against such an environment the caste system
gave small individual security, and life required the further
fortress of the joint family.

In general the joint family consisted of a man, his wife, his
parents, his brothers together with their wives and children,
his sons together with their wives, and his grandsons together
with their wives. This social molecule ideally provided a great
deal of individual security; it supported those who were too old
to work and nourished those who were otherwise too young to
afford children; it avoided the fragmentation of land holdings
through inheritance and marshalled the labour resources of the
family for united effort. Yet the system depended too much on
individual restraint; too often its very functions promoted its
failure. A contemporary account, despite – or rather because
of – the distinctive Hindu pessimism of its tone, lists causes of
disintegration that must have operated throughout the centuries.

Evil-minded as Man is, it is very difficult for him to live up to the high ideals of the joint family system, and so the joint family splits up ... Often a family splits up after the death of the father, when the brothers seek separation and division of property, but cases of separation between fathers and sons are not absent. The villagers as a whole strongly accuse women of causing the break-up of families, and they are justified in their condemnation. Many a man leaves his parents and settles down in a separate house as soon as he is married, or at the latest within two or three years of his marriage. This is an almost universal feature of family organization in the village. The men are instigated by the womenfolk to ask for a division of property ... The women of the family always quarrel. The quarrels may not be of a serious nature, but the constant bickerings make life unpleasant. Quarrels are often due to very trivial causes such as a woman giving more food to her children than to other children in the family. The other women look upon such partiality with indignation and the result is a quarrel. Finally these quarrels get on the nerves of the menfolk and force a separation.[1]

Considering the traditional place of women in the family, the inculcated qualities of reticence and submission, one may doubt that wives have ever possessed quite as much destructive power as the late Professor Majumdar claims. 'In 99 cases out of 100, separation from the joint family was brought about by women,'[2] he reports, and it comes as no surprise to discover that all his village informants were men. It seems more probable that, as with sexual relations, the men feel guilty for having failed to live up to the ideal pattern of behaviour and transfer the blame to their wives. But whichever sex is primarily responsible for the disintegration of the joint family, the system itself is today, as it was in the past, clearly inadequate to withstand the stresses placed upon it. Whether evil-minded or merely human, man has shown himself in the main incapable of the effort and sacrifice essential to make the joint-family system a success. Besides, this further fortress, even when its inhabitants have been united, has given only a limited

[1] *Caste and Communication in an Indian Village*, p. 203.   [2] Ibid.

protection against the assaults of the Indian environment. It has not been proof against epidemics or famine or the exactions of conquest, let alone the casualties of endemic want and disease. Like the caste system, the joint family may have fortified endurance, but it has not been able to eliminate suffering. And suffering has been, as Hindu pessimism has reflected, the major component of life.

Inevitably, therefore, like the Jews in the Diaspora, the Hindus have sought to escape from the cruelties and deceptions of the human condition in a supernatural communion. Conflict is intrinsic to the relationship between mother and child and between husband and wife. Duties contradict duties. The very survival of Hinduism requires the sexual act, while the sexual act saps the material of vigour and flouts the disciplines of Hindu piety. Everywhere men reveal their fallibility. Friends betray, brothers fight, children desert. When the family cannot survive the jealousy of women, the greed of brothers, the despotism of fathers and the rebelliousness of sons, what security is there in more distant relationships? One can be sure only of oneself, and the need to find one's own road to salvation. Each man possesses an *atma* or soul which is a spark of that Great Soul or *Parmatma*, God Himself, and the highest duty of all is to blow that spark, through ceaseless devotion and obedience to the commands of the sacred scriptures, into the flame which will merge at last with the divine fire. In that ultimate absorption lies the only escape from the otherwise interminable miseries of life, death and rebirth. The logical conclusion of Hindu pessimism is a retreat from life altogether.

Of all the great figures in recent history, Mahatma Gandhi may reasonably be supposed to have been the most generous and self-denying, a perfect blending of the saint and the public servant. He did more than any other man, by precept and by act, to establish the humanity of the outcaste millions and secure for them at least a constitutional recognition of their rights to political, social and economic equality. Yet in some of his important personal relationships he seems to have been careless and even cruel. The history of his struggle towards *brahmacharya* or continence began when, at the age of sixteen, he lay with his wife while his father was dying. 'Ashamed and miserable' that his 'animal passion' should have made him miss his father's final moments, he set himself to escape the 'shackles of lust',[1] and in 1906, at the age of 37, he at last took a vow never to have sexual relations again. In doing so, he later explained, he was 'drawn to woman as the mother of man. She became too sacred for sexual love.'[2] His vow, however, was never an easy one for him to keep, and to the end of his life he struggled to discipline himself. In February 1947 he told a prayer meeting that his aspiration was to become 'a eunuch not through operation, but to be made such through prayer to God'. Unhappily, he did not confine himself to prayer. Nirmal Kumar Bose, who worked closely with him during the months of 1946–7 when he was trying to still communal violence in Bengal and Bihar, discovered that Gandhi was putting himself to the test, without sufficiently considering the effect of his actions on those, including his young granddaughter Manu, whom he employed for the purpose. Bose wrote to a troubled follower:

When I first learnt in detail about Gandhiji's *prayog* or experiment, I felt genuinely surprised. I was informed that he sometimes asked women to share his bed and even the cover which he used, and then tried to ascertain if even the least trace of sensual feeling had been evoked in himself or his companion. Personally, I would never tempt myself like that; nor would my respect for woman's personality permit me to treat her as an instrument of an experiment undertaken only for my own sake.

But when I learnt about this technique of self-examination employed by Gandhiji, I felt that I had discovered the reason why some regarded Gandhiji as their private possession; this feeling often leading them to a kind of emotional unbalance. The behaviour of A, B or C, for instance, is no proof of healthy psychological relationship. Whatever may be the value of the *prayog* on Gandhiji's own case, it does leave a mark of injury on the personality of others who are not of the same moral stature as he himself is, and for whom sharing in Gandhiji's experiment is no spiritual necessity.[3]

[1] M. K. Gandhi, *An Autobiography* (Navajivan Publishing House, Ahmedabad, 1959 edition), pp. 22–3.
[2] *Harijan*, November 4th, 1939.
[3] *My Days with Gandhi* (Nishana, Calcutta, 1953), p. 174.

Bose showed Gandhi the letter before sending it, and Gandhi replied that his self-examination was part of his *dharma*. It did not imply any assumption of woman's inferiority.

> I have believed in woman's perfect equality with man. My wife was 'inferior' when she was the instrument of my lust. She ceased to be that when she lay with me naked as my sister. If she and I were not lustfully agitated in our minds and bodies, the contact raised both of us.
>
> Should there be a difference if it is not my wife, as she once was, but some other sister? I do hope you will acquit me of having any lustful designs upon women or girls who have been naked with me. A or B's hysteria had nothing to do with my experiment, I hope. They were before the experiment what they are today, if they have not less of it.
>
> The distinction between Manu and others is meaningless for our discussion. That she is my granddaughter may exempt me from criticism. But I do not want that advantage.[1]

No one knowing anything of the character and work of Gandhi would suppose that, under cover of his reputation for sanctity, he was engaging in sexual orgies with his disciples. He was no hypocrite, and the readiness with which he admitted and even publicly discussed his experiments underlines that they were nothing more than he claimed them to be – tests of his difficult determination and so measures of his progress towards God. As he wrote to Bose: 'For me, *brahmacharya* is that thought and practice which puts you in touch with the Infinite and takes you to His presence.'[2] What must, however, be concluded is that his search was a deeply self-centred one, in which the consequences of his conduct for others were never a material consideration. What damage he did to the minds of those who participated in his experiments, or came under the influence of his singular asceticism, cannot, of course, be measured. But Bose is not alone, among those who followed, admired and even loved Gandhi, in claiming that the effect of his close association with women was frequently harmful. There were several of Gandhi's former associates who told me during my interviews with them in India how neurotic many of the

[1] *My Days with Gandhi*, p. 177.   [2] Ibid., p. 176.

women around Gandhi had been, how few of them married or ever again led normal or apparently contented lives.

The concentration of traditional Hinduism upon the personal relationship to God, with the distrust of the real world and its deceptive, contradictory experiences, must naturally lead to an obsession with self and a fundamental indifference to the feelings of others. That a man of Gandhi's imagination and stature should so easily have used other people for his private purposes provides sufficient indication. Evidence of more commonplace indifference is abundant in the writings of psychologists like Dr Carstairs.

Onlookers would interrupt a patient to discuss his symptoms, and often his private life, with a seeming disregard for his feelings. It seemed to me that the patients were sometimes quite painfully embarrassed by this, although they did their best to appear indifferent ... There was the same disregard for others' physical as well as emotional sensitivity: several helpers would roughly demonstrate a patient's ulcer or abscess for my inspection. Whenever anyone accidentally stumbled, or injured himself, this invariably provoked laughter, but of a constrained 'social' kind, as if to cover up the lapse from dignified behaviour ...

A further evidence of insensitivity towards each other was observed in conversations with groups of Hindu friends. Usually, two or three people would be talking at once, and talking in intermittent monologues: no one troubled to listen to his fellows' point of view, but interrupted impatiently to assert his own.

Girdari Lal was one of the first to impress upon me the connection between this solipsism and the Hindu religious life. 'When she dies,' he said, pointing to his elderly wife while three of his children listened respectfully, 'I'll become a wandering *saddhu.*'

'But, these sons and daughters, won't they miss you?'

'Why should they miss me? I am on my way to God, that's all.'

Daulmal also spoke of becoming a wandering holy man, undeterred by the fact that he had a wife and a young child, and many debts: 'You don't think of anything else at all, you think of God only: you just feel assured that your family will get whatever is fated for them.'[1]

Of this self-centred view of life, a firm belief in astrology is a natural part. Each man is concerned with his own relationship to God and the universe which God pervades, so it is only natural that the stars and planets should exercise a unique influence on his career. The horoscope is often enough proved wrong, but that cannot erode popular confidence in its necessity; astrology is a complicated science, and only the most expensive of astrologers, who are far beyond the ordinary villager's capacity to pay, can be expected to provide a horoscope that will correspond exactly to a client's destiny. The average Indian must make do with the astrologer he can afford, and he does so happily enough, acknowledging the possibility of error but prepared to trust in his horoscope all the same.

It is not, of course, the villagers alone who consult their astrologers at regular intervals and especially on important occasions. Rich and largely Westernized industrialists seek astrological advice before negotiating deals, and many of the most senior politicians have their horoscopes cast at the breath of an emergency. One Cabinet Minister is reputed never to take the shortest journey by train without first consulting his astrologer, and some of his colleagues, just before Nehru's rumoured Cabinet reshuffle of July 1963, made the long journey to Benares, the holy city on the Ganges, where astrology is practised by celebrated experts with an abundance of ritual.

Not surprisingly, it is at betrothal time that the astrologer is most in demand, and most Indian parents will require favourable horoscopes from those whose marriage to their children they are contemplating. The matrimonial columns of the newspapers, both English-language and vernacular, commonly contain requests for astrological testimonials.

A Bachelor non-Srivatsa Iyengar, 28–31, with good salary, B.E., M.B.B.S., or double-graduate required for a fair, slim, girl of decent family. Early decent marriage. Correspond with horoscopes. Box …

[1] *The Twice Born.*

Wanted suitable match getting Rs. 200 and above monthly for Baradhwaja Vadama girl, slim, very fair, beautiful and educated. Daughter of a Gazetted Officer. Please send horoscope and family particulars to Box ...[1]

Such advertisements display the importance attached by Indians not only to horoscopes but to colour. Candidates for marriage are carefully described not only as slim or beautiful or educated, but, where possible, as fair and even very fair. Certainly, there are few words of disparagement as powerful as 'dark', and it is often used as a ready term of abuse. Most Africans studying in India claim to have encountered hostility because of their colour, and there have been several embarrassing disturbances in university cities by Africans unhappy at the loneliness of student life and angry at the jeering of crowds in the street. Perhaps they exaggerate; perhaps the more sensitive often mistake indifference for contempt; Africans are in general more spontaneous than Indians; but it is difficult to believe that all their stories are not true, or that street scenes for which the government itself felt it necessary to apologize never took place. Besides, the experiences that African students claim to have had because of their colour fit well enough with the thinly disguised contempt which so many light-skinned Indians have for their own darker countrymen.

This obsession with colour in India – and obsession is not too strong a word – springs from no desire to approach the whites as closely as possible, which is so often the aim of coloured people in southern Africa, the United States and parts of Latin America. Indians are all deeply aware of their past, the village carpenter no less than the Calcutta advocate. Their sacred books, their folklore, and, most of all, their caste structure make real and essential to them events that took place thousands of years ago. The peasant in Orissa or Bihar may not know when the Aryans came or from where, but he will probably know that they came, with light skins and sacred books in Sanskrit, to rule over other peoples weaker and darker than they. He may not know the complex character or function of caste, but he probably knows from his sacred books how

[1] *The Hindu*, January 14th, 1963. Published in Madras and one of India's influential English-language national newspapers, read in the main by members of the Westernized middle class.

castes are supposed to have arisen, and he certainly knows –
nothing better – that there are higher and lower castes, with
those of the higher castes generally lighter-skinned than those
of the lower. For him the Aryan and the high-caste and the
light-skinned are synonyms of the superior, and he will inevitably
try to approach the superior, at least in appearance, as closely
as possible. Negro women in Chicago who buy special creams
to lighten their skins do so to make themselves as white as they
can manage; Indian women who use such creams hope to
seem as Aryan and high-caste as possible. It is natural enough.

The Indian is more than merely aware of his past, however.
He is proud – too often, inordinately proud – of it. His very
awareness of how ancient are his beliefs and social institutions
encourages him to stay as he is – for when things have always
been as they are, how can they change? – giving him some
sense of security in an existence so insecure, and a sense of
meaning and importance in an existence of such common
degradation. The Africans studying in India who complain
that they are despised because of their colour, complain also
that their culture is persistently disparaged. 'They talk as
though we were just down from the trees,' Ugandans in
Madras, Rhodesians in Delhi, and Ghanaians in Calcutta told
me. And I accepted what they said, for throughout my stay in
India I met people of urbanity and broad education who
spoke of Africans with a delicate patronage; I could easily
enough imagine how the less urbane and educated expressed
their views. Such pride is not only silly, because it concerns the
achievements of the dead – indeed, the very long dead – not
the living, and ignorant, because Africa's past is no less
momentous than India's, but dangerous, because it confirms
within India itself the resistance to change. How can a people
move into the future, let alone the present, when they lock
themselves so proudly to the past?

Yet there are few more creative and resourceful communities
than those of the emigrant Indians in Africa and the Americas.
South Africa itself provides a vivid illustration, for there an
Indian community of half a million people, descended in the
main from indentured labourers, has, despite unremitting persecution from white authority, developed a vigorous commercial
and intellectual life, changed slums into suburbs with schools

and libraries, hospitals and cinemas, meeting halls and social centres, produced a unity of struggle against racial subjection and in the process rolled up the blinds of individual indifference. It is as though the departure from India had been a departure from the past, with its caste protectiveness, its resignation and pessimism, its self-centred flight from the real. The Indian poor of the sugar-plantations and city backstreets in South Africa are still poor beyond European imagining, but it is a different poverty from the poverty of the poor in India; it is a poverty of rejection and protest, of desire and demand.

How is India itself to emigrate from its past? For nothing less is likely to make of national independence something more than just another in those distant shifts of power that alone separate the centuries. Even Gandhi's leadership in the movement of resistance to British rule only grazed the skin of India's multitudes. The most successful of the civil disobedience campaigns involved directly less than one in every two hundred Indians; is it credible that British power could have long survived the disciplined rebellion of two million, let alone twenty million, or two hundred million of its subjects? The struggle for independence may have sporadically stirred the masses, but it never in fact became a mass struggle, and the achievement of independence, not unconnectedly, has not yet assumed a mass meaning. Of course, there have been changes since the last viceroy left for home. Not the least of them is that over one hundred million Indians now go regularly to the polls and in electing their government express their immediate preferences. But how far do those preferences reflect the resolve or the energy, even the desire, to remake the real world of India? The evidence suggests, very little as yet.

Vishnu and Śiva know the problem is formidable enough, and no government, let alone the distracted and irresolute one that Congress offers at present, would find it easy to tackle. For it involves no less than changing the ageless character of Indian custom, of making vital to the Indian people the community and not the caste, all India's bodies and not each separate soul, the world of the gutter and the dam and not the world of the shrine and the horoscope. It means no less than moving India from the past into the present, to the living and the dying from the dead. And it can come only with the insurrection of desire, with the turning from submission and indifference to rejection and demand. I for one do not begin to have an idea of when and how such a revolution in Indian history will come about. But that it must come I have no doubt. I believe the alternative to be finally unendurable.

CHAPTER FOUR

THE ECONOMIC PRECIPICE

THE overriding characteristic of India is its poverty, a poverty so profound and pervasive that it seems to be an aspect of nature itself, like the heat. It commands submission and jeers at the endeavour to diminish it. It is not a poverty that results from gratuitous inequalities. India is not South Africa, where need is merely the requirement of surfeit and distribution of the country's wealth would supply a general sufficiency. India's poverty is absolute, and though there are those who are rich and daily grow richer, they are relatively no more than the surf at the edges of want.

India has too many people for too few developed resources. It has a mere 2·2 per cent of the world's land area, yet supports more than 14 per cent of the world's population. It is only a seventh the size of the Soviet Union, between a quarter and a third the size of China, Canada or the United States, almost a third the size of Brazil, and little more than the size of Argentina. Yet it is the second most populous country on earth – surpassed only by China – with more than twice the population of the United States or the Soviet Union, seven times the population of Brazil, and well over twenty times the population of Canada or Argentina. Its population density is on a level with Switzerland's, many times that of the United States, the Soviet Union, Brazil or Canada, more than four times that of Nigeria, Africa's most densely populated state, and more than twice that of China. It is exceeded only by some of the highly industrialized states like the Netherlands, the United Kingdom, and, in Asia, Japan.

The highly industrialized societies can afford high population densities; they are able to pay for their massive imports of food from a largely agricultural world with their exports of manufactured goods, and they have mechanized their own agriculture to produce high yields. India not only possesses a high

Table 3

Country	Size in sq. miles	Population	Population per sq. mile
Canada	3,851,000	18,000,000	5
Brazil	3,287,000	63,102,000	19
U.S.S.R.	8,648,000	208,827,000	24
U.S.A.	3,628,000	179,500,000	49
Ghana	92,000	6,691,000	53
Nigeria (late Cameroons)	373,000	32,433,000	87
China	3,758,000	640,000,000	170
Switzerland	15,000	5,400,000	360
India	1,138,000	438,000,000	368
U.K.	94,000	51,680,000	550
Japan	142,000	92,970,000	650
Netherlands	12,000	11,095,000	885

REF.: Cassell's *New Atlas of the World*, 1961.

population density, but an overwhelmingly agricultural economy, with yields amongst the lowest in the world. An analysis of occupational patterns shows India's agricultural emphasis as dangerously great, not only in relation to the rich white world, but even in relation to other poor non-white societies.

Table 4

Country	Working population	Year used	Agriculture, forestry, fishing & hunting	Mining & quarrying	Manufacturing & construction	Commerce & finance	Transport	Services, gas, electricity, water	Unclassified
					(percentages)				
U.K.	23,620,000	1959	4·5	3·5	46	13	7	26	—
U.S.A.	67,342,000	1959	10·5	1	29	30	——18——		11·5
U.S.S.R.	54,600,000	1958	12	——36——		0·5	11·5	20	20
Ghana	277,000	1957	15	12	24	10·5	9·5	29	—
Switzerland	2,156,000	1950	16·5	——47——		11·5	4·5	17	3·5
Netherlands	3,458,000	1957	29	2	42	——26——			1
Japan	43,120,000	1958	37	1	25	17·5	—19·5—		—
China*	—	—	48·1	—	32	15·5	4·4	—	—
Brazil	17,117,000	1950	61	——13——		6	4	16	—
India	101,175,000	1951	70	0·5	10	6	2	11·5	—

REF.: Cassell's *New Atlas of the World*, 1961.

* Sources of National Income.

Not only is the Indian economy overwhelmingly agricultural; it is less productive, land measure for land measure, than the agricultural economies of most other states. Too many people struggle to wrest survival from the earth, and the earth yields far too little in return.

Table 5

YIELDS OF MAJOR CROPS IN INDIA AND OTHER SELECTED COUNTRIES

WHEAT

	1948–49 – 1952–53	1960–61
India	6·7	8·5 (8·8)*
U.S.A.	11·2	17·6
Canada	12·8	14·2
Argentina	11·5	11·0
U.S.S.R.	8·4	10·6
France	18·3	25·3
Italy	15·2	14·9
Australia	11·2	13·1
China Mainland	(6·9)†	(13·0)†

MAIZE

India	6·9	9·2 (9·1)*
U.S.A.	24·5	33·5
Canada	32·0	35·8
Argentina	14·8	17·7
U.S.S.R.	13·7	16·7
Netherlands	32·5	38·1
Italy	18·4	32·1
Australia	17·6	21·2
Yugoslavia	13·4	24·0

RICE (PADDY)

India	11·3	15·2 (15·1)*
Japan	40·0	48·6
Burma	14·6	16·2
Thailand	13·1	13·7
United Arab Republic	37·9	50·1
Australia	48·6	61·1
China (Mainland)	21·7	25·4

Eastern Economist, 1963 Annual (Quintals per hectare)

* These figures refer to 1961–2.
† These figures refer to 1959–60.

The stark consequence is that India produces only enough to feed at all adequately a little less than two-thirds of its population. In 1960–1, with the population at 438 million, food production reached 78 million tons. Together with 3 million tons of imported food, this permitted an average consumption of 16½ ounces a day, or 8½ ounces less than the essential minimum recommended by nutritionists. If a diet necessary to sustain health was provided for as many people as possible, therefore, some 150 million people in India would have nothing whatsoever to eat. If everyone received the same amount of food, 438 million people would be eating less than two-thirds of what their bodies required. As it is, a few are able to buy more food than they need, some can just afford the necessary diet, most live in constant – if manageable – want, and many – no one knows how many, but they are certainly to be numbered in tens of millions – exist·in a state of unrelieved starvation.

No nutritional expert in the world has recommended a diet that yields less than 2,500 calories a day for an adult. The Food and Nutrition Board of the United States suggests 2,500 calories a day for a sedentary worker and 4,500 calories a day for an active one, while the British Medical Association suggests 3,400 calories a day for an average adult. Oshima, the Japanese nutritionist, has recommended 3,000 calories a day for an adult doing light work, and 5,500 calories a day for an adult doing hard work. For adult Indians, the Joint Committee of the Indian Council of Medical Research and the Indian Council of Agricultural Research has recommended a diet yielding 2,700 calories a day; the U.N. Food and Agriculture Organization has recommended 2,550–2,650 calories a day; and Dr V. N. Pahwardhan, an Indian nutritional expert, after 137 surveys involving 14,000 people, has recommended a daily diet of 2,500 calories.[1]

The actual calorie intake of the average Indian is far less than the recommended essential and hardly half that of the Briton or North American. Recent figures[2] reveal an average calorie consumption for Great Britain of 3,270; for the United States, of 3,150; for Canada, of 3,140; for Japan, of 2,110; and for

[1] N. C. Agrawal, *The Food Problem of India* (K. K. Vora, Vora & Co., Bombay, 1951), pp. 75–7.
[2] *Times of India Directory and Year Book*, 1962–3, p. 279.

India, of 1,880. Furthermore, it is not enough for a human being to consume a specific number of calories a day; he must consume them in the proper proportion of sources. Sound physical development requires a diet in which less than half the intake of calories comes from carbohydrates – rich foods like cereals – and the balance is composed of foods like meat, milk, eggs and vegetables, rich in proteins and vitamins. The Indian not only eats less food than the European or North American; he eats much more of the wrong sort.

Table 6

calorie intake per person per day

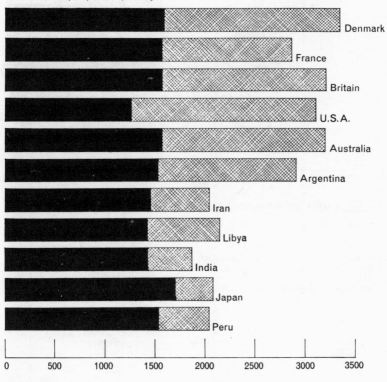

calories from cereals starchy roots and sugar

FOOD AND POPULATION

Distribution of the population of the world according to daily intake of calories

Size of country in proportion to population

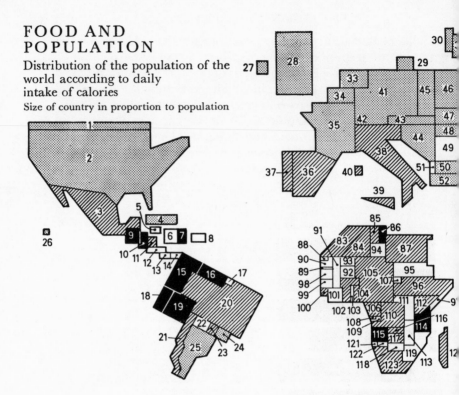

SOURCE: Food and Agriculture Organization, Maps of Hunger

OVER 2,700 CALORIES   2,200–2,700 CALORIES

1. Canada
2. United States
3. Mexico
4. Cuba
5. Jamaica
6. Haiti
7. Dominican Republic
8. Puerto Rico
9. Guatemala
10. El Salvador
11. Honduras
12. Nicaragua
13. Costa Rica
14. Panama
15. Colombia
16. Venezuela
17. Guianas
18. Ecuador
19. Peru
20. Brazil
21. Chile
22. Bolivia
23. Paraguay
24. Uruguay
25. Argentina
26. Hawaii
27. Ireland
28. United Kingdom
29. Denmark
30. Norway
31. Sweden
32. Finland
33. Netherlands
34. Belgium
35. France
36. Spain
37. Portugal
38. Italy
39. Sicily
40. Sardinia
41. Fed. Rep. of Germany
42. Switzerland
43. Austria
44. Yugoslavia
45. Eastern Germany
46. Poland
47. Czechoslovakia
48. Hungary
49. Rumania
50. Bulgaria
51. Albania
52. Greece
53. U.S.S.R.
54. Turkey
55. Syria
56. Lebanon
57. Israel
58. Jordan
59. Saudi Arabia
60. Yemen
61. Iraq
62. Iran
63. Afghanistan

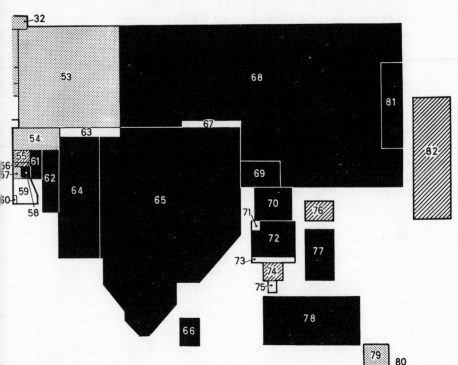

■ BELOW 2,200 CALORIES ☐ DATA NOT AVAILABLE

64. Pakistan
65. India
66. Ceylon
67. Nepal
68. China, Mainland
69. Burma
70. Thailand
71. Laos
72. Viet-Nam & N. Viet-
    Nam
73. Cambodia
74. Fed. of Malaya
75. Singapore
76. China, Taiwan
77. Philippines
78. Indonesia
79. Australia
80. New Zealand
81. Korea & N. Korea
82. Japan
83. Morocco
84. Algeria & Sahara

85. Tunisia
86. Libya
87. United Arab Re-
    public
88. Mauritania
89. Gambia
90. Senegal
91. Mali
92. Upper Volta
93. Niger
94. Chad
95. Sudan
96. Ethiopia
97. Somalia
98. Guinea
99. Sierra Leone
100. Liberia
101. Ivory Coast
102. Ghana
103. Togo
104. Dahomey
105. Nigeria

106. Cameroun
107. Central African Re-
     public
108. Gabon
109. Congo-Brazzaville
110. Congo-Leopoldville
111. Uganda
112. Kenya
113. Ruanda-Urundi
114. Tanganyika
115. Angola
116. N. Rhodesia
117. S. Rhodesia
118. Nyasaland
119. Mozambique
120. Madagascar
121. S.W. Africa
122. Bechuanaland
122. Basutoland
122. Swaziland
123. South Africa

The average inhabitant of the rich, industrially developed states – all but a few of them in Europe or North America – consumes some 3,000 calories a day, of which 40 per cent comes from animal products and only 35 per cent from cereals, starchy foods and sugar. In India, the daily average intake of calories is below 2,000, and the starch and sugar content exceeds 80 per cent.

Maps and tables, the rigid shapes of statistics, depersonalize meaning, producing patterns out of people. They communicate abstractions, hunger and sufficiency, health and disease. But hunger is not the hungry, nor disease the diseased. And so it is not enough to say that 1,800 calories a day are 800 or 900 calories short of the necessary number for sustaining health. The meaning is in the dull sunken eyes of peasant women, in the unregarded dying of Calcutta streets. It is not enough to know that India can adequately feed less than two-thirds of its population; one must know also that tens of millions of separate people are slowly starving to death because there isn't enough food to keep them alive. And this starvation is fortunate, the accomplishment of good harvests and shiploads of food from abroad. A wayward monsoon, a plague of pests, and want can quickly become famine. I have seen photographs of the 1943 Bengal famine, of dogs eating dead bodies undisturbed and of the still living so reduced that they seemed to be held together only by ragged pieces of cloth. Yet such images are not the memorials of a distant escape; they are, in nearly every Indian's mind, an ever-present threat wrapped up in the arrival of the rains.

It is not as though the risks of famine have been slowly shrinking over the years, or the numbers of the starving significantly diminished. The average Indian in the 1950s was much further from sufficiency than the Indian of the 1870s. True, the development of railways and roads, the existence of aircraft and the responsibilities of a popularly elected government have lessened the possibilities of an isolated local famine. But the margin of safety between food resources and survival consumption has decreased under the mounting pressures of population. In 1878–9 food production in British India, with a population of some 181 million, amounted to 51,530,000 tons, or an average of 27·9 oz. of food per person per day. With daily average food consumption running at a rate of 25·7 oz. per person, there was accordingly a surplus of 2·2 oz. per person per day, or an annual total of 4,360,000 tons.[1] Some seventy years later, in 1951–2, independent India, with a population of some 361 million, produced 51,140,000 tons of food, which seed and cattle-feed requirements together with wastage reduced to a total of 42,100,000 tons available for consumption, or 14·3 oz. per person per day. Only the provision of 5,276,000 tons from abroad allowed an average consumption figure of 16·1 oz. per person per day, or less than two-thirds of the amount consumed in 1878–9. Indeed, on the dietary level of the population in 1878–9, there was in 1951–2 a national deficit in food-grains of 33,500,000 tons, swollen to 40,700,000 tons by proper seed and cattle-feed requirements. Moreover, since protein-rich food like meat, milk, butter and eggs, and vitamin-rich foods like vegetables and fruit are generally scarcer and more costly than food-grains, it can be securely assumed that the consumption of these foods during those seventy years showed an even greater decline.

Another view of the Indian food crisis may be caught by considering average income figures in relation to living costs. The average *annual* income, at current prices, of an Indian in 1955–6 was estimated at 352 rupees (or some £27 sterling); at market prices then ruling, a reasonably balanced daily diet would have cost, with necessary salt and spices (a minor item), 356 rupees a year. By this accounting, a balanced diet would be available to all Indians today – for the position has changed little since 1956 – provided that they

> consent to go naked, live out of doors all the year round, have no amusement or recreation and have nothing else except raw food. But if they want some fuel to get their food cooked, and require some clothing, however coarse it may be; some house-room, however wretched; some distraction, however primitive; and want to fulfil some of their essential wants, they will have to cut their expenditure on the consumption of their food at least by half.

> Even this minimum, which cannot be considered sufficient for civilized human existence, is possible only when the whole national income is distributed equally

[1] Indian Famine Commission Report, 1880.

amongst all the people, which is not the case. A sizable portion of the national income is distributed amongst a small percentage of the people while the majority has to remain content with a smaller portion. This wide disparity in the income of the people further tend[s] to reduce even that minimum which has been considered insufficient for civilized human existence.[1]

There is simply not enough food, nor enough money to buy enough food, for all the Indians there are. Constantly, unremittingly, the population presses upon the country's resources, increasing every year to consume every increase in resources. The 1951 census registered a population of 359,220,000, and the government Planning Commission in New Delhi sieved its statistics to estimate that the population would grow during the 'fifties – roughly the period of the First and Second Five Year Plans – at an annual rate of 1·2 per cent.

By 1960–1, therefore, it was supposed, India's population would total 408 million. Instead, the 1961 census registered a population of 439,235,000, or an annual growth rate of 2·15 per cent. There were over 30 million more mouths to feed than the government had been led by its experts to expect.

Table 7

Year	Population	Decennial growth in numbers	Decennial growth in %
1901	236,281,245	—	—
1911	252,122,410	15,841,165	+ 5·73
1921	251,352,361	− 770,149	− 0·31
1931	279,015,498	27,663,237	+ 11·01
1941	318,701,012	39,685,514	+ 14·22
1951	361,129,622	42,428,610	+ 13·31
1961	439,235,082	78,105,460	+ 21·50

SOURCE: 1961 Census. Paper No. 1 of 1962

At the current rate of increase, some 9,400,000 people, or rather more than the total population of Belgium, are added each year to the demand for food. It is not that mothers are bearing more children, though every year, of course, there are

[1] *The Food Problem of India*, pp. 68–9.

more mothers to bear; the birth-rate has remained fairly constant in the last ten years. It is the death-rate which has moved significantly, dropping every year under the assaults of modern medicine and efficient transport. While mass preventive measures have reduced dramatically the incidence of malaria, smallpox and cholera, the country's traditional scourges, the development of storage and communications has reduced the risks of localized famine. More children survive their infancy, and adults live longer.

Table 8

	ANNUAL AVERAGE		
	1941–51	1951–6	1956–61
Birth rate (per 1,000)	39·9	41·7	40·7
Death rate (per 1,000)	27·4	25·9	21·6
Infant mortality:			
Male (per 1,000 live births)	190·0	161·4	142·3
Female (per 1,000 live births)	175·0	146·7	127·9
Expectation of life at birth:			
Male (years)	32·5	37·8	41·7
Female (years)	31·7	37·5	42·1

SOURCE: *Statistical Outline of India*, published by Vora & Co., Bombay, 1961, for Tata Industries, p. 8.

If the population growth continues at its current rate, the country will have some 800 million people by the late 'eighties and 1,000 million before the end of the century. Even the most pessimistic forecasts of growth in the 'fifties have already been outstripped, and the rate shows no signs of declining. Nor is the problem one of numbers alone; it is a problem also of age. The diminishing figures for infant mortality, and in lesser measure the diminishing death-rate of the old, means that those of working age will have from year to year to support a growing proportion of the population unable to provide for itself. In order to feed its population at the present very low level of diet, India must increase its food yield by at least 2·15 per cent a year, and this it did on an average, with little to spare, in the years from independence to 1960–1, or the end of the Second Five Year Plan.

But the margin of safety was narrow, and easily crossed by the

Table 9

INDEX NUMBERS OF AGRICULTURAL PRODUCTION IN INDIA: 1950–1 TO 1961–2 (*base*: 1949–50= 100)

	Weight	1950–51	1955–56	1956–57	1957–58	1958–59	1959–60	1960–61	1961–62
Food-grains	66·9	90·5	115·3	120·8	109·2	131·0	126·8	135·6	135·2
Rice	35·3	87·9	114·2	120·4	105·7	128·4	125·3	136·2	136·0
Wheat	8·5	101·1	131·3	140·7	118·5	147·4	151·7	162·7	174·8
Maize	2·1	84·4	112·3	132·8	135·9	135·5	146·5	144·5	146·2
Pulses	8·6	91·7	118·4	122·9	103·0	136·0	120·0	128·6	121·1
Gram	3·7	98·0	138·9	159·8	125·8	180·3	143·5	162·3	152·7

The *Eastern Economist*, 1963, Annual Number.

weather. In 1961–2 the yield was slightly lower than that of the year before, the harvests of 1962–3 were disappointing, and the harvests of 1963–4, in consequence of a prolonged cold spell in northern India during the first few months of 1964, are likely to be worse. Provisional estimates suggest that food production will be no higher in 1963–4 than in 1960–1, though there will be an additional 28 million people to feed. Already there are reports of extensive food-hoarding, a dangerous rise in food prices, and depleted stocks of imported food, with the country's financial reserves unable to meet the cost of substantial new imports.

The constant crisis of survival is common to almost all the poor, or – as they are more politely termed – 'underdeveloped' countries, and if the crisis appears starker in India than in most of the others, it is because India reveals the characteristics of 'underdevelopment' more starkly than they do. Like them, though on a much more massive scale, India has a low average income for its inhabitants; small access to mechanical energy; a subsistence sector, mainly agricultural, which cannot generate a surplus for investment and so stagnates or deteriorates, yet which constitutes the major portion of the economy; and an organized, mainly industrial sector, which can produce profits for investment but which constitutes a minor portion of the economy. Such a society is not only poor, it tends irretrievably to grow poorer. The techniques of modern medicine, the decline in internal disorder, the development of centralized authority, all encourage a population increase that is unmatched by an increase in economic resources. Agricultural yields are low and fall even further as more and more people crowd their tiny ancestral plots; only large-scale mechanized farming, with the employment of fertilizers and pesticides, would increase yields significantly, but for this there is neither the land organization nor the capital. The subsistence farmers are too poor to nourish themselves, let alone the soil which they work, too poor to replace exhausted equipment or buy new and more efficient implements, too poor to support beyond subsistence the village pedlars, artisans and shopkeepers. Producing and earning no more than can provide them with their essential food and clothing, they cannot save and spend and so promote a market for the consumer goods on which a dynamic industrial sector might develop; such industry as exists does so despite rather than because of them.

It is a vicious circle of impoverishment, squandering human as well as natural resources. The United Nations Report on 'Measures for the Economic Development of Underdeveloped Countries' has estimated that many regions of India and Pakistan – as well as parts of the Philippines and Indonesia – possess a surplus agricultural population of somewhere between 20 and 25 per cent of the total. One out of every four or five agricultural workers, in other words, is unnecessary and even burdensome, consuming without adding anything at all to the productivity of the whole. Since in India the rural population constitutes over 80 per cent of the total, or some 360 million people, anywhere from 72 to 90 million people exist as economic parasites. Transferred to another sector of the economy, they might be made productive, while the farming community, relieved of its burden, even if producing no more would consume much less, spend more, save and invest more, and so in the end produce more. Yet the farming community cannot unburden itself till the unneeded workers have somewhere else to go, and the only other place they can go is the organized, mainly industrial sector. But the small organized sector cannot absorb them, and would be able to do so only if it could be developed by the spending power of a prosperous farming community. The problem seems insoluble. A subsistence economy can only progress to a dynamic one by producing profit for investment in industry and mechanization; yet the essence of a subsistence economy is that it cannot produce profit. A poor society can only grow rich by utilizing its labour force productively; yet a productive labour force requires the diversification, the capital equipment and the consumer demand which a poor society cannot afford.

There exist only two means of escape. A poor society can acquire the capital for its development from abroad, through loans and gifts from rich societies; or it can generate its own by organized sacrifice. The first method is at the same time easier and rarer. Rich societies do not generally lend or give money unless they can profit by doing so; they expect returns, in the form of strategic involvement, political subservience or economic advantages; and whatever their motives, they seldom lend or give enough to produce more than a peripheral effect. The second method entails suffering, discipline and co-ordination, sometimes voluntary, often enforced. A subsistence economy can be made to yield surpluses by lowering the level of consumption, whatever the human costs; a society that produces 1,800 calories a day for average consumption can try to feed its citizens on 1,600 calories a day, export the resultant agricultural surplus, and purchase capital equipment with the receipts. Whether this is done with the intention of establishing in the process a system of economic equality or of 'free enterprise', the surpluses must be produced somehow, and the proceeds of its sale not fruitlessly consumed, but productively invested in the materials of industrial and agricultural advance.

Two men above all others influenced the course that India was to pursue with independence: Gandhi and Nehru; and though they worked closely together in the Congress movement and had for each other a strong affection and regard, they differed radically in their objectives and programme for change. Gandhi was by temperament, manner and belief far closer to the Indian villagers, their faith, traditions and culture. He wanted to preserve village India; to liberate it from foreign rule so that it might develop, undisturbed, a moral democracy, economically self-sufficient, with its members needing to exploit neither each other nor anyone else.

Industrialization is, I am afraid, going to be a curse for mankind. Exploitation of one nation by another cannot go

on for all time. Industrialism depends entirely on your capacity to exploit, on foreign markets being open to you, and
on the absence of competitors ... In fact, India, when it
begins to exploit other nations – as it must if it becomes
industrialized – will be a curse for other nations, a menace
to the world. And why should I think of industrializing India
to exploit other nations?[1]

I have been saying that if untouchability stays, Hinduism
goes; even so I would say that if the village perishes India
will perish too. It will no more be India. Her own mission
in the world will get lost. The revival of the village is possible
only when it is no more exploited. Industrialization on a
mass scale will necessarily lead to passive or active exploitation of the villagers, as the problems of competition and
marketing come in. Therefore, we have to concentrate on
the village being self-contained, manufacturing mainly for
use. Provided this character of the village industry is maintained, there would be no objection to villages using even
modern machines and tools that they can make and can
afford to use. Only they should not be used as a means of
exploitation of others.[2]

Gandhi, of course, more than any other man, recognized,
reproved and, in his singular way, worked against the want and
degradation of the Indian poor, but his method, as his objective,
was a moral one. Committed to non-violence in the broadest
sense, he saw the eradication of injustices and crude inequalities
as the consequence of individual conversion; socialism for him,
and he called himself a socialist frequently, was not so much a
system of government as a spiritual revolution. It was in demonstrating this attitude that he proclaimed his view of the
rich as trustees of the people's goods, a view from which he
never – despite widespread criticism – swerved. He did not
believe in class war, and maintained that it could be avoided.

When the people adopt it [non-violence] as a principle
of conduct, class war becomes an impossibility ... By the
non-violent method we seek not to destroy the capitalist,
we seek to destroy capitalism. We invite the capitalist to

[1] *Young India*, November 12th, 1931.   [2] *Harijan*, August 19th, 1936.

regard himself as a trustee for those on whom he depends for the making, the retention and the increase of his capital... Immediately the worker realizes his strength, he is in a position to become a co-sharer of the capitalist instead of remaining his slave. If he aims at becoming the sole owner, he will most likely be killing the goose that lays the golden eggs. Inequalities in intelligence and even opportunity will last till the end of time. A man living on the banks of a river has any day more opportunity of growing crops than one living in an arid desert. But if inequalities stare us in the face, the essential equality too is not to be missed. Every man has an equal right for the necessaries of life even as birds and beasts have.[1]

Nehru was Gandhi's apparent antithesis. By temperament, manner and belief he was closer to the cities of the world than to the villages of India, his culture as foreign to the peasants as his scepticism was far from their constant god-awareness. Where Gandhi heard the hum of the spinning-wheel, Nehru heard the crash of huge modern machines; he did not want to preserve ageless village India, he wanted to oust it, mechanizing agriculture and promoting rapid urban industrial growth. He acknowledged the antagonism between Gandhi's ideas and his own, and he stated it.

The khadi movement, hand-spinning and hand-weaving, which is Gandhiji's special favourite, is an intensification of individualism in production, and is thus a throw-back to the pre-industrial age. As a solution of any vital present-day problem it cannot be taken seriously, and it produces a mentality which may become an obstacle to growth in the right direction ... Gandhiji has said repeatedly that he is not against machinery as such; he seems to think that it is out of place in India to-day. But can we wind up the basic industries, such as iron and steel, or even the lighter ones that already exist? It is obvious that we cannot do so. If we have railways, bridges, transport facilities, etc., we must either produce them ourselves or depend on others. If we want to have the means of defence we must not only have

[1] *Young India*, March 24th, 1931.

the basic industries but a highly developed industrial system. No country to-day is really independent or capable of resisting aggression unless it is industrially developed.[1]

Where Gandhi wanted an India with as decentralized a government as possible, an economic democracy of the village, Nehru looked beyond even India, to an international government, an economic democracy of the world.

It is possible, I think, that in an agricultural country like India, so very low is our present standard, that there might be a slight improvement for the masses with the development of village industries. But we are tied up, as every country is tied up, with the rest of the world, and it seems to me quite impossible for us to cut adrift. We must think, therefore, in terms of the world, and in these terms a narrow autarchy is out of the question. Personally I consider it undesirable from every point of view. Inevitably we are led to the only possible solution – the establishment of a socialist order, first within national boundaries, and eventually in the world as a whole, with a controlled production and distribution of wealth for the public good.[2]

Gandhi, of course, sought to change the individual; Nehru sought to change the society. For Gandhi, the arena was the spirit and the enemy was sin; for Nehru, the arena was power and the enemy was privilege, the possession – and so inescapably the pursuit – of individual wealth.

Gandhiji wants to improve the individual internally, morally and spiritually, and thereby to change the external environment. He wants people to give up bad habits and indulgences and to become pure ... Of course he detests all this violence and degrading conflict. But are they not inherent in the acquisitive society of to-day with its law that the strong must prey on the weak? ... The profit motive to-day inevitably leads to conflict. The whole system protects and gives every scope to man's predatory instincts; it encourages some finer instincts, but much more so the baser instincts

---

[1] *Jawaharlal Nehru: An Autobiography* (The Bodley Head, London, and the John Day Company Inc., New York, 1958 edition), pp. 523, 526.
[2] Ibid., pp. 522-3.

of man ... If these motives and ambitions are encouraged by
society and attract the best of our people, does Gandhiji
think that he can achieve his ideal – the moral man – in
this environment?... it is clear that the good of a nation or of
mankind must not be held up because some people who
profit by the existing order object to the change. If political
or social institutions stand in the way of such a change,
they have to be removed.[1]

In consequence, where Gandhi spoke of conversion, Nehru
spoke also of force. For Gandhi, non-violence was an alternative
to class war; for Nehru, non-violence was a useful instrument
of struggle in the very conduct of class war.

The non-violent method, in order to justify itself, must be
dynamic and capable of changing such a régime or social
order. Whether it can do so or not I do not know. It can, I
think, carry us a long way, but I doubt if it can take us to the
final goal. In any event, some form of coercion seems to be
inevitable, for people who hold power and privilege do not
give them up till they are forced to do so, or till conditions
are created which make it more harmful to them to keep
these privileges than to give them up. The present conflicts
in society, national as well as class conflicts, can never be
resolved except by coercion...[2]

Nehru's thought owed much to Marxism, and Nehru himself made no effort to conceal the debt. Indeed, he advertised
his agreement with the Marxist interpretation of history[3]
and accepted the need for a revolutionary rather than a reformist change in India's basic structure. He admitted the appeal
of Soviet Russia, and though he condemned 'the ruthless
suppression of all contrary opinion, the wholesale regiment-
ation, the unnecessary violence,'[4] he considered violence to be
the very foundation of the acquisitive society, and he maintained that Soviet violence at least was aimed at peace and a
'real freedom for the masses'.[5] Yet he saw that the Indian
Communists misunderstood the role of Gandhi, and he himself stressed the need for a united national struggle against

---

[1] *Jawaharlal Nehru: An Autobiography*, pp. 521–3.   [2] Ibid., p. 551.
[3] Ibid., pp. 362–3.   [4] Ibid., p. 361.   [5] Ibid., p. 362.

foreign rule. He recognized that it was Gandhi who had shaken the masses awake, and that anyone who deserted Congress would cut himself 'adrift from the vital urge of the nation' and condemn himself to an 'ineffective adventurism'.[1] So he accepted Gandhi's leadership, in the hope that the struggle for independence would itself release mass energies requiring and accomplishing social change.

In January 1948, a handful of months after India had achieved its independence, Gandhi was assassinated, and soon afterwards Sardar Vallabhbhai Patel, Home Minister and Deputy Prime Minister, the leader of the Congress right wing – whose ideas on industrialization were very close to Gandhi's[2] – and the only effective political rival that Nehru had for national leadership, suffered a heart attack. Patel never regained his health and died three years later. From 1948, therefore, Nehru was in effective command of Congress policy, and from 1951 without a serious contender for rule. Seldom in history did the leader of a democratic society enjoy so much power. Whatever pattern of social and economic progress India would pursue was Nehru's to determine.

Of the escape ways open to a poor state, Nehru himself closed one all but completely. The United States alone was at that time able to supply aid in sufficient quantities to make much impact on a country the size of India, and Nehru's foreign policy, based on a rejection of any alignment with East or West in the Cold War, made small appeal to an American administration obsessed by the military threat of Communism and eager for strategic alliances. Whether the United States would otherwise have provided India with enough capital to secure its substantial economic advance may endlessly be disputed; what is certain is that India's foreign policy substantially reduced such aid as the United States was able – and, in other relevant instances, willing – to provide.

During the eight fiscal years 1949–50 to 1956–7, India received from abroad a total of $1,325 million in loans and grants, or an average of $165 million a year. Of this total, some $1,000

[1] Ibid., p. 365.
[2] 'True socialism lies in the development of village industries. We do not want to reproduce in our country the chaotic conditions prevalent in the Western countries consequent on mass-production.' Patel speaking at Ahmedabad on January 3rd, 1935.

million came from the United States government – an average of $125 million a year – mainly in the form of loans for the supply of wheat and other commodities, while the bulk of the money from other sources was provided, in the form of high-interest-bearing loans, by the International Bank.

Then, from 1957 onwards the United States was joined by other countries in the provision of loans and grants to India, with funds coming from East as well as West. The United Kingdom, West Germany, Australia, New Zealand, Norway and Japan, the U.S.S.R., Roumania and Czechoslovakia all

Table 10

INTERNATIONAL ECONOMIC AID TO SELECTED UNDER-DEVELOPED COUNTRIES FOR TWO YEARS 1958 AND 1959

Country	Population (in millions)	Total aid (in U.S. $ million)	Per capita aid (in $)
Jordan	1·6	108·9	68·1
Libya	1·2	60·2	50·2
Israel	2·0	93·5	46·8
Korea, Rep. of	22·5	643·5	28·6
Lebanon	1·6	43·8	27·4
Costa Rica	1·1	22·3	20·3
Formosa (Taiwan)	9·9	173·6	17·5
Bolivia	3·4	56·0	16·5
Chile	7·3	109·0	14·9
Peru	10·2	133·0	13·0
Liberia	1·3	16·1	12·4
Colombia	13·5	153·9	11·4
Guatemala	3·5	37·4	10·7
Nicaragua	1·4	14·6	10·4
Panama	1·0	10·1	10·1
Paraguay	1·7	13·6	8·0
Iran	19·7	142·2	7·2
Honduras	1·8	12·5	6·9
Argentina	20·2	105·6	5·2
Ceylon	9·4	42·4	4·5
Mexico	32·3	128·4	4·0
Uruguay	2·7	10·4	3·9
Pakistan	85·6	322·9	3·8
Thailand	21·5	65·2	3·0
India	397·4	622·7	1·6

U.N. Statistical Yearbook, 1960.

contributed. Yet the United States remained by far the largest source of aid, providing 44 per cent of the total, while the World Bank supplied 16 per cent, the U.S.S.R. 18 per cent, and all other donors together 22 per cent. India was unable to get anywhere near the extent of assistance required for the transformation of her economy, nor even anywhere near the assistance that many other poor societies – with less objectionable foreign policies – proportionately received.

There isn't much that a country can do with a total foreign investment equivalent to 80 cents (or about 5s. 6d.) for each inhabitant a year. India was forced to find the means of development from her own resources.

Long before independence, Congress had set its face both against development by chance – the productive investment of 'free enterprise' – and development by the coercion of popular sacrifice. A National Planning Committee of Congress had been established under Nehru's chairmanship in 1937, and this had defined planning 'under a democratic system' as 'the technical co-ordination, by disinterested experts, of consumption, production, investment, trade and income distribution, in accordance with social objectives set by bodies representative of the nation. Such planning is not only to be considered from the point of view of economics, and the raising of standard of living, but must include cultural and spiritual values, and the human side of life.'[1] It was the hand of Nehru and the voice of Gandhi.

Independence itself struck a serious blow to the already weak Indian economy with the establishment of Pakistan. India retained 77·7 per cent of the pre-partition population but only 73·1 per cent of the pre-partition area, 72·5 per cent of the rice acreage, 70 per cent of the wheat acreage, and 70 per cent of irrigated land. The new frontier divided the cotton and jute mills of India from their sources of supply in Pakistan, the consumers of manufactured goods in Pakistan from the factories of India. Moreover, political relations between the two states, bad enough on the morrow of independence, rapidly deteriorated to the point of armed collision, and a boundary became a barrier. A clear policy for the economic development of India became increasingly urgent.

[1] H. Venkatasubbiah, *Indian Economy Since Independence* (Asia Publishing House, 1961), p. 292.

On April 6th, 1948, the National Government proclaimed a comprehensive industrial policy, aimed at establishing specific spheres for government and privately owned undertakings and indicating the broad lines of state regulation and control. Industries were divided into four main categories: (i) those required for defence, including the manufacture of munitions, the production of atomic energy, and the ownership and management of railway transport, which were to be the exclusive monopoly of the state; (ii) basic and key industries, such as iron and steel, coal, aircraft manufacture and shipbuilding, which were to be in the government-controlled sphere, with all new undertakings to be owned and operated by the government and those already under private ownership and management subject to possible nationalization after ten years; (iii) twenty other important industries including heavy chemicals, sugar, textiles, cement, paper, salt and machine tools, which were to be run by private enterprise but controlled and regulated by the state; and (iv) residual industries to be run by private enterprise under the general control of the state.

It was a blue-print for the mixed economy, a compromise between the reformist, 'spiritual' attitude of Gandhi, dominant in the early definition of planning made by the National Planning Committee of Congress, and the revolutionary, 'secular' disposition of Nehru himself. Not surprisingly – as was to happen again and again in the future – government policy fell flat on its face between two stools. The threat of nationalization after ten years disturbed the private entrepreneurs, who postponed any expansion and replacement of their plant and equipment in the basic and key industries, and within two years of having announced its policy the government reassuringly declared that it might not find it possible to nationalize all the existing units in the second category even after the ten-year period. The apostles of economic revolution grew cynical about the government's true intentions, and the private industrialists were emboldened to believe that they could indefinitely delay nationalization by tactics of timely inaction. Furthermore, in declaring that all new undertakings in the category of basic and key industries were to be owned and operated by the state, the government made provision for exceptions – allowing the co-operation of private enterprise 'in the national interest' –

and it soon became clear that the exceptions were more to be followed than the rules. Though 'mineral oils' had been listed as a basic or key industry, the government permitted three private foreign firms – Standard-Vacuum, Burmah-Shell and Caltex – to establish petroleum refineries in India during 1951–3, and the small part of their capital that was opened to Indian subscription was taken up not by the government but by private investors. After long delays over the establishment of government steel plants, the government instead forced the amalgamation of two existing private units – the Steel Corporation of Bengal and the Indian Iron and Steel Company – and their expansion with a loan from the World Bank in 1952. When, towards the end of 1953, the government did at last decide to establish a steel plant of its own, it did so in partnership with the German firm of Krupp-Demag, which was to bear up to a third of the total investment and enjoy corresponding representation on the board. As one Indian economist has tartly written: 'If there was to be no private capital in the agreement for a second state steel plant signed with the Russian Government early in 1955, that was because there is no private enterprise in Russia.'[1] Where the 1948 statement of industrial policy did commit the government unequivocally to immediate state ownership and management, it dealt with the self-evident. No one expected the government to hand back the railways to company management, to allow suddenly the private manufacture of armaments, or to allure private industrialists into undertaking the development of atomic energy. By making a virtue of the obvious, the government only succeeded in appearing absurd.

In March 1950 the Indian Planning Commission was established, with Nehru as Chairman, to organize the planned development of the Indian economy, and in July 1951 the Commission presented the draft outline of the First Five Year Plan, covering the period from April 1951 to March 1956. The general objective, as proclaimed in the draft outline, was to increase national and average individual income by systematic capital investment, and the view taken was of twenty-five years, with the doubling of national income in seventeen and the doubling of average individual income in twenty-two years as

[1] H. Venkatasubbiah, *Indian Economy Since Independence*, pp. 92–3.

the targets. The First Five Year Plan was itself modestly conceived within the context of a mixed economy, on the supposition that 'public and private sectors should function side by side as integral parts of a single organism'.[1] The government would endeavour progressively to widen the public sector, but this did not imply a programme of nationalization, and the private sector would be allowed to expand within a limited field. In keeping with the tone of the 1948 statement of industrial policy, nothing revolutionary was projected or planned. War and partition had left the country with industrial production well below capacity, a badly run-down transport system, the need to rehabilitate large numbers of displaced persons, inflationary pressures within the economy and an adverse balance-of-payments position. The government resolved upon consolidation and repair before expansion.

Agriculture received the greatest attention in the Plan, since there was an acute food shortage in the country and a programme of intensive industrialization would in any event require an increased and secure supply of food and raw materials. As high as 42·1 per cent of the total Plan provision, or a sum of 1,001 crores of rupees (1 crore, or 10 million rupees, is equivalent to £750,000), was set aside for agriculture, community development, irrigation and power projects, and significant if unspectacular progress was registered. Overall agricultural production recorded an increase of 18 per cent during the Plan period, while food production rose from 50 million tons to 65 million tons, an overall increase of 30 per cent or an annual average increase of 6 per cent. An area of 8,500,000 additional acres was irrigated, and the installed capacity of electricity generation rose by over 50 per cent.[2] Industrial production increased by some 40 per cent or an average of 8 per cent a year, with substantial rises in cement output – from 2,700,000 tons in 1950–1 to 4,600,000 tons in 1955–6; cotton cloth – from 4,076 million yards in 1951 to 5,307 million in 1956; paper and paper board – from 132,000 tons in 1951 to 193,000 tons in 1956; bicycles – from 114,000 tons in 1951 to 664,000 tons in 1956; sewing machines – from 44,000 in 1951 to 130,000 in

[1] Alak Ghosh, *Indian Economy – Its Nature and Problems* (World Press, Calcutta, 1962), p. 57.
[2] From 2,300,000 to 3,400,000 kilowatts.

THE ECONOMIC PRECIPICE

1956; and important chemical products, like sulphuric acid –
from 107,000 tons in 1951 to 164,000 tons in 1956. Finally,
some 570 crores of rupees, or over £427 million, were spent
during the Plan period on transport and communications; thirty
major bridges were built, 4,000 miles of existing road improved,
and 636 miles of linkage constructed, while 380 miles of new
railway line were added and 430 miles of dismantled line
restored.

External financing constituted less than a tenth of the Plan's
total requirements, and indeed of the 296 crores made available from sources abroad for development programmes in the
public sector, only 188 crores were utilized, leaving 108 crores
available for additional expenditure under the Second Plan.
Over the five years of the First Plan period, national income
increased by 17·5 per cent, while *per capita* income rose by 10·5
per cent. Most impressively, millions of refugees from Pakistan
were absorbed into the economy without undue dislocation;
many of them were found productive employment in the cities
and many settled with success on the land.

Yet all in all the achievements of the First Five-Year Plan
fell substantially short of the country's needs. The increases in
agricultural production were largely the result of unusually
good weather, as the balance of payments was assisted by the
thriving commodity markets of the Korean war and its after-
math: there was a rise in output from the existing potential, but
little increase in new sources of production as envisaged by
programmes of irrigation, land reclamation and the distribution of fertilizers, manures and improved seeds. There was
no systematic and comprehensive crop-planning, and little
was done to reform the wasteful and unjust rural structure, with
its absentee landlords, voracious moneylenders, indebted
peasantry and sub-subsistence landless labourers. On the
surface of ageless village India the first experiment in democratic
planning stirred hardly a ripple.

Industrial progress resulted from the larger availability of
raw materials, the employment of spare capacity and the heavy
investment of the private sector rather than the state. The
industrialists, consoled by official denials of any real intent to
nationalize, measured the profits to be made by feeding the
hunger for consumer goods and set out to realize them. The

government did not excite economic advance so much as allow it. Indeed, the public sector provides less investment than the private one – of the total 3,100 crores invested during the five years of the Plan, the public sector accounted for slightly less than half, at 1,500 crores, while the private sector produced close on 1,600 – and in the sphere of manufacturing industry the private sector accounted for 233 of the total 293 crores invested. The results achieved by the Plan were between 85 and 90 per cent of those envisaged, but the targets were themselves far less than the requirements of a growing economy. The development of power was just sufficient to meet the increasing demand, and little attention was paid to the development of mineral resources. In short, the First Five Year Plan accompanied a vaguely guided economic advance, rather than exciting a co-ordinated and necessarily vast economic expansion. As Nehru himself later admitted, when he addressed the National Development Council in September 1957: 'We had rather an easy time in the First Five Year Plan, because really we had not stretched ourselves. We had not made any particular effort. We just took what was there and called it a Plan.'

At the beginning of April 1956 the Second Five Year Plan was launched, with four main objectives: (i) a sizeable increase in national income so as to raise living standards in the country; (ii) speedy industrialization, with especial emphasis on the development of basic and heavy industries; (iii) a large expansion of employment opportunities; and (iv) a reduction of inequalities in income and wealth, with a more even distribution of economic power. The First Plan had left the Indian masses little better off than it had found them; had concentrated on agriculture to the neglect of heavy industry, without which massive industrialization would have to remain a vision; had generated direct employment for some 4,500,000 people, but left some 5,300,000 still unemployed; and had made many of the rich a great deal richer, without noticeably affecting the condition of most of the poor. The Second Plan proposed to make a start at remedying these defects. It calculated on raising the national income by 25 per cent over the five years of its operation, with an increase in agricultural production of some 30 per cent, since half the national income originated in the agricultural sector. In promoting heavy industry, the Plan

aimed at three steel plants in the public sector, each with a
capacity of one million tons a year, as well as the expansion of
two main producers in the private sector; a rise in coal production, from both private and public sectors, from 38 million
to 60 million tons a year; an increase in cement production from
4·3 to 13 million tons a year; and expansion of traffic capacity on
the railways to meet the requirements of the industrial programme. The Planning Commission estimated an addition to
the country's labour force during the Second Plan period of
some 10 million people, and it therefore planned on creating
10 million new jobs. In this it proposed a mere holding operation, since it made no provision for the 5,300,000 unemployed
left at the end of the First Plan period; the backlog was left
for the massive solution of subsequent Plans. Finally, the Second
Plan set a 'socialist pattern of society' as the broad objective of
economic policy.

On April 30th, 1956, soon after the launching of the Second
Plan, the Indian parliament adopted an Industrial Policy
Resolution, which was less vapid than its predecessor of 1948
had been on the role of the state in an industrial economy. It
declared:

> The adoption of the socialist pattern of society as the
> national objective, as well as the need for planned and rapid
> development, requires that all industries of basic and
> strategic importance, or in the nature of public utility
> services, should be in the public sector. Other industries
> which are essential and require investment on a scale which
> only the state, in present circumstances, could provide,
> have also to be in the public sector. The state has therefore
> to assume direct responsibility for the future development
> of industries over a wider area.

The 1956 statement of industrial policy divided industries
into three broad categories, instead of the four in the 1948
statement. The first category consisted of industries whose
future development would be the exclusive responsibility of the
state, and though these included some self-evident segments like
the manufacture of munitions and the production of atomic
energy, they also included iron and steel, heavy machinery,
coal and mineral oils – the foundation of the country's in-

dustrial structure. Indeed, this new first category merged the
first and second categories, the strategic and the basic industries,
in the 1948 statement; but in contrast to the 1948 policy, the
1956 statement carried no threat to nationalize the existing
units in the private sector. In the second category of the new
statement were industries which were to become progressively
state-owned; the state would generally take the initiative in
establishing new undertakings, but private enterprise would be
expected to supplement such efforts. Comprising such important
industries as aluminium, ferro-alloys, machine-tools, fertilizers,
synthetic rubber and antibiotics, this category emphasized the
government's continued allegiance to a mixed economy, with
the simultaneous expansion of public and private sectors, and
with the state's bearing the responsibility for establishing new
undertakings wherever private enterprise, motivated solely by
considerations of profit, refused to do so. The third category
corresponded to the fourth category in the 1948 statement of
policy, covering residual industries whose future development
would be left to the general initiative of the private sector; but
it went one step further by proclaiming the power of the state to
start new undertakings in the residual category if such were
considered necessary to the public interest and the successful
execution of the Five Year Plans. The 1956 statement of policy
also aimed at reducing disparities in industrial development
among different regions of the country, and for this purpose
promised to provide power, water and transport facilities to the
backward. It noted the need for training adequate technical and
managerial personnel, for education in business management
and for the proper regulating of industrial relations, and it
stressed the importance of cottage and small industries in
providing immediate employment, in ensuring a more equitable distribution of national income, and in mobilizing idle
resources of capital and skill.

Now whatever might be said of the 1956 Industrial Policy
Resolution, it was certainly a far cry from the revolutionary
barricades in the thought of pre-Independence Nehru. Here
was no assault on 'the profit motive', which 'inevitably leads to
conflict', which 'protects and gives every scope to man's pre-
conflicts' by coercion, because 'people who hold power and pri-
datory instincts'. Here was no attempt at resolving 'class

vilege do not give them up till they are forced to do so'. The Resolution echoed the old dedication to an industrial India, to the pounding of steel mills. But it echoed also an accommodation to the hum of village spinning-wheels, even, it seemed, to the hum of the 'trustee'. Gandhi had not left the impression of his doctrines on the flag of independent India alone. Of course private enterprise raised an outcry against the promise of more state initiative in industry. Merchants and industrialists in India always cry out against state initiatives, and never – the conclusion is irresistible – so shrilly as when the initiatives threaten to be of profit to them. It is as though they cannot believe their luck and cry out to be reassured. For the government in its 1956 statement of policy was not pronouncing the decline of private enterprise in India, it was proclaiming a multitude of new opportunities. Development in the public sector would excite development in the private one. The state would itself be establishing those heavy industries which were essential to the growth of the whole economy but whose huge investment costs and distant profitability discouraged private risk; and once established these state-owned heavy industries would provide privately owned light industries with the raw material of profit. The steel and power plants in the public sector, for instance, would present firms in the private sector

Table 11

PROGRESS OF PUBLIC LIMITED COMPANIES

	1955	1957	1958	1959
		Rs. Crores		
Total income	1,624	2,040	2,126	2,293
Disposal of profits:				
Profits before tax	118	108	121	161
Tax provision*	50	52	56	59
Profits after tax*	68	56	65	102
Dividends	39	43	47	64
Retained profits	29	14	18	38

NOTE: Compiled from the Reserve Bank's study of a sample of 1,001 public limited companies. The sample accounts for 17% of the paid-up capital of the category of companies covered.

* Figures for 1958 and 1959 are not strictly comparable with those for the earlier years owing to the changes in the system of company taxation introduced by the Finance Act, 1959.

with the means to increase production of consumer goods. The 'socialist pattern of society' was in practice to give India's capitalists more 'power and privilege' than they were likely to have possessed if left to their own devices.

From 1955 to 1959, during the five years which covered most of the Second Five Year Plan period, the public limited companies as a whole did extremely well, even by the standards of a society wholly dedicated to capitalism.

Foreign investment, cajoled by the profits that Indian private industry was making and reassured by repeated government declarations, continued moving into India, but still only as a tentative trickle, while it poured into other countries more ruthlessly practising the virtues of 'free enterprise'. Compared with the £1,800 million of Western investment in South Africa, the extent of foreign business participation in the Indian economy remained pitifully small.

Table 12

FOREIGN BUSINESS INVESTMENTS IN INDIA

	End of 1955	End of 1957	End of 1958	End of 1959
	Rs. crores (one crore = £750,000)			
Industry-wise				
Plantations	87·2	86·6	96·0	95·1
Mining	9·6	9·8	12·4	13·0
Petroleum	104·0	134·1	118·4	120·7
Manufacturing	131·8	184·0	218·6	250·7
Services	123·5	128·5	127·2	131·2
TOTAL	456·1	543·0	572·6	610·7*
Net inflow	16·3†	50·0	27·7	38·1
Source-wise				
United Kingdom	376·8	398·8	398·8	400·1
United States	39·9	57·5	60·0	82·0
Switzerland	6·6	6·7	6·8	7·6
West Germany	2·5	3·5	3·8	5·4
World Bank	2·7	46·9	72·2	83·0
Others	27·6	29·6	31·0	32·6

* *Direct Investments* Rs. 447·9 crores, and *Portfolio Investments* Rs. 162·8 crores.

† Annual average of 1954 and 1955.

REFERENCE: *Statistical Outline of India* (Tata Industries, 1961), p. 36.

India was inevitably getting the worst of both worlds. Openly
dedicated to a 'socialist pattern of society', the government could
never entice foreign capital in the quantity that the country
required; and careful to conciliate private investment at home
and abroad, it was able neither to take real command of the
economy nor inspire popular enthusiasm for self-sacrifice. It
confirmed instead of dispelling general cynicism.

The Second Five Year Plan failed substantially to attain many
of its major targets. Massive investment generated a purchasing
power which was inadequately controlled and which conse-
quently led to a dangerous rise in prices. The cottage and small-
scale industries, with their outdated techniques and equipment,
could not meet the demand for basic consumer goods; hoarders
and black-marketeers took advantage of a smaller-than-anti-
cipated rise in agricultural production to create, in the absence
of stern government measures, a largely artificial food shortage;
and the readiness of the commercial banks to supply speculators
with funds increased the already strong inflationary pressures
of large-scale deficit financing. Over the five-year period of the
Second Plan, wholesale prices rose by some 30 per cent and
foodstuffs alone by 27 per cent; industrial raw materials by
45 per cent; and manufactured articles by over 25 per cent.
With the general level of prices rising by an annual 6 per cent,
and foreign exchange reserves reduced to near exhaustion by
excessive purchasing from abroad, only a scaling down of Plan
targets prevented a runaway crisis. In the end, though all the
4,600 crores of rupees allocated were spent, inflation had significantly reduced their value, and only four-fifths of the Plan was
actually achieved. The shortfall in finished steel was some 40
per cent (2·6 million tons instead of 4·3 million), in cement over
30 per cent (8·8 million tons instead of 13 million), and in
ammonium sulphate some 57 per cent (125,000 tons instead of
290,000); coal production reached 54 million tons instead of
60 million, and electricity 5·8 million kilowatts instead of 6·9
million. Only in jute, sugar, petroleum refining, glass and
woollen textiles, among the significant measures of progress
that it had set itself, did the Plan attain or slightly exceed its
objectives. Significantly, instead of the 10 million new jobs
outside of agriculture that the Plan had set out to produce for
the expanding population, it generated only 6,500,000, leaving

3,500,000 new unemployed to be added to the backlog of 5,300,000.

In large measure it was the insufficiently ordered production and consumption of the business community which distorted the progress of the Plan. The unprecedented profits made by the industrialists, the merchants and the pure speculators created an enormous demand for luxury consumer goods like quality furniture and fabrics, modern bathroom and kitchen equipment, air-conditioners and automobiles, and these commodities competed with projects of fundamental importance to the economy for scarce resources like steel, cement, power, foreign exchange and technical skills. As one careful Indian economist described it:

> During the Second Plan period a serious diversion of resources took place for the benefit of the privileged Upper Classes sector (i.e. the U-sector), and it is highly probable that this tendency was assisted by the inequality in distribution of incomes resulting from the planned investment process which produced increasing accruals of profit and salaried incomes to the U-sector. The result is that at the present moment the U-sector, with its effective demand, is controlling the market forces towards its own benefit.[1]

It is in the light of this that official figures for any growth in general prosperity must be considered. The Second Plan increased the national income by just under 20 per cent – or 5 per cent less than the objective – but since the population had meanwhile risen by some 10·5 per cent, the increase in average income for all Indians was something like 9 per cent for the five-year period. This, while disappointing, would still have been a sign of progress, however slight, had the increase in national income been equally shared by all Indians; but since a clearly disproportionate amount went to the already rich, it is not unreasonable to conclude that most Indians were no better off at the end of the Second Plan than they had been at the beginning, and that many may even have suffered, with the sharp rise in prices, a further drop in their already low living standards.

The necessity for rural reform, both to remove the more glaring economic injustices and to increase agricultural pro-

[1] Alak Ghosh, *Indian Economy – Its Nature and Problems*, p. 93.

ductivity, had been canvassed, as a major argument against continued British rule, by the Congress leadership for many years before the achievement of independence. The Congress election manifesto of 1946 called for 'the removal of intermediaries between the peasant and the state', and a ceiling on individual land holdings became Congress policy at the end of 1947. 'Land to the tiller' had been the cry of Congress struggle, and became the promise of Congress rule. An amendment to the Constitution in 1951 protected from judicial attack the abolition of rent-collecting landholder or *zamindari* rights, with the fixing of compensation by the government, and by the middle of 1954 legislation for the removal of intermediaries had been enacted by almost all the Indian states. Compensation – which totalled about 450 crores of rupees or some £335 million – was on a sliding scale, with a small portion paid immediately in cash and the balance in annual instalments or through the issue of low-interest-bearing and eventually redeemable bonds; there was a rising element of simple expropriation as the size of the landholding increased, but in the main the compensation was generous, and this essential first measure of reform was anything but punitive.

The government also embarked on a programme of tenancy reform, and in the First Five Year Plan recommended to the states the enactment of legislation to reduce rents, provide greater security of tenure, and encourage the purchase of land from the larger landowners by their tenants. Action was certainly urgent, for the prevailing rate of rent was as high as half of the gross produce, with the tenant bearing almost all the costs of cultivation, and the Plan proposed a reduction to a third or a quarter of the gross produce, according to whether the land was irrigated or not. The landowning class, however, exercised considerable influence in state even more than national politics, and threatened or cajoled the Congress administrations into less precipitate reform; in Andhra, for instance, the ceiling on rent was set at 40 per cent, and in Madras at 45 per cent. Furthermore, where significant changes were enacted – in Bombay (now the states of Gujarat and Maharashtra) the rent ceiling was set at merely a sixth of the gross produce – landowners ejected their tenants and cultivated the land themselves through hired labour. By the end of the Second Plan, the state administrations had almost all been pressed by the national leadership of Congress to enact security of tenure, but in most states there was a virtually total lack of enforcement, and landowners openly disregarded the new tenancy laws. Nowhere was this more manifest than in the evasion of restrictions on individual land holdings. State after state set a ceiling on the amount of land – usually between 25 and 50 acres – that might be owned by any one person, but the landowners merely divided their holdings up among members of their family or turned the excess into fruit gardens and so profitably escaped the application of the law. It was soon apparent that in agriculture no less than in industry, the rich – by trickery, influence or corruption – were able to circumvent the intentions of the government.

A redistribution of land holdings was in any event only one of the major reforms which Indian agriculture required; the whole antiquated system of marketing and rural credit, which directed peasant productivity through the fingers of middlemen and moneylenders, demanded change. For the policy of 'land to the tiller' would have little meaning if the tiller himself could neither market his produce profitably nor acquire loans for seed, fertilizer and essential equipment to develop his new holdings.

The immediate task of the government was to overhaul marketing methods, for much of agricultural production was being sold by the peasants in the villages themselves at low prices to travelling traders, who frequently doubled as moneylenders and so could dictate terms to their debtors. Inadequate storage facilities forced the cultivators to sell their produce straight after the harvest, when prices were depressed, while the lack of cheap and easy transport kept them from the competition of organized markets. Even those few who evaded the clutch of the travelling traders and took their produce to market were frequently defrauded through ignorance of prevailing prices and the deliberately bewildering multitude of strange weights and measures used there. The government set about regulating the markets themselves and by the early 'sixties had dealt with some two thirds of the 1,800 in the country, establishing management committees on which producers and traders were both represented. Further measures, however, were – as usual – more impressive in project than in execution. The Second Five Year

Plan recommended the urgent creation of co-operative marketing societies, and over 1,700 of these were duly organized – with
financial help of less than £4 million. In 1956 parliament passed
special legislation to further the construction of warehouses,
and by the end of the Second Plan period thirty-eight had been
built by the central government, with a storage capacity of
64,000 tons; the Third Plan has allotted some £6 million for
further warehouse construction, but past performance suggests
that only part of this small sum will in the end be spent.

Far worse is the state of massive peasant indebtedness. The
All India Rural Credit Survey of 1951–2 estimated that 70
per cent of rural credit was provided by moneylenders, 23 per
cent by traders, landlords and relatives, 3 per cent by government agencies, 3 per cent by co-operatives, and a mere 1 per
cent by the commercial banks; moreover, the major portion of
the money lent by co-operatives went to the larger agriculturists, while the other cultivators, constituting some 70 per cent
of the total, received what they could of the residue. Nor were
the debts in the main being incurred for productive purposes;
less than a third of the money borrowed was invested in the land,
while almost a half went into paying the exorbitant interest on
old loans and providing for current expenditure on such neces-
sities as dowries, marriage celebrations and religious ceremony.
The moneylenders themselves had no real competition from
alternative sources of credit, could accordingly charge what
interest rates they liked, and to secure their loans frequently
took control of the peasant's crops – which they then bought at
a nominal price – his land and even his movements. Inevitably
the peasant sank ever deeper into debt, losing all efficiency and
initiative, neglecting improvements to his land which would
serve only to enrich the moneylender. No real development of
Indian agriculture, and so no real progress of the Indian economy, could be expected until the problem of rural credit was
solved.

The Survey stated the difficulties succinctly enough: 'the
agricultural credit that is supplied falls short of the right quantity,
is not of the right type, does not serve the right purpose, and by
the criterion of need (not overlooking the criterion of credit
worthiness) often fails to go to the right people.' A vast rescue
operation had rapidly to be mounted, and the Survey itself

proposed a general plan. The stranglehold of the moneylender had first of all to be loosened, and that could be achieved only by the provision of large-scale, cheap and easy credit; the government should supply, through a national state-run bank, the co-operatives with adequate resources, and ensure that they did not become the preserve of the richer cultivators, while the co-operatives themselves should give loans on the security of anticipated crops instead of solely on land. Then marketing and credit should be joined as far as possible, so that the repayment of loans at harvest time might be facilitated through the sale of produce to the marketing society, while the wholesale construction of warehouses would enable the cultivator to sell his crops most profitably and borrow meanwhile on the collateral of a storage receipt.

The government at first gave some support to the recommendations of the Survey. By nationalizing the Imperial Bank it created the State Bank of India, which started functioning at the start of July 1955 and reached the target of 400 new branches in rural areas within five years. It created a special fund for agricultural credit in 1956, with an initial gift of 10 crores and an annual subsidy of 5 crores or £3,750,000, and established with the Indian Reserve Bank a Central Committee for Co-operative Training. Then suddenly, in 1958, the government reversed its policy, in the belief that the state should interfere as little as possible in the co-operative movement, which was to be based, as tradition required, on the principles of 'free association' and 'mutual help'. State intervention had merely dampened the popular spirit of self-reliance, and led to increasing calls on official time and energy. Future development, therefore, would concentrate on the spread of small, especially single-village co-operatives, and the larger societies, covering several villages, would be introduced into backward areas alone.

It is astonishing that the Indian government should have decided that the need was for less rather than for more state participation, that the Indian peasant – by doctrine and tradition drained of initiative and distrustful of his fellows, heavily in debt and still lacking the most basic equipment for increasing the yield from his tiny ancestral plot – was able or willing to change his condition by a mere acceptance of the need for self-reliance and community effort. The tenets of 'liberal democracy' were being applied to a society still fundamentally feudal. What the government might more profitably have considered was a policy of drastic reform amounting to rural revolution, by which the money-lending class would have been uprooted from the countryside altogether and state-directed co-operatives with massive financial resources planted in its place. If some coercion were required, Nehru himself had long before accepted the necessity for it, and in any event it could hardly be greater than that already exercised against many millions of peasants by the moneylenders themselves for the least productive of purposes. The official figures give instead the dreary account of once again too little done far too slowly. The Survey of 1951–2 had estimated the rural credit need at 750 crores of rupees, or some £560 million. But this figure applied to immediate requirements, and each year increased it by the rise in prices and population. Moreover, any serious attempt to deal with agricultural backwardness by mechanization and the wholesale provision of fertilizers would swell the credit need a great deal further.

How much of the money lent by the co-operative movement has in fact reached those most in need of it cannot be established with any accuracy, but the rise in membership of agricultural

Table 13

PROGRESS OF PRIMARY AGRICULTURAL CREDIT SOCIETIES – FIRST AND SECOND PLANS

Period	Societies (numbers)	Membership (in millions)	Short and medium-term loans advanced (in crores of rupees)
First Plan			
1950–1	104,998	4·4	22·9
1955–6	159,939	7·8	49·6
Second Plan			
1956–7	161,510	9·1	67·3
1957–8	166,543	10·2	96·1
1958–9	182,905	11·9	125·5
1959–60	203,172	14·4	169·1
1960–1 (estimates)	210,000	17·0	200·0

SOURCE: Third Five Year Plan Report (1961).

credit societies has clearly not kept pace with the increase in money advanced, and it may not unreasonably be supposed that, despite the findings and recommendations of the Rural Credit Survey, most of the loans have continued to be made to the richer cultivators. With something like 100 million cultivators in the country, agricultural credit societies involve only 17 per cent, while the average loan works out at 117 rupees, or £9 sterling, a year.

The cultivators constitute only part of the rural problem, however, for there are also over 31 million hired labourers, or some 23 per cent of the agricultural working population,[1] most of whom are totally landless. Two special Agricultural Labour Inquiries were ordered by the government to probe their condition, the first in 1950–1 and the second in 1956–7, and together they tell a story of deep and deepening degradation. Of the 16,300,000 'agricultural labour households' – or families for whom agricultural wages constitute the major source of income – existing in 1956–7, 73 per cent were 'casual' or employed at daily rates for short and unspecified periods, while 27 per cent were 'attached' or employed on contract for a specified period. (The proportion of 'attached' labourers almost tripled from 10 per cent in 1950–1, as landlords evaded tenancy regulations and revenue intermediaries like the *zamindars* escaped expropriation by assuming personal cultivation of their estates with the help of permanent wage-paid labourers.) Nor are only adults employed; in 1950–1 there were 2 million children, and in 1956–7, 3 million working as agricultural labourers.

The average daily wage of adult male hired labourers, in both cash and kind, declined from 190 naye paise (100 naye paise = 1 rupee, or about 1s. 6d.) in 1950 to 96 naye paise in 1956, with women and children earning substantially less and the differential growing; indeed, one of the major findings of the Second Inquiry was that the total income of hired-labour households had fallen by some 11 per cent between 1950–1 and 1956–7. The average annual income of an agricultural labour family was 447 rupees (about £34) in 1950–1, and 437 rupees, despite a significant rise in food prices meanwhile, in 1956–7, while the average *per capita* income fell from 104 rupees (£8)

[1] 1961 *Census of India*, Paper No. 1 of 1962.

to just over 99. Since the national *per capita* income in 1956–7 was 295 rupees, the *per capita* income of agricultural labourers and their dependants was accordingly a mere third of the already low national average. Inevitably agricultural labour families could not survive at all on their earnings – as the Agricultural Inquiries established, average expenditure in 1956–7 was 617 rupees a year, or 180 rupees more than income – and the shortfall was met from savings, the sale of primitive possessions or stock and loans; when such resources were exhausted there could only follow, inexorably, starvation and death.

The Agrarian Reforms Committee of 1950 declared that 'to leave out the problem of agricultural labour in any scheme of agrarian reforms as has been done so far – is to leave unattended a weeping wound in the agrarian system of the country.' During the First and Second Plans most of the state governments, under pressure from the Congress leadership, passed legislation to fix minimum wages for agricultural labour. But the labourers themselves generally belong to outcaste or low-caste backward communities, are accustomed to suffering social disabilities and economic exploitation, and even when aware that they are protected by law – which is seldom enough – do not know how to enforce their rights. There are far more landless labourers than there is labour for, and those few who have heard of the minimum wage and demand it, soon find themselves without even casual employment. Some landowners even reacted to the new laws by paying the pittance laid down – usually little more than one rupee a day for adult males – withdrawing all customary gifts of food and clothes, and pressing for repayment of loans or refusing any further ones; inevitably their labourers soon returned to the traditional relationship. The central government itself, for all its stated recognition of the need to settle landless labourers on their own smallholdings, provided only 1½ crores of rupees, or little more than £1 million, for the purpose during the five-year period of the First Plan, and just under 5 crores, or £3,750,000 to establish 20,000 agricultural labour families on 100,000 acres of land during the five years of the Second Plan. A greater sense of urgency informed the Planning Commission in drafting the Third Five Year Plan, and a Central Advisory Committee on Agricultural Labour, appointed by the Commission, has announced efforts to settle

100,000 landless families on an area of 5 million acres; the states are to spend 4 crores, and the central government 8 crores, on the settlement schemes. The border conflict with China, however, has led to the projection of a huge armament programme, and this must erode expenditure on measures of social welfare; when I was in India during the emergency, such proposals as I heard from members of the government for increasing and modernizing the equipment of the armed forces invariably sacrificed sums already allotted for schemes of social change and rural reform. And even were the progress in settling agricultural labour on land holdings as promised in the Third Plan to be fully achieved, the annual population increase would swallow it up and still swell the numbers of the landless.

There remains an extraordinary failure by the Indian government to recognize the extent of the emergency existing not on the northern borders but throughout the country. Imaginative projects of reform are generated in New Delhi with undiminishable fertility, but they either starve to death because their financial nourishment is neglected, or are sent into the streets to earn their own living without proper preparation, and soon succumb to indifference or despair. The heaviest of these was the Community Development Programme, launched in October 1952 to transform the whole of agricultural India by an intensive and co-ordinated campaign to increase productivity, utilize surplus labour in rural industry, and overcome peasant listlessness and inefficiency by education, better housing and health, recreation, and the establishment of village democracy. Basic project areas were selected and each of them divided into three development blocks, with the average block comprising one hundred villages, a total population of 60–70,000, and some 50,000 acres of cultivated land. For each project area an executive officer was appointed, with three block-development officers, twelve technical experts, and – the pivot of the whole scheme – five or six dozen village-level workers, each to keep in constant touch with the inhabitants of the four or five villages under his control. The government allotted 90 crores or some £67 million for the five years of the First Plan, but only 46 crores, about half the amount, was in the end spent; the Second Plan proposed an expenditure of 200 crores or £150 million, but – despite the serious drop in money value during the period – no more than 194 crores were spent.

That something was accomplished cannot be denied. Irrigation and power projects helped to develop agriculture, establish new industries and extend transport facilities; millions of peasants were instructed in the use of fertilizers and pesticides. But the programme fell far short of its objective. The village level worker, a matriculate with two years' additional training of which hardly a third was devoted to agriculture, was overloaded with unnecessary work; required to collect savings, keep records and make innumerable reports, he had little time for his main job of teaching new agricultural techniques. Moreover, like most educated Indians, he generally objected to working with his own hands, and, inexperienced himself in practical agriculture, had constant difficulty in vanquishing the scepticism of his older and hardened peasant pupils. The village *panchayats* or councils, which the government diligently established in the belief that village democracy would lead to communal initiative, moved in the clogs of caste; elections simply formalized and confirmed the traditional authority of the higher castes and the subjection of the lower ones. The vast development programme, aimed at co-ordinated peasant effort, was itself largely uncoordinated. One farmer, finally convinced of the value of fertilizers, would find that they were unobtainable when he needed them; another, applying to a co-operative agency for a loan to buy a bullock, would get only half of what he needed and so spend the money on clothes or ceremony instead; a third, uninstructed in the proper use of irrigation waters, would ruin his fields before being told precisely what he should not have done. Cultivators would frequently receive improved seed that had been badly stored and was useless; or, once having increased productivity by hard work and the application of new methods, would find themselves, in the absence of price guarantees, no better off than before and so returned to their former ways. Agricultural yields in some project areas certainly increased, but the overall picture was one of merely marginal improvement, cancelled out, as so many other efforts, by human fertility.

The government's own Programme Evaluation Organization, set up by the Planning Commission independently to measure the progress of the Community Projects, issued in 1957 a report critically reviewing the first four years of performance. It complained that many villages had not seriously undertaken irrigation, land reclamation, soil conservation and the consolidation of land holdings, all steps essential to any real increase in agricultural production. Above all, the basic weakness of the whole development programme lay in the widely disparate benefits it distributed. Within individual development blocks there were disparities between accessible and remote villages; within individual villages, between the cultivating and other classes; among the cultivators themselves, between those with the larger land holdings and financial resources, to whom the benefits of state aid in the main accrued, and others whose need was greater but whose security and influence were less. The organization's evaluation report of 1958 revealed that the average income available to the village *panchayats* was pitiably inadequate for the development functions that they were expected to undertake, while the projects had had no significant effect in extending co-operative credit agencies. Together the reports stressed the two main shortcomings of the Community Development Programme; that the contact established by the government through its officials had been not with communities but with a few families in the various villages assigned to development, and that the richer cultivators had benefited disproportionately, if not indeed at the expense of the poorer ones.

I attended a conference of village-level workers in a district of Gujarat one stifling afternoon and listened to a discussion on fruit-growing. At a table in front of the audience sat the visiting expert with two of the largest cultivators in the area, both of whom wore Gandhi caps and khadi, held important positions in the co-operative movement of the area, and – I was told – were influential members of Congress. My Punjabi companion stared at the party boss in the centre of the group, an old man with vibrating gums, and remarked sourly: 'One can see that he has been sucking at the public nipple for thirty years.' It was hardly kind, but if faces betray character at all – an admittedly moot point – it was devastatingly exact. The village level workers themselves seemed much more hopeful, and they brought to the questioning an obvious eagerness. 'Is it better to dust insecticide, or spray it?' 'How does one treat coconut-leaf disease?' But, after a while, I felt a stirring of distrust. Most of the questions were asked and answered in English, and when some members of the audience used Gujarati a ripple of translation would run along the seats. I wondered how much of the enthusiasm I saw was transmitted direct to the peasants and how much had to be channelled through translators or the larger landholders who spoke the language of the raj.

Congress itself was slow to acknowledge the shortcomings of the Community Development Programme, but it did so at last and at its Nagpur meeting in 1959 accepted a new co-ordinated land policy – for which Nehru himself was largely responsible – in what has become known as the Nagpur Resolution. This projected co-operative farming as the basis of land reform and an all-out national effort to increase agricultural productivity. As a preliminary, legislation to limit the size of individual landholdings was to be enacted in all the states of the Indian Union, surplus land vested in the *panchayats* or village councils for co-operative management, and temporary service co-operatives with a voluntary membership organized throughout the country to supply good seed, fertilizers, equipment and advice to cultivators. To assure a fair return to the tiller, a floor price was to be fixed for each crop in reasonable advance of the sowing season, and wholesale state trading in food-grains introduced to eliminate hoarding, profiteering and the dominance of the middleman. At last – and it was hoped that this stage might be reached within three years – full-scale joint farming would be introduced. Village co-operatives – a number of which might form themselves into a union for greater efficiency – would be established, with all villagers, whether owners of land or not, eligible for membership, and these, provided with adequate powers and resources, would be responsible for introducing improved cultivation techniques, encouraging cottage industries, providing credit, and organizing the joint storage and marketing of agricultural produce. The land itself would be pooled for joint cultivation, with the farmers retaining their individual property rights, and taking a share of the produce in proportion to the size of their holdings; but the landless labourers would also participate, receiving a share commensurate with the work that they did.

The new agricultural policy was denounced by the Indian right wing, both within Congress and without, as surrendering the pass to Communism. In Madras I had breakfast with a highly emotional Bombay businessman, formerly a prominent member of Congress and now a leading organizer of the 'free enterprise' Swatantra Party. It was difficult to digest even porridge at half-past seven in the morning to the accompaniment of such alarming propositions. With the Nagpur Resolution Nehru, under the influence of Krishna Menon, had finally made Congress an agent of international Communism, and the government would attempt to collectivize agriculture on the Soviet pattern; but the Indian farmer was no less hostile than his Russian counterpart had been, and blood would flow in the fields when the policy was forced on him. My own contention – that the new policy seemed no more likely to be efficiently promoted than its predecessors – was casually dismissed by my companion; like so many of those in Indian public life, both loyally within Congress and in open opposition, he was more excited by what the Congress leadership said than by what it did.

Nehru himself recognized a crucial weakness in the Nagpur policy, but characteristically did no more than warn against it; the pivot of co-operative farming would be the village councils or *panchayats*, and experience had already revealed them as riddled with caste preoccupations and almost rotten with political jobbery. When late in 1959 the state of Rajasthan introduced local council control of community development, the celebrated *panchayat raj*, Nehru admonished all those involved to 'beware of politics and groupism creeping in';[1] it might have been more constructive had he considered injecting a different force altogether into agriculture and the whole project of co-operative farming. If cultivators with an unequal possession of land, money and influence are to be persuaded to farm together for the welfare of the whole community and not merely private profit, the persuaders are unlikely to be the very people who believe that they have most to lose by the success of the scheme; to place the establishment and initial administration of co-operative farming in the hands of the village councils, dominated as they are by the richer cultivators, is to

[1] *The Hindu*, October 4th, 1959.

give urban landlords the responsibility for setting up and staffing an equitable rent tribunal.

Despite the outcry of Bombay businessmen, what Indian agriculture needs is not less 'Communism', but more, if the chasm between rich and poor is to be crossed, if a sense of community and so of national effort is ever to be induced, if enough food is to be grown to feed the multitude of starving, and if the alternative of Stalinist violence is in the long run to be escaped. To propose, as a few radical members of Congress have done, that Congress itself should imitate Communist practice and recruit from the countryside party cadres, with the background, enthusiasm and ability to communicate the purpose of co-operative farming to the peasants, is not to destroy democracy in India, but to develop it. There is little point in attempting to eliminate the traditional tax-collecting intermediaries and preserving the traditional political ones; and it is nonsense to call the securing of privilege the protection of liberty. If co-operative farming is ever to flourish, it will have to be fostered and, initially at least, managed by peasants especially trained to appreciate and to transmit its advantages in the pursuit of a national progress; and to suppose that this can be done without injury to the interests of the larger landholders is unreal. Some coercion will inevitably be needed, and it is the function of a party dedicated to democracy and socialism to ensure that the minimum is employed commensurate with the purposes of economic advance and social justice. The alternative, an even further impoverishment of the poor who compose the vast majority of the Indian people, bears no real relation to democracy or freedom. If a small minority of dissidents must be coerced into co-operative farming, there is coercion on a far greater scale in the very inequalities of present-day rural India. Are the landless labourers, and the small cultivators sunk in debt and unable to scratch even a subsistence for themselves and their families, not endlessly coerced? What must be avoided is coercion of the peasant masses themselves, and the existence of free and regular national elections can provide the insurance against this.

The question, it seems to me, is not whether peasant cadres should be recruited as soon as possible and entrusted with their emergency task, but whether the government or the party in power should do the recruiting. It is obviously better for a government to raise a permanent civil service than for a party; trained civil servants cannot, with any profit to the state, be changed with electoral swings. Peasant cadres, however, would not be part of the permanent civil service; they are an emergency measure, and one which the sole conceivable alternative government of India at present, a right-wing coalition, would on achieving power immediately discard. Short of a Communist Party seizure of control, improbable in the short run, co-operative farming is inseparable from Congress rule. Furthermore, despite the muddle and timidity, the bright packaging and shoddy content of its policies, the Congress party is still closer to the Indian peasantry than the government, which retains the image of the alien and oppressive. It is not inconceivable that Congress, as the movement of struggle against British power, could re-establish itself in popular confidence as the party of change; the government could not, and its servants would be distrusted on sight.

The relationship between Congress and the peasant cadres would be conducive not only to the reform of Indian agriculture, but to the reform of Congress itself. The party would find it difficult to hold a militant peasantry and the political bosses, its idealists and profiteers, together for long; the corruption of Congress has in major measure been marked by its submission to the control of the machine men, the political élite serving the interests of – where it is not the same as – the economic one. It would do Congress no harm to return to the countryside through the channel of its peasant cadres; it might rediscover its purpose and the source of its ultimate strength. In any event, prudence would propose the separation of management and control. Were the government to raise, employ and command the peasant cadres, it would the more easily permit the corruption of power. Despite the dominance of Congress in the representative institutions of India, there remains a distinction between party and government, and it is a distinction that can only safeguard the mass of Indians from the gratuitous compulsions of authority. A movement, no less than a person, should not be judge in its own cause. But whatever the precise form of peasant recruitment, Congress – and the government of India – cannot afford any further confusion, delay or inertia. Nothing could be worse in the condition of India today than for co-operative farming to be tried and wastefully to fail.

The Third Plan, India's most substantial experiment in controlled development, was given its final shape at the beginning of June 1961 and is to cover the five years from April 1st, 1961, to March 31st, 1966. Its main objectives are to achieve a growth in national income of over 5 per cent a year and increase domestic saving for investment to an annual rate of 11·5 per cent; to achieve self-sufficiency in food-grains at 100 million tons, or some 30 per cent more than the output at the end of the Second Plan; to expand the basic industries like steel and chemical manufacture so that the requirements of further industrialization can be met within ten years mainly from the country's own resources; to expand employment opportunities so as to provide 14 million new jobs; and to reduce disparities in income and wealth, establishing a more even distribution of economic power. The public sector outlay is set at 7,500 crores

Table 14

MAIN HEADS OF EXPENDITURE IN THE SECOND AND THE THIRD PLANS, IN CRORES OF RUPEES

Head	SECOND PLAN		THIRD PLAN – PROVISIONS	
	Total expenditure	Percentage	Total	Percentage
Agriculture and community development	530	11	1,068	14
Major and medium irrigation	420	9	650	9
Power	445	10	1,012	13
Village and small industries	175	4	264	4
Organized industry and minerals	900	20	1,520	20
Transport and communication	1,300	28	1,486	20
Social services and miscellaneous	830	18	1,300	17
Inventories	—	—	200	3
TOTAL	4,600	100	7,500	100

SOURCE: Third Five Year Plan Report, 1961.

of rupees, compared to 4,500 crores for the Second Plan and 1,960 for the First, and there is an increase in the proportion of expenditure devoted both to Power and to Agriculture and Community Development, with a slight drop in the expenditure on Social Services and a substantial one in the expenditure on Transport and Communication.

The Third Plan proposes to achieve an output of 10·2 million tons of steel ingots, compared to the 2·6 million tons achieved by the Second Plan, through an expansion of existing plants in the public sector and by the erection of a fourth state-owned and managed steel plant. The core of the plan, however, is to be the rapid development of the machine-tool and engineering industries; two new machine-tool plants are to be established in the public sector, while substantial expansion in the production of machine tools by private industry is also to be encouraged. The private sector, indeed, is expected to play a crucial role in the success of the plan, and predictions that the share of the public sector in the output of organized industry will rise from less than 10 per cent in 1960–1 to some 25 per cent in 1965–6 seem unlikely to be fulfilled.

The Third Plan, more ambitious than its predecessors, reveals like them a concentration on objective at the cost of method. The public sector programme for agriculture, irrigation and community development entails an expenditure of over 1,700 crores of rupees, or some £1,275 million, as high as 25 per cent of the total budget for the Third Plan, compared to an expenditure of 950 crores, or some £712 million, 20 per cent of the total budget, spent on similar items in the Second Plan. While such a programme is aimed at increasing the rate of growth in the agricultural sector, to an average 6 per cent a year, the Planning Commission itself is not sure how the aim is to be achieved. It proclaims that the development targets cannot be reached by the organizational approach followed in the First and Second Plans; yet while stressing the need for new detailed planning at the village and district level, it offers no proposals on how such planning should be undertaken. The conclusion is inescapable that the government is once again embarking on a project that will consume vast resources of men and money but is impossible of fulfilment in the absence of appropriate method. No less significant is the Commission's treatment of the foreign exchange difficulties. The bulk of India's foreign reserves was spent, often unproductively, in the spree of the Second Plan, and the acquisition of essential machinery and raw materials from abroad must for the most part now be met by a favourable balance of trade. But there is no surplus at all on current account, and the condition of Indian trade is itself critical; far from increasing its share of world trade during the first ten years of planned development, India suffered a decline from 2·1 per cent in 1950–1 to 1·1 per cent 1960–1. The Planning Commission stresses the urgency of expanding exports and suggests that foreign exchange should be allocated in favour of industries producing entirely or substantially for the export market; yet it nowhere proposes a programme for export promotion. In the end it seems that the success of the whole Third Plan will depend on the readiness of other countries to provide aid in much larger measure than they have so far done or show the slightest intention of doing.

As though to confess their anticipation of failure, the drafters of the Third Plan leave a gap of 600 crores or some £450 million between the cost of the programme they propose for the public sector and the amount of money that they expect to be raised in the five-year period of the Plan. Since they stress themselves that the objectives they have formulated can only be attained by the full outlay that they advise; and since they do not show how the full outlay is to be found, the observer can only suppose that their accounting is incompetent or that they do not take seriously the consequences of failure. Their response to the mounting problem of the unemployed merely confirms such an impression. According to the calculations of the Planning Commission itself, some 17 million newcomers will be added to the country's labour force during the five years of the Plan; yet the Plan aims at creating only 14 million new jobs, leaving 3 million to be added to the backlog of 8,800,000 unemployed at the end of the Second Plan. The Commission makes no effort to propose a systematic and co-ordinated policy for eliminating the new backlog of nearly 12 million unemployed, and its own prediction of 14 million new jobs must, on past performance and its own scanty evidence, be suspect. The Third Five Year Plan is less a programme for disciplined development than an intricate exercise in wishful thinking.

Even the muddled half-measures of the Third Plan, however, are threatened by the Indian government's reaction to the border conflict with China. Succumbing to pressure from within Congress itself and the shrill recriminations of the right-wing opposition, it has agreed to a costly armament programme, the final measure of which has not been determined but which will certainly deflect resources from economic development and erode – despite official denials – the investment projected in the Third Plan, if only by increasing the pressures of inflation. With Chinese armament expenditure running at 5 per cent of the national income, influential organs of opinion inside India[1] press for a raising of the country's expenditure from 2·5 per cent to 7 or even 8 per cent, in order to match the military power of China. Such a policy would be dangerous and self-defeating. China can spend a smaller percentage of its national income on defence and yet spend more than India for as long as its national income is greater; the way of increasing Indian power is not to invest vast sums in armaments at the cost of economic development, but to promote economic development so that heavier defence expenditure may be borne without requiring sterile popular sacrifice and distorting the whole economy. It may even be reasonably argued that India should spend not more on defence at the moment but less, since the country is not able to defend itself effectively against China and will be unable to do so for some time to come; either China intends to conquer India, in which case the raising of expenditure on defence to 8 per cent or even more will make no difference in the short run, or China does not, in which case India will be assuming a gratuitous – and, in its present condition, dangerous – economic burden by sacrificing planned development to defence. Certainly no Indian policy would better serve the interests of China, if China does contemplate the conquest of substantial Indian territory, than one which would feverishly devote resources to arming and starve economic development into collapse. The significant struggle between the two countries is not in defence but in the production tables.

Though China, with an estimated 750 million, has a population some 60 per cent greater than that of India, its agricultural production, despite the calamities of drought and flood during

[1] See, for instance, the *Eastern Economist*, Annual Number, 1963.

the past four years, is generally considered to be double, while its production of electric energy is almost three times, and its output of a crucial industrial commodity like steel almost four times as great. This is all the more significant since at the end of the 'forties Indian production was greater than Chinese in crude petroleum, cotton yarn, cement, pig-iron, crude steel, and electric energy, all important indices of economic strength which are now much higher in China than in India; and though the coal output of both countries was then more or less the same, China's output is now seven times greater than India's. In almost every aspect of industrialization, the method of economic progress chosen by India itself, China has advanced further and faster than India; moreover, it has done so during the last few years with shrinking aid from abroad, while the foreign aid given to India has steadily increased.

It does not, of course, follow that India should adopt the Chinese political system or imitate every gesture of China's economic programme. The development of modern China has not, even by sympathetic accounts, been without its blunders and unnecessary cruelties. But despite the claims of China's committed assailants, it is difficult to believe that the country's economic development during the last fourteen years could have been accomplished in the absence of massive popular enthusiasm, let alone in the presence of massive popular hostility. No number of Five Year Plans can achieve fundamental change in India without the recruitment of voluntary popular effort. Yet no popular participation in economic advance is probable while the already vast disparities between rich and poor continue to widen. A government that attempts to conceal economic inequalities with the incantations of socialism may reassure itself of its ultimately noble intentions, but is likely to strain too far the faith of the starving.

A comparison between taxation rates in India and selected economically more advanced countries, or between the pattern of estate duty in India and in Britain, is a strange commentary on the dedication of Congress to militant socialism.

At the lower levels of the rich (for in India, with 60 per cent of the population enjoying an annual income of less than 264 rupees or some £20 a head, a family income of £1,000 a year is riches), Indian taxation is lower than Britain's or Norway's

Table 15

CHINA

Product	Measure	1953	1954	1955	1956	1957	1958	1959	1960	1961
Wheat	Thousand metric tons	18,300	23,350	22,950	24,800	23,650	28,950	31,294	—	—
Rice	"	11,250	70,850	78,000	82,450	86,800	88,000*	80,000*	85,000*	—
Cottonseed	"	2,350	2,130	3,040	2,890	3,280	4,200	4,820	—	—
Fish catches	"	1,900	2,294	2,518	2,640	3,120	4,060	5,020	—	—
Coal (inc. lignite)	"	69,680	83,660	98,300	110,360	139,730	270,200	347,800	420,000	—
Crude petroleum	"	622	789	966	1,163	1,460	2,264	3,700	5,500	—
Sugar	"	638	693	717	807	864	900	1,260	1,260	1,200
Cotton yarn (pure)	"	744·5	834·1	719·8	951·6	844·8	1,106·5	1,496·5	1,632·6	—
Sulphuric acid	"	260	344	375	517	632	740	1,100	—	—
Metallurgical coke	"	3,500*†	4,000*†	4,500*†	5,500*†	6,685*†	18,000*†	22,000*†	25,000*†	22,000*†
Cement	"	3,877	4,600	4,503	6,393	6,860	9,300	12,270	16,000†	14,000†
Pig-iron and ferro-alloys	"	2,234	3,114	3,872	4,826	5,936	13,690	20,500	27,500†	22,000†
Crude steel	"	1,774	2,225	2,853	4,465	5,350	11,080	13,350	18,450	15,000†
Electric energy	Million kWh	9,195	11,001	12,278	16,593	19,340	27,530	41,500	58,500	—

INDIA

Product	Measure	1953	1954	1955	1956	1957	1958	1959	1960	1961
	Thousand metric tons									
Wheat		7,526	8,014	9,042	8,768	9,403	7,997	9,958	10,251	10,992
Rice	,,	42,904	38,272	41,311	43,555	38,269	46,031	46,953	51,297	51,223
Cottonseed	,,	1,403	1,511	1,422	1,674	1,686	1,666	1,308	1,916	1,600
Fish catches	,,	819	828	839	1,012	1,233	1,064	823	1,164	961
Coal (inc. lignite)	,,	36,557	37,471	38,839	39,910	44,204	46,075	47,833	52,640	56,129
Crude petroleum	,,	263	300	335	384	429	426	471	445	523
Sugar	,,	1,457	1,208	1,785	2,161	2,286	2,166	2,303	2,814	3,086
Cotton yarn (pure and mixed)	,,	682·7	708·1	739·5	758	807·4	764·5	781·5	787·9	862·3
Sulphuric acid	,,	111	153	169	168	199	230	297	360	414
Metallurgical coke	,,	1,981	2,290	2,638	2,546	2,606	3,072	4,299	4,778	6,226
Cement	,,	3,841	4,468	4,559	5,008	5,691	6,186	6,936	7,845	8,231
Pig iron and ferro-alloys	,,	1,804	1,993	1,925	1,989	1,942	2,135	3,108	4,192	4,999
Crude steel	,,	1,531	1,712	1,732	1,766	1,742	1,842	2,473	3,287	4,071
Electric energy	Million kWh	8,681	9,669	10,877	11,972	13,757	15,415	17,794	20,041	22,683

NOTES: The source is the *United Nations Statistical Yearbook* of 1962. Figures with * behind them are estimates accepted by the *Yearbook*, and figures with † estimates made by the U.S. Bureau of Mines. The selection of products is my own, but conditioned by the scarcity of comparative statistics; there is no point, for instance, in giving the figures for the production of manganese in India, because the *Yearbook* has no figures for Chinese manganese production; nor in giving the figures for Chinese tin production, since the *Yearbook* has no figures for the production of tin in India. The 14 products in the tables measure progress in vital sectors of agriculture, mining, industry and power.

Table 16

TAX AS PERCENTAGE OF EARNED INCOME

(For a married person with two children)

Income (Rs.)	(£s)	India 1960–1	Britain 1960–1	Norway	Japan
13,333	1,000	6·4	7·7	11·4	15·6
26,666	2,000	16·5	18·8	30·8	23·0
40,000	3,000	26·3	25·1	42·1	27·5
53,333	4,000	34·5	30·4	49·1	30·6
66,666	5,000	40·7	35·4	54·6	33·3
80,000	6,000	46·0	39·6	58·3	35·3
93,333	7,000	49·8	43·3	60·9	37·2
106,666	8,000	53·1	46·2	62·8	38·8
120,000	9,000	55·7	48·9	64·4	40·1
133,333	10,000	57·9	51·2	65·6	41·1
200,000	15,000	64·2	62·0	69·2	45·7
266,666	20,000	67·4	68·7	71·0	48·0
333,333	25,000	69·3	72·7	72·1	50·4

SOURCE: *Taxation and Private Investment*, a publication of the Indian National Council of Applied Economic Research.

Table 17

ESTATE DUTY

INDIA		BRITAIN	
Value of estate	% Rate of duty	Value of estate	% Rate of duty
On the first Rs.50,000 (£3,750)	Nil	–£5,000	Nil
On the next Rs.50,000	7½	£5,001 –£6,000	1
On the next Rs.50,000	10	Rising gradually to	
On the next Rs.100,000 (£7,500)	12½	£15,001 –£17,500	10
		Rising gradually to	
On the next Rs. 200,000 (£15,000)	15	£35,001 –£40,000	24
		Rising gradually to	
On the next Rs.500,000 (£37,500)	20	£60,001 –£75,000	40
		£75,001 –£100,000	45
On the next Rs.1,000,000 (£75,000)	25	£100,001–£150,000	50
		£150,001–£200,000	55
On the next Rs.1,000,000	30	£200,001–£300,000	60
		£300,001–£500,000	65
On the next Rs.2,000,000 (£150,000)	35	£500,001–£750,000	70
		£750,001–£1,000,000	75
On the balance (from almost £375,000)	40	Over £1,000,000	80

and less than half that of Japan's; at the summit it is higher only than Japan's, though Britain at least has had for more than a decade a government committed to 'free enterprise'.

Even worse, for a society pledged to eliminate inherited privilege, the rates of estate duty are half those of Britain's. The Indian rich are able not merely to continue increasing their riches, but to transfer the major part of them to their heirs.

The crisis of Indian poverty and backwardness is not a distant one. As these words are being written in the middle of July 1964, food prices are rising rapidly, with an estimated shortfall in essential food supplies of 11 million tons, and there are reports of hunger marches and attacks on government food shops from many parts of the country. Popular anger is nourished by the belief that the crisis is in large measure due to Indian's endemic hoarders and profiteers, whom the Congress government is accused of protecting because its most cherished political associates are the richer peasants and traders. In the middle of the massive Third Five Year Plan, the economy of India – and with it all political stability – is close to collapse. The Communist Party has already announced plans for mass civil disobedience, demonstrations and strikes, against hoarding and high prices, while opposition parties to the right of Congress, like the Jana Sangh in the north and the Tamil separatist D.M.K. in the south, are making similar plans. A magnanimous monsoon, with bumper harvests in the autumn, may temporarily retrieve the situation; but mean or extravagant rains would be calamitous. That this should be so, after thirteen years of planned economic development, under a regime committed to eliminating poverty and hunger, privilege and exploitation from India, promises a terrifying future. India has been living too long on a ledge of the economic precipice, frightened both to climb and to fall. But the ground is crumbling beneath her, and if she does not begin speedily to grope her way upwards she must soon fall below.

CHAPTER FIVE

POLITICS – THE GREAT HIATUS

FIVE days after my arrival in New Delhi at the start of my stay in India I had lunch at the home of a British newspaper correspondent. The principal guest was a state Chief Minister, whose reputation for aggressive enterprise was matched by the easy flamboyance of his manner. Here was a professional of the type I thought I knew, and I listened with eagerness to his carefully careless comments on the Indian political scene. Under Nehru's government, he declared, power had steadily been flowing from the centre to the states, whose Chief Ministers increasingly controlled their own citadels and exercised influence in the capital as leaders of their state delegations within the Congress party. The emergency of the border war with China had arrested and even reversed this process, but it would not last, and when Nehru went, his successor would probably be chosen by a coalition of strong Chief Ministers.

It seemed to me then a diagnosis almost mannered in its cynicism. After all, the flow of power in nearly all the newly independent states was towards the centre, and even those which had emerged from colonial status with federal elements in their constitutions had rapidly discarded these, if not on paper then in practice. Both economic advance and political stability appeared to demand a strongly centralized government, and India, faced by such vast problems of poverty and backwardness within, as well as by formidable hostility without, needed a national command and effort no less, if not more, than any other of the recently imperial possessions. Yet, as I was soon enough to discover, the Chief Minister's diagnosis had been dismayingly accurate. Within a few months of the Chinese withdrawal from the edge of the Indian plains, the Chief Ministers were once more extending their local sway, and when Nehru died in the middle of 1964, his successor, Lal Bahadur Shastri, was selected by a coalition of Chief Ministers, led by

K. Kamaraj, the President of Congress and former Chief Minister of Madras whose influence in the far south has remained supreme.

Everywhere in India are signs of the great hiatus between need and resources, claim and reality, intention and achievement. At the very moment when national unity is vital, regional separatism flourishes; politicians pretend a simplicity and self-sacrifice while advancing their bank accounts or the careers of their relatives with speculation or jobbery; innumerable plans to promote everything from village sanitation to economic equality are announced with intermittent trumpeting and promoted with inadequate resources or organization, so that they seldom, if ever, succeed; the statute books are packed tight with laws of social and economic reform, most of them safely disregarded by those whose interests they unfavourably affect.

'We the people of India', the Indian Constitution proclaims in its Preamble, 'having solemnly resolved to constitute India into a SOVEREIGN DEMOCRATIC REPUBLIC and to secure to all its citizens:

'JUSTICE, social, economic and political;

'LIBERTY of thought, expression, belief, faith and worship;

'EQUALITY of status and of opportunity; and to promote among them all

'FRATERNITY assuring the dignity of the individual and the unity of the Nation;

'IN OUR CONSTITUENT ASSEMBLY this twenty-sixth day of November, 1949, do HEREBY ADOPT, ENACT AND GIVE TO OURSELVES THIS CONSTITUTION.'

Part IV of the Constitution then outlines certain directive principles of State policy – not enforceable by any court – submitted for the guidance of the legislatures, the government and the judiciary. Apart from the general indication of a desire that the State should promote the welfare of the people – a re-phrasing of the Preamble itself – this section promotes the attainment of certain specific aspirations. Under Article 39, the State is called upon to direct its policy towards securing, amongst other objectives: (a) that all citizens have the right to an adequate means of livelihood; (b) that the ownership and control of the community's resources are distributed so as best to serve the common good; (c) that the operation of the economic system does not result in the concentration of wealth and means of production to the common detriment; (d) that equal pay should be given to both men and women for equal work; and (e) that childhood and youth, men and women, are protected against exploitation or moral and material abandonment. Articles 41, 42 and 43 direct the State, within the limits of its economic capacity and development, to secure the right to work, to education, and to public assistance for the unemployed, aged, sick and disabled; to secure proper conditions of work and maternity relief; and to secure by suitable laws or economic organization for all workers a living wage and full enjoyment of leisure: while Article 45 calls upon the State to provide, within a period of ten years, free compulsory education for all children up to the age of 14 years.

The whole of this constitutional section embodies the spirit of Congress struggle against British rule, the promise of a better life for everyone – or everyone but the already privileged – with the enjoyment of political freedom. Here is captured the idealism of the Congress leadership in the hangover of battle, and especially the secular idealism of Nehru himself, who as Prime Minister played a crucial role in the Constituent Assembly. But the secularism of Nehru was not to be the only component. The influence of Gandhi and – or, for the two were occasionally in conflict – of traditional Hindu values is translated into several Articles. Article 46 calls upon the State to concentrate upon promoting the educational and economic interests of the weaker sections of the people, in particular the tribes, lower castes, and outcastes, protecting them from social injustice and all forms of exploitation; Article 40 instructs the State, in conformity with the importance of village *panchayats* or councils in ancient India, to organize such local authorities and provide them with the powers enabling them to function effectively as units of self-government; and Article 43 stresses the need to promote cottage industries on an individual or co-operative basis in rural areas. Article 47 dedicates the State to raising the level of nutrition and the standard of living as a primary duty, with an attempt to prohibit the consumption, except for medicinal purposes, 'of intoxicating drinks' and injurious drugs; while Article 48 calls for the preservation and improvement of cattle breeds and the prohibition of their slaughter.

The Preamble and Directive Principles of the Constitution – disregarding the special injunctions of religious or Gandhian inspiration, like the prohibition of cattle-slaughter or the development of cottage industries – do no more than propose the normal aspirations of a civilized society. Yet in the context of India's material circumstances, such dedications are no less than revolutionary. In a country where starvation is no mere climatic calamity but the only real citizenship which tens of millions enjoy; where the distance between rich and poor is so enormous as almost to produce two different species; where epidemics that belong in other parts of the world to history or fiction still carry off thousands of Indians each year; where every now and then, more than a century after its legal prohibition, devout villagers thrust a widow on to the burning funeral pyre of her husband; and where thousands of young girls married only to be widowed have their heads shaven and spend the rest of their lives as evil omens, the ordinary objectives of the developed secular and democratic welfare state demand nothing short of national upheaval.

The Constituent Assembly of the Indian people, which so conscientiously formulated its aspirations, thereby projected a standard by which the success of Indian independence was to be measured. In the event, a great deal has been attempted; but accomplishment has lagged far behind, and in relation to what was to be done, and the need to do it quickly, a dangerous amount still resides in the realm of ambition. The Indian people resolved upon a revolution; their progress since has been at best a slow evolution, which has not yet outstripped the problems running alongside it.

The hiatus everywhere evident in Indian life exists within the Constitution itself. India is technically a federation, but one in which there is provision for such centralized control that it should be considered ultimately a union; in the uncertain distance between, there is room in practice for both the strongest and weakest of centres, the most or least dependent of parts. The country possesses all the usual characteristics of a federation: a written constitution; a dual political composition, with power distributed between the national government and the governments of the constituent states; and an independent judiciary to interpret the constitution and adjudicate in matters of conflict between authority at the centre and authority in the various parts. Such a federation, however, has generally resulted from a decision by separate and independent communities to unite for particular and common purposes. In India the unity existed before the units, and the act of federation, which established the constituent states, was a process of dispersal rather than of coalescence. On the other hand, because authority rested with the centre and not with the still-to-be-constituted parts, the centre secured for itself far more substantial power in relation to the parts than exists in any other federation, where the parts possessed all the power to begin with and retained a significant measure as a condition of unity.

The constituent Indian states – of which there are now fifteen, with six 'union territories' administered by the centre – have governments of limited and specified powers; the central government also has its own limited and specified powers, but under certain circumstances possesses a final authority over the state governments, and – in times of emergency, proclaimed by the President – may take all or any power that it wishes.

In both the Australian and American federations, the powers not specifically given to the centre belong to the parts; in India, the powers of both the central and the state governments are carefully enumerated in three legislative lists, with all residuary power assigned to the centre. In most federations, as in the United States, there exists dual citizenship – a citizenship of the whole and a citizenship of each constituent state; India has only one citizenship, that of the whole, and every Indian has the same citizenship rights, no matter to which state he belongs. In other federations, as in the United States, all state authorities – legislative, executive and judicial – are subject to their particular state constitutions as well as to the constitution of the whole; in India, there is only one constitution, that of the whole, to which the entire territory and all its constituent parts are alike subject. The usual federation has a legislature of two chambers, with the lower one elected by the citizenry of the whole divided into equal constituencies, while the upper secures the equality of the federating units by providing them with equal representation, regardless of size and population; in the Indian upper chamber, or Council of States, representation is firmly based on the population of each constituent unit. Finally, although the central and state governments in India are each organized separately and independently for the performance of their various functions, they are integrated to function also as a single entity; unlike many other federal structures, as that of the United States, the Indian federation is provided by its constitution with uniformity in all basic aspects of administration – one judiciary, a uniform code of fundamental civil and criminal laws, and a central civil service for strategic posts at both the centre and in the constituent parts.

The government of India is a parliamentary one, with a President as the executive head – corresponding in his general functions to the British monarch – and the actual executive power exercised by a Council of Ministers, collectively responsible to the House of the People, or Lok Sabha. The President himself is elected for a period of five years, with the possibility of re-election, by a special electoral college which consists of the elected members of both central legislative bodies, the House of the People and Council of States, and the elected members of the various state Legislative Assemblies. On paper he enjoys enormous authority – as, in theory, does the British monarch – and no Bill may become law without his assent; but in practice he acts, and is expected to act, on the advice of the Council of Ministers through the Prime Minister, who is himself the hinge of the whole political system. Article 74 of the Constitution provides specifically for a Council of Ministers with the Prime Minister at its head, to aid and advise the President in the exercise of his functions, and though the Prime Minister is in the first instance appointed by the President, he enjoys his appointment, and retains it, only through the support that he possesses in the House of the People. As the British monarch, the President has the function of securing government in conformity with the wishes of the people and so is armed with the power of dismissing Ministers and, in the last resort, of dissolving Parliament itself to obtain the verdict of the electorate; but once this verdict has been conclusively expressed, he has no choice but to accept it.

The Upper House, or Council of States (Rajya Sabha), consists of 250 members, 12 of whom are nominated by the

President for their special knowledge or practical experience in such matters as literature, science, and social service, while the remaining 238 are elected by the Legislative Assemblies of the various states, through a system of proportional representation, on the basis of population. The Lower House, or House of the People (Lok Sabha), on the other hand, consists of more than 500 members, chosen by direct election from territorial constituencies all of which as far as possible must contain the same number of electors. Every citizen who is no less than 21 years of age and is not otherwise disqualified because of insanity, or crime, or corrupt practice, is entitled to be registered as a voter for elections to the House of the People. The Council of States is not subject to dissolution, and its members are elected for six years, with one-third of them retiring every second year; the House of the People, unless sooner dissolved, has a maximum duration of five years from the date appointed for its first meeting. In all significant respects the procedure, powers and privileges of both Houses correspond to those of the British Parliament.

All Bills, other than a Money Bill, may originate in either House and require the consent of both Chambers, with provision made for a joint sitting – at which questions are determined by a majority of the members – in the event of deadlock. Money Bills, however, may only originate in the House of the People on the recommendation of the President – in other words, on the responsibility of the Cabinet – and though the Council of States may discuss its provisions and return it for reconsideration within fourteen days, the House of the People may then pass it again, ignoring all recommendations, and the Bill becomes law as though voted so by both Houses. The power to tax and spend, therefore, is the sole preserve of the Lower House.

In order to prevent the despotism of a government which might use its parliamentary power to flout the interests of minority opinion and deny basic civil liberties to the individual citizen, the framers of the Indian Constitution inserted a number of fundamental rights together with guarantees against their violation. The State would be prohibited in normal circumstances from passing any law which would abridge or deny those rights, and an independent judiciary was established to ensure that they would be properly protected. For citizens of India, there may be no discrimination on grounds of religion, race, caste, sex, or place of birth; all are promised equality of opportunity in public employment; freedom of speech, of assembly and of association; freedom to acquire property or assume any occupation, trade or business; the right to reside or settle in any part of India; the right to conserve a distinct language or culture; and the protection of all minority interests. To all who live in India, whether citizens or not, the Constitution promises the protection of life and personal liberty; equality before the law; security against retrospective penalization; protection against slavery and enforced labour; freedom of conscience, with the right to profess, practise and propagate any religion; and the right to constitutional remedies against infringement of their rights.

As may have been expected, the relevant courts of India were cluttered for years after the adoption of the Constitution with applications from individuals who claimed that their fundamental rights had been infringed by legislation of social and economic reform. The Indian Supreme Court in a whole series of judgments made clear that 'equality before the law' did not literally mean that all citizens should be treated equally by law, but that all should have the equal protection of law and should not be subjected to arbitrary or unreasonable treatment.

The provisions of the Constitution relating to fundamental rights have special significance in a society which by religious tradition has discriminated against women, especially widows, and outcastes, the so-called 'untouchables'. The guarantee against discrimination on grounds of religion, race, caste, sex, or place of birth was extended specifically to a prohibition upon any limitation of access to public restaurants, hotels, and places of entertainment, or the use of wells, tanks, sacred bathing places, roads, and places of public resort maintained by the State. In particular, under Article 17, the practice in any form of untouchability was forbidden, and the enforcement of any disability arising out of that condition made a punishable offence. Though it would take many years for the directives in the Constitution to be reflected significantly in public practice – there is still widespread discrimination against untouchables in India today – it was now at last made a crime for caste villagers to prohibit outcastes from using the village wells, or restaurants from refusing to serve them. Moreover, the constitutional provisions on equality of opportunity were qualified by the generally recognized need to advance the condition of the socially and educationally backward classes, the lower castes, the outcastes, and those still living in a tribal state of society. By the Constitution (First Amendment) Act of 1951, Parliament acquired the power to make laws discriminating in favour of any backward class of citizens for appointment in the public service if, in the opinion of the State, such class was not adequately represented.

Watching over the fundamental rights guaranteed by the Constitution, as well as the whole machinery of government in India, is the judiciary, independent both of the legislature and of the executive, and entrusted with the function of interpreting the Constitution, securing its provisions, and adjudicating in any constitutional disputes between the central government and the government of a constituent state or between the various state governments themselves. Unlike the United States and other federations, India has no dual system of courts, one to administer national laws and the other state laws; all the courts of the country belong to a single system of judicial authority with the Supreme Court at its head. Provision is made in the Constitution for the appointment of a Chief Justice and, by subsequent amendment, thirteen other judges of the Supreme Court by the President, and none may be removed from office except by order of the President himself, made after a decision of each House of Parliament – passed by a majority of at least two-thirds of those members present and voting – on the grounds of proved misbehaviour or incapacity. The privileges and allowances, together with other rights such as those of residence and pension, enjoyed by the judges are guaranteed by the Constitution, and their salaries, a charge on the Consolidated Fund, are not subject to vote by Parliament. Finally, the Supreme Court is a court of record and has all the powers of such a court, including the power to punish for contempt of itself. Since the Indian Supreme Court is the highest court of appeal in the land for normal judicial processes, as well as being solely responsible for interpreting the Constitution, it may be said to exercise a degree of control – on the national, state and individual citizen level alike – which no similar organ of authority, even in other federations like Australia, Canada or the United States, possesses.

The organization of government at the centre of the Indian Union – for so, despite its federal character, it officially describes itself – is largely recapitulated in the government of its constituent parts. Each state executive is, like the executive at the centre, parliamentary, with a Governor – corresponding to, and appointed for five years by, the President – acting as executive head on the advice of his own state Council of Ministers. The Council of Ministers itself, which functions as Cabinet government on the British pattern, is headed by a Chief Minister, who corresponds on the state level to the Prime Minister at the centre, and who is, with his Council, responsible to the Legislative Assembly of the state. As with the central government, the decisions of which are taken in the name of the President, all state decisions must bear the signature of the Governor and be issued in his name. Each state, too, has its own popular legislature, with a majority having two Houses, the Lower called the Legislative Assembly and the Upper the Legislative Council. Each Legislative Assembly, which must consist of not more than 500 and not less than 60 members, is elected from single-member constituencies as far as possible the same in population, while the Legislative Council, which must be no greater in membership than one-third that of the Assembly, is composed of members elected by local authorities, those specially elected by university graduates and teachers, those nominated by the Governor for their knowledge of or practical experience in such matters as literature, science and social service, and members elected by the Legislative Assembly itself. The procedure, privileges and functions of the state legislatures are similar to those of the central parliament within the limitations of the authority provided by the Constitution, and each state, furthermore, has a High Court, the members of which are appointed by the President and enjoy office and remuneration on terms similar to members of the Supreme Court.

In any federation, it is the distribution of powers between the centre and the parts which constitutes the crux. The Indian Constitution divides the subject-matter of legislation into three Lists, with Parliament enjoying exclusive powers to make laws

on all matters enumerated in the Union List, the state legislatures possessing exclusive power over matters in the State List,
and both Parliament and the state legislatures having the right
to legislate on all matters in the Concurrent List. The pattern
behind this distribution is that Parliament should legislate for
the whole or any part of India, while the state legislature
should make laws merely for its particular state or any part
of it. Yet the framers of the Constitution were well aware of
the dangers inherent in a division of powers, and so, wherever
possible, stressed the supremacy of the centre. In matters on the
Concurrent List, it is Parliament that must be paramount in
any conflict between national law and state law, and it is
Parliament which enjoys any residual power over matters not
specifically enumerated in the three Lists. Moreover, since such
matters as the production, supply and distribution of goods,
included in the State List, may assume national importance,
Parliament possesses the power to legislate on any matter in the
State List provided that the Upper House or Council of States
has decided, by not less than two-thirds of the members present
and voting, that it is necessary or expedient in the national
interest for Parliament to do so. No other federal constitution
in the world gives the centre such absolute reserve powers,
even when an emergency has not been declared, over the
constituent states, and the inclusion of such a provision in the
Indian Constitution is the clearest indication of the degree to
which the framers desired a strong central government.

A dual government is by its very nature weaker than a single
one, and the weakness is no more evident than at a time of
national emergency, when co-ordinated action must be taken
without delay for the whole territory and all its people.
Provision is accordingly made in the Constitution for Parliament to legislate on any matter in the State List once a
Proclamation of Emergency has been declared by the President;
indeed, under a Proclamation of Emergency the government
of India becomes in terms of the Constitution a unitary one,
with extraordinary powers vested in the centre not only over the
constituent states but over individual citizens, whose fundamental rights may be disregarded and cease to be enforceable
by the judiciary. The procedure for declaring an emergency is
in itself simple enough: if the President is satisfied that the

security of India or any part of its territory is threatened by external aggression or internal disturbances he may, by proclamation, establish a state of emergency which operates for two months without the approval of Parliament; if Parliament agrees, the emergency may be indefinitely extended. While such an emergency is operating, no limit applies to the laws that Parliament may pass, or to the executive power of the centre, which may command the executive power of any constituent state. Such emergency powers may be used not only in times of invasion and war, but even to maintain proper government in the constituent states. If the President is satisfied that a situation has arisen in which the government of a particular state can no longer be carried on in accordance with the Constitution, he may by proclamation assume all the executive powers of the state and give its entire legislative authority to Parliament. The constitutional provision for such action is by no means academic; it was used to dismiss the Communist government in Kerala and substitute President's rule until the holding of elections produced a Congress-dominated administration.

The government of India, therefore, is fundamentally a unitary one with federal trappings – though its unitary character depends on the willingness and practical ability of the centre to make use of its many reserve powers – operating as a parliamentary democracy on the British model. What this model is seen to be by authoritative Indian opinion itself is reflected in the report of the Joint Select Committee on Indian Constitutional Reform (para. 20).

Parliamentary government, as it is understood in the United Kingdom, works by the interaction of four essential factors: the principle of majority rule; the willingness of the minority for the time being to accept the decisions of the majority; the existence of great political parties divided by broad issues of policy, rather than by sectional interests, and finally the existence of a mobile body of political opinion, owing no permanent allegiance to any party and therefore able, by its instinctive reaction against extravagant movements on one side or the other, to keep the vessel on an even keel.

The central issue of Indian democracy today is the degree
to which, in fact, these four essential aspects of parliamentary
government in Britain apply to India. The principle of majority
rule, if by this is meant rule by a duly elected parliamentary
majority, is unquestionably pursued at the national level. In
the Lok Sabha, Congress – the governing party – held 364
seats out of 489 as a result of the 1951–2 general election,
although it polled only 45 per cent of the total votes; 371 seats
out of 494 after the election of 1957, when it polled 47·78 per
cent of the votes; and 356 out of 489[1] seats after the election
of 1962, when it polled 45·02 per cent of the total votes. The
government majority in the Lower House is, of course, much
greater than the popular vote for the party in power warrants;
but this is no less true of the British House of Commons, where
a party polling a minority popular vote may yet enjoy a
workable majority in Parliament, and where only a small
majority in the popular vote may be swollen into a crushing
parliamentary dominance. If Congress has accomplished this
dominance with an overall minority vote, it is because the
opposition is fragmented, and under the normal constituency
system the candidate with the most – as distinct from the
majority of – votes is victorious. On the state level, too, the
principle of majority rule in the legislative sense has been
generally accepted, but only – one may reasonably conclude
from the dismissal of Kerala's Communist government by the
President – because the governing party at the centre has on
all but one occasion, lasting little more than two years, been
the governing party in all the constituent states.

Less certain is the willingness of the minority to accept for
the time being the decisions of the majority, if by this is meant
submission to constitutional forms of opposition. Direct mass
action began during the nationalist struggle against British
rule, for there were few channels of constitutional struggle
available and it was only by mobilizing large numbers in the
streets, for civil disobedience or strikes or demonstrations, that
Congress could hope to shatter British intransigence. This
tradition is still very much alive in Indian politics, and has
been re-enforced not only by the seeming unvanquishability of

---

[1] Excluding four seats from Himachel Pradesh and one seat from the
Punjab which were filled by election at the end of April 1962.

Congress at the polls, but also by the signal success with which mass action, on sufficiently widespread a scale, has been met. The towering majority of Congress in parliament, accomplished with no real sign of erosion in three general elections over a period of fifteen years, has excited opposition groups to believe that the speediest way of accomplishing their immediate purposes and simultaneously discrediting the government is by organizing street pressures against it. And the eventual collapse of the government to such pressures on significant occasions has enormously invigorated this view.

It was mass disorder in the Telugu-speaking areas of Madras State, following upon the fast to death in 1952 of Potti Sriramulu, a prominent Gandhian disciple who demanded provincial autonomy, that led to the establishment of Andhra as a separate state and subsequently to the whole reorganization of Indian states along linguistic lines. In the words of *Crossroads*, a Communist periodical, of January 11th, 1953: 'Railways, postal and telegraphic communications and all transport stopped. Mass demonstrations were held, in which people died and many were injured by police firing. The people made it impossible for government machinery to move until an Andhra province was granted.' It was the Communist Party that, more than any other political group, was responsible for marshalling the successful unconstitutional pressures in Andhra; it was against the governing Communist Party of Kerala that similar methods were used successfully by a coalition of Congress, the Praja Socialist Party, the Muslim League and the Christian Churches. In April 1957 the Communists had won the state elections in Kerala and formed a government; by July and August of the following year, in declared opposition to the Education Bill which would advance state control of the many Church- and caste-run private schools, there was a series of mass demonstrations and strikes in many parts of the state. The President declared a state of emergency and new elections were eventually held, in which a coalition of opposition parties gained victory at the polls.

Even Bombay State, left intact by the linguistic reorganization of 1956, fell victim to street pressures despite the frequently proclaimed intention of the Congress national government to withstand all demands for partition. Riots between Marathi-

and Gujarati-speaking citizens led to a division of the state into Gujarat and Maharashtra in April 1960.

The Socialist Party, led by Dr Lohia, has constantly furthered – and still does – the campaign to make Hindi the sole national language of India by organizing mass civil disobedience; thousands have been imprisoned for defacing public notices in English or otherwise breaking the law.

This revolt against authority has been sometimes dramatically reflected in what is commonly called 'student indiscipline'.[1] In the struggle against the British, student demonstrations were condoned and even encouraged by the Congress leadership, and both government and educational authorities were harassed by protest meetings, strikes and – despite Gandhi's known displeasure – the destruction of school and college property. Yet with the attainment of Indian independence, student rebelliousness, far from diminishing, has increased. Serious disturbances led to the closing of Lucknow University in 1953 and Benares Hindu University in 1958, while police fired on students at Patna in Bihar, in Gwalior (1950) and Indore (1954). In 1959 students at Amritsar were arrested while demonstrating in favour of Hindi; in Calcutta students abandoned their examination; in Jaipur students launched a mass movement against an increase in their fees; and in 1960 major disturbances broke out once again in Lucknow and at Allahabad. The Ministry of Education early on listed the causes as 'loss of leadership by teachers, growth of economic difficulties, general loss of idealism, absence of social life, a sense of fear and insecurity, and unhappy living conditions'.[2] On several occasions, most markedly during the disturbances at Benares, students used violence, stoning police and destroying property.

Violence, of course, is not limited to students, and has repeatedly occurred, in the city of Calcutta at least, since Independence. Shops have been attacked, police assaulted, and trams overturned and burnt. Yet the violent disturbances have in the main been middle- and not working-class in character;

[1] See the chapter on 'Students' in *The Politics of Scarcity* by Myron Weiner (Asia Publishing House, 1963), pp. 170–99.

[2] *Education in Universities in India, 1951–52* (Government of India Press, 1954), p. 3.

strikes have been generally peaceful, as have the many demonstrations by refugees; but protests against an increase in tram fares or agitation for an increase in teachers' salaries have soon flared into violence. One reason is certainly the tradition of violent resistance in Bengal; terrorism, usually middle-class in leadership, against British rule persisted in the area long after Gandhi's influence had eliminated it elsewhere. Another is that the middle class in India, especially in the professional ranks, still controls the important political movements, both in power and in opposition; the urban workers and above all the peasants, who constitute the vast bulk of the population, are seldom stirred from their traditional resignation.

Yet this is not the whole story. In 1956 the Indian Institute of Public Opinion conducted surveys in Calcutta, Delhi, and Travancore-Cochin (now the state of Kerala) to discover what problems were regarded as most pressing by the public and whether government or private industry was the better agency to tackle them. More than half the replies (53·1 per cent) considered the rise in food prices as the most urgent issue, 21·6 per cent chose unemployment, 10·3 per cent a ceiling on income, 6·3 per cent the low standard of living, and the remainder (8·7 per cent) seven other issues like housing (0·9 per cent) and refugee rehabilitation (1·8 per cent). On almost every issue, a clear majority of the replies held government to be responsible for taking action. In Calcutta, as elsewhere in India, the articulate, vigorous middle class – which has the status but nowhere near the income or amenities of its counterpart in the industrialized world – requires the government to act and when the government does not, responds by returning to the past and employing the desperate pressure of the streets. The very success of such methods confirms their use.

Since Independence, more sober attempts to influence public policy have often failed whereas the chief minister of West Bengal, many of his ministers, and his administrative personnel have frequently proved more responsive to mass pressure ... Only when public order is endangered by a mass movement is the government willing to make a concession, not because they consider the demand legitimate, but because they then recognize the strength of the group making the demand and its capacity for destructiveness. Thus, the government often alternates between unresponsiveness to the demands of large but peaceful groups and total concession to groups that press their demands violently.[1]

The masters of Congress, from their long control of Indian public opinion, now often talk and act as though the public does not really know its own mind or, if it does, is in any event mistaken. For all their genuflections to democracy, they feel that they know what is best for the people they govern, without having to ask, and they treat any popular initiative as an ignorant affront. When fifteen million peasants quietly petition, the Congress leadership cannot hear, and when fifteen hundred rioters loot shops and fire trams, it stirs to respond. Thus, when it should attend, it ignores; when it should measure, it resists; and when it should resist, it succumbs.

'If I hate anything in public life,' Dr B. C. Roy, a lifelong friend of the Nehru family and for several years Chief Minister of West Bengal, once declared, 'it is the creation of political sectors or groups for the sake of controlling public opinion. I am convinced that this universally practised political manoeuvring cannot lead to the greatest good of the greatest number, and abuses, nepotism and dishonesty follow.'[2] So, he might properly have added, does democracy. Between such Congress leaders and the mass of the Indian people exists a clear hiatus in communication – due as much to attitude as to background – which only periodic rebelliousness seems able to cross.

Of equal significance to the strength of parliamentary democracy in India is the lack of great political parties divided by broad issues of policy rather than by sectional interests. To begin with, there is only one great party in terms of tradition, consistent popular appeal and parliamentary representation on the national level, and that is Congress itself. The largest opposition group, the Communist Party of India, has no more than 29 seats in a Lok Sabha of some 500 members, and has no

[1] *The Politics of Scarcity*, pp. 215–16.
[2] Quoted by K. P. Thomas, *Dr. B. C. Roy* (West Bengal Pradesh Congress Committee, Calcutta, 1955), p. 189.

parliamentary representation at all in the states of Assam, Gujarat, Madhya Pradesh, Maharashtra, Mysore, Orissa, the Punjab, and Rajasthan, or in eight of the fourteen main constituents of the Indian union. Other opposition parties are similarly restricted to regional support: the Praja Socialist Party has no parliamentary representation whatsoever in seven of the fourteen states; the Jana Sangh, in ten; and the Swatantra Party, in nine. Congress itself is in many ways both government and opposition parties wrapped together. When India achieved independence, Congress represented a national movement and included within itself all shades of opinion united by a common cause. The Jana Sangh on the extreme right and the Communist Party on the extreme left were already in possession of their own identities, but the other significant opposition groups – the Praja Socialist Party, the Socialist Party, and the Swatantra Party – emerged from Congress itself. There are, indeed, still more self-proclaimed socialists in Congress than in either of the two socialist parties, and more apostles of 'free enterprise' there than in the Swatantra Party. The opposition groups have not so much affected policy by their overt activity in the legislature as by their pressures upon groups within the Congress party itself, which in turn have fought each other for control under the arbitration of Nehru. The propaganda of the socialist parties has encouraged Congress formally to proclaim socialist programmes; the Swatantra Party has strengthened the pressures for restraint from the capitalist wing; and the Jana Sangh has added force to the group of Hindu communalists. Parliamentary democracy in India, therefore, is less a system of great parties fighting for electoral support and so legislative control, than a one-party system, in which the one party changes its policies according to the pressures exerted upon it by articulate public opinion and by relatively small groups of organized opposition in intermittent conflict with it and with each other.

The danger to parliamentary democracy in India is that the rivalries within the one party monopolizing government have increasingly assumed the aspect of factionalism rather than genuine differences of policy. Office has inevitably brought material rewards, along with the enjoyment of prestige and the exercise of patronage, while success and time have together eroded the idealism of the struggle against alien rule. Gandhi himself had been enough of a realist to see and say this long before the repeated victories of Congress at the polls. Congress-men, he claimed, were not sufficiently interested in constructive work: 'We must recognize the fact that the social order of our dreams cannot come through the Congress party of today.'[1] Whether his own brand of idealism would have satisfied the needs of modern India may be doubted; but he certainly saw how necessary idealism would be in the new struggle to recon-struct India, and he foresaw the speed with which it would be evaporated by power. For power, rather than its employment in a particular constructive cause, has become for many Congress leaders the ultimate objective, the final virtue of independence. And precisely because Congress is the only great party in the State containing within itself so many different pressure groups of opinion, policy has taken second place to position. It has increasingly become a matter not of why, but of whom, not of whether one or other programme would be the right one for the country to follow, but of whether one or other faction would benefit from its adoption.

For this devaluation in the political currency of Congress, the party's leadership itself has been notably to blame. It has guided its followers by its own examples of cynical manoeuvring in the pursuit of power, its repeated sacrifices of principle to immediate electoral expediency. The seduction of seats has promoted alliances which Congress, as a party committed to secularism, socialism and national integration, should never have considered and would, in any other party, strenuously have denounced: with the Sikh separatist Akali Dal in the Punjab, for the 1957 elections; with the Muslim League against the Communist Party in the Kerala state elections of 1960; with the Ganatantra Parishad, the party of the princes, to form a coalition government in Orissa after Congress had lost its absolute majority in the 1957 state elections. Furthermore, in order to steal the clothes of its opponents, Congress has in-creasingly at election time given nominations to those whose only aptitude for office was potential electoral support of the most primitive kind – to princes in Rajasthan and to Muslims

---

[1] Quoted in 'Ethics and Electoral Democracy' by P. C. Chaudhuri, *Seminar* No. 30 (February 1962), p. 32.

in Muslim areas – whether or not this has inevitably meant nourishing reaction or communalism. Such tactics have been most menacingly evident in the encouragement which Congress has given to caste politics.

Cocooned in their air-conditioned offices at New Delhi or in the state capitals, the Congress leaders constitute a modernized and professional political élite far removed from the voting masses of rural India. Such a distance can be closed in one of two ways: by the promotion of a clear and constructive policy, capable of generating mass enthusiasm, productively utilizing the prestige and organizational force of Congress, and in the process developing an intermediate élite, modern in outlook and dedicated to change; or by the employment of the traditional élite, itself in contact with the peasant masses, as an indefinite holding operation. Congress has since independence chosen the second, despite the implicit – and frequently explicit – hostility of its own leadership and programmes to the authority of caste. This traditional élite – the male elders in each caste and sub-caste – has been a source of popular power throughout Indian history, and far from being forced to loose its hold with the coming of universal suffrage, has actually tightened it. For historically the caste system was a rigid institution with a hierarchy seldom susceptible to significant shifts. The power bestowed by democracy upon large numbers of votes, however, promoted competition between various castes, which were consequently available to manipulation by – and which could attempt to manipulate in turn – the political parties. Caste and party came more and more to depend upon each other: the caste dependent for the opportunities that the party could give it to exercise political influence and so even change its place in the traditional hierarchy; the party dependent for the votes it could receive in response to the right candidate or the appropriate promises.

Such mutual dependence has had three important consequences: (i) the choice of party candidates at elections is determined by the predominant caste affiliation of each constituency; (ii) caste politics influence party politics, since if one caste gives support to a particular party, its rival will give support to the rival party; and (iii) alliances and counter alliances are formed between minority castes and sub-castes to offset the predominance of a particular caste.[1] Not surprisingly, the numerically important castes have enormously increased their power – often at the expense of other castes which have dominated them in the past, or of lower castes which need government intervention to promote their social and economic advance. Election to parliament has become much less the victory of a particular programme at the polls than the successful manipulation of caste rivalries and allegiances.

There is indeed a wide gulf between caste as an endogamous and ritual unit, and the caste-like units which are so active in politics and administration in modern India. But between these entities there is not only connection but much communication. Village level leaders cultivate ministers for privileges and for a variety of favours, and the ministers in turn need the help of village leaders during elections. Many if not most Ministers at the State level are also leaders of their castes, and through this, of their regions also ...[2]

The principle of caste is so firmly entrenched in our political and social life that everyone including the leaders have accepted tacitly the principle that, in the provincial cabinets at any rate, each major caste should have a minister ... In the first popular cabinet in Mysore State, headed by Shri K. C. Reddy, not only were the ministers chosen on a caste basis, but each had a secretary from his own sub-sub-sub-caste. And today in Mysore State this principle is followed not only in every appointment, but also in the allotment of seats in schools and colleges.[3]

This headlong retreat from the politics of policy, promoted by the factionalism within Congress, has in turn sustained and encouraged that factionalism further. There have been countless instances of splits within Congress at the local and even state level; between Congress state organizations and Congress state governments; within Congress state committees, between one

[1] See 'Background and Possibilities' by Jitendra Singh in an examination of 'The Emerging Leadership', *Seminar* No. 51 (November 1963), p. 15.
[2] M. N. Srinivas, *Caste in Modern India and Other Essays* (Asia Publishing House, 1962), p. 6.
[3] Ibid., p. 72.

caste group and another; within individual constituencies, between those supporting the official candidate and those, for caste or linguistic or personal reasons, supporting an unofficial candidate, or even an opposition-party nominee. In such a welter of factional disagreements, such coherent policy as Congress at one or other time assembles can only with the greatest difficulty be projected to a mass electorate.

The virtually unassailable possession of government by Congress for so many years has had a further dangerous effect in the blurring of the line, kept scrupulously – or almost scrupulously – distinct in the British model, between the politicians and the civil service. Congress has a clear, if concealed, hold over those who owe their employment and prospects of promotion to government; and the Congress political machine, to the Cabinet Minister level, has made marked and frequent use of this advantage. In a country where communications are generally so poor and where vast distances have to be covered by election campaigners, government transport – planes and trucks – have been freely used by Congress candidates and officials, and civil servants have been delicately prodded into helping with the organization of meetings. This is natural enough in a country where the governing party lacks a proper mass organization and the government possesses one; the need for such activity would decrease were Congress to establish an effectively popular administrative base of its own; but meanwhile the consequent corrosion of public trust in the impartiality of the civil service cannot be sufficiently stressed. Nor does Congress as the party with power restrict its pressures to government employees. Influential local figures are cajoled into lending their support and helping in the persuasion of others by administrative bribes, the promise of sympathetic treatment for an application long delayed, or the suggestion of a community project with all its attendant possibilities for patronage.

Moreover, Congress enjoys, despite the foundation of the big-business-backed Swatantra Party, by far the largest access to money for political purposes – less through the generosity of its mass support, for the poor in India are far too poor to provide any significant subsidy, than from the merchants and industrialists in pursuit of government contracts, import licences, and administrative jobs for members of their families. During the ascetic days of Congress struggle against British rule, the display and possession of wealth – despite the friendship of Gandhi himself with particular men of enormous riches like Birla – was generally an electoral disqualification, and such money as came from the business community was used in a national campaign by a national movement. Today vast industrial concerns not only give substantial sums to Congress for its election funds, but carefully advertise their gifts, and the Congress leadership is stolidly unembarrassed by such contributions. Lal Bahadur Shastri, now Prime Minister and when Minister of Commerce and Industry, declared in Parliament: 'I candidly admit that Congress has collected funds from these rich people who wanted to give funds. I do not want to deny the fact, but we do not feel that we have done anything wrong. Mass collections take place and sometimes in that mass are included Messrs Birlas, Tatas, Dalmias – they are all there.' The disclaimer is too innocent: it strains credulity too far to suggest that such contributions from the major Indian industrialists, men of proved wiliness and self-interest, are spontaneous manifestations of political sympathy, on the level of the rupee contributed by a primary school teacher; that such funds come unsolicited and go unrewarded. Of course, India is not the only democratic state in which money is profitably employed at election time and where a significant discrepancy exists between the financial resources of one party and another; despite the financial superiority of the Republican Party in the United States, the Democratic Party has in modern times usually succeeded at the polls, and despite the financial power and expenditure of the Conservative Party in Britain, the Labour Party achieved a spectacular victory in 1945. Yet the discrepancy between the Republican and Democratic Parties in the United States, and between the Conservative and Labour Parties in Britain, is so different in degree from the discrepancy between Congress and the other political parties in India as to constitute a difference in kind.

Congress, of course, is not unaware of the advantages which its overwhelming financial dominance gives it. Though the law lays a limit of 9,000 rupees (just under £700) for a candidate's campaign expenditure for a state legislative seat, one 'modest'[1]

[1] 'Money and Votes' by Kewal Varma, a financial journalist, in *Seminar* No. 30 (February 1962).

estimate suggests an average expenditure of 20,000 rupees (or over £1,500) for a rural constituency and 10,000 rupees (over £750) for an average urban one. The safeguards in the Representation of People's Act are virtually useless. There is no ceiling whatsoever on the expenditure of political parties themselves in election campaigns, and the Act was so amended in 1956 as to render the account of election expenses for individual candidates – to quote the Election Commission on the Second General Elections – 'practically nugatory'. Since the accounting of expenses was made to cover only the period between the date of poll notification and the date of declaration, there was exempted all expenditure incurred by a prospective candidate for most of his canvassing effort. The Election Commission noted the consequences:

> An unscrupulous candidate is, therefore, legally free to flout the legal maximum of election expenditure by adopting several subterfuges. He may, for example,
> (i) buy up and pay for all the petrol needed by him for his election campaign before the date of notification;
> (ii) hire all vehicles needed for the campaign and pay for them in full before that date;
> (iii) pay the bulk or the whole of his printing and publicity charges before that date;
> (iv) engage and pay all his workers and agents in advance before that date, stipulating that they will render their services to him later during the election campaign; and
> (v) he may pay large sums of money to his party and to his friends before that date on the understanding that they will spend the amounts on his behalf before and during the election campaign without any further specific reference to him in respect of each individual item of expenditure.

No one who visits India today can escape hearing on all sides the charges of corruption with which Congress is assailed. Even senior members of the government, as though to absolve themselves from any such activity, hint at the underhand dealings of colleagues: the favours that they have secured for their sons if not for themselves; their intrigues and hypocrisy. Corruption[1] is certainly widespread, though it is improbable

[1] See Chapter 6 on 'Corruption and the New Raj'.

that its prevalence in Congress is quite on the scale that general gossip suggests; there are leaders of undoubted integrity holding positions of power in the party, and the tradition of popular service has not altogether collapsed. Many of the votes that Congress can poll at election time are the ready rewards of a political party that has done something measurable – if not as much as it should or it could – to dig India out of the entombment of its past. Accusations of corruption, hypocrisy and nepotism come strangely from national newspapers owned by industrialists whose acquaintance with such activities is only too close; the business community which attacks Congress for corruption is itself the principal source of temptation and the principal beneficiary. What cannot, however, be discounted are the consequences of the general belief in widespread political corruption, the cynicism not only of the urban middle class but of the peasantry. Any system of government is in part an act of faith, but democracy perhaps more than any other. The research workers of Lucknow University who investigated conditions and attitudes in a typical north-Indian village reported an unexpected response to the experience of independence.

> Comparing the present government with the British rule, some villagers say that under British regime they lived peacefully and the government did not interfere in their affairs unnecessarily. Further at the time of British rule, they say, justice was meted out with fairness and the wrong-doer was punished, but now, often the wrong-doer escapes and the innocent is punished, for there is much corruption and bribery among those in power.[1]

Doubtless this is a sentimental view of the British raj; the past acquires attractions in proportion to its distance. But the belief of peasants in widespread administrative corruption today, in independent India, is a different matter, and cannot but erode confidence in the democratic experiment.

Even more damaging than cynicism is its companion, the feeling of helplessness. What, after all, is the point in supporting an opposition group? Many of those who would be at home in

[1] D. N. Majumdar, *Caste and Communication in an Indian Village*, p. 299.

the Praja Socialist Party consider it futile to join a movement that has no prospect at all of accomplishing power; yet their lack of confidence in the socialist determination proclaimed by Congress keeps them from supporting the government and so out of active politics altogether. Inevitably, the same retreat is beaten by others with different political ideas. The extent of Congress dominance offers no feasible organized alternative, and the purpose to which such dominance is put encourages a withdrawal from constitutional activity. The greater the withdrawal, the more Congress falls into the possession of the political careerists, and the more that Congress falls into their possession the greater does the withdrawal by those who can best serve the party become.

With the death of Nehru, Congress and democracy in India face a pressing challenge. While Nehru reigned, the political bosses of Congress were able to rule in the radiance of his popular prestige and the tradition of Congress struggle for national independence which he embodied. The cult of the 'good man', above the squalor of contest and ambition, is strong in India and fortified by Hindu tradition. Nehru, for all his secularism, was widely held to be such a man even by orthodox Hindus, partly through his association with Gandhi and the known regard in which Gandhi had held him, partly through his own reticent, even arrogant, always patently elevated character. The scandals that lapped his family or friends did not affect his own reputation with the masses; the 'good man' is traditionally tormented by disappointing human relationships. Were not Gandhi's own sons a cruel trial to him? With Nehru gone, and no 'good man' of similar status to succeed him, Congress is for the first time on its own, to be judged by its policies and not by the personality of its leader. While Nehru lived, he could contain the various factions within Congress and, when he thought it necessary – which, unhappily, he did not do nearly often enough – impose his will upon them. Indeed, such a radical image as Congress periodically projected was in major part the consequence of his will; the left faction in the party is a minority one which always depended upon Nehru himself to promote its programme.

Now, with Nehru no longer there to hold them together, the factions may well go their natural and separate ways – the economic right wing attaching itself to the Swatantra Party, the Hindu communalists finding a home in the Jana Sangh, and the left dividing, with some members joining the Communist Party and others, perhaps in conjunction with the existing Socialist Parties, producing a new socialist force – while Congress itself attempts to survive as a party of the centre. Such a disintegration in the direction of policy could only serve democracy and India itself well. The alternative is that Congress should attempt to survive as it is, held together not by a common allegiance to a coherent policy, but by a common appetite for the perpetuation of power. In such an event, if it does not meet at the polls the rejection which its basic confusion and inability to deal with India's problems demand, the factionalism, the corruption, the cynicism and the helplessness can only grow, till the whole system of democratic government is finally discarded.

The fourth character of the British model, carefully noted by the Indian constitutionalists, was 'the existence of a mobile body of political opinion owing no permanent allegiance to any party and therefore able, by its instinctive reaction against extravagant movements on one side or the other, to keep the vessel on an even keel'. Perhaps the greatest promise of Indian democracy lies in the existence of just such a body of opinion in India, not only within the middle class but among the Indian masses themselves. In a series of by-elections, even before Nehru's death, during the second half of 1963, Congress was unexpectedly defeated at the polls in spite of – and, there is reason to believe, partly because of – blatant attempts by the Congress political machine to manipulate caste and communal allegiances. As the late Professor Majumdar, head of the Lucknow University team investigating village life, reported – in the face of his otherwise harsh and frequently dismaying conclusions:

Villagers do realise the importance of elections, and know that they have the power to a certain extent of selecting or rejecting those who are to be in authority. Social awareness has been increasing and the villagers today are becoming increasingly conscious of their political rights. The freedom with which some of the villagers express themselves shows their dissatisfaction, and their preferences augur well for the future of Indian democracy.[1]

It is in large measure a question of time. Given several years of peaceful development, and a government sufficiently concerned with the gravity of India's problems to take radical and efficient steps for their solution, the grip of democratic practice would doubtless so tighten as to leave no room for authoritarian alternatives. But there is little or no time left, and to the endemic crisis of poverty, superstition and mass inertia, communalism and the mounting political power of caste, corruption and the cynicism that it feeds, must now be added the threat to the integrity of the Indian union that regional quarrels present. There can be no doubt that, despite his clear appreciation of the menacing consequences, Nehru permitted, and with increasing laxity over the years, not only the establishment of regional entities with separate claims to popular allegiance – as in the 1956 reorganization of states along linguistic lines – but also the drift of power from New Delhi to the state capitals. Armed with the unitary emphasis of the Indian Constitution and his own national dominance, he could – at the cost certainly of a struggle, but one which would have been the easier successfully to conclude, the earlier it had been undertaken – have arrested the centrifugal forces of India. His early rival for supreme power, the right-wing Sardar Patel, showed a vigour and consistency of will in integrating the princely states during the early years of independence which set a profitable precedent for Nehru to follow. His failure to do so must be accounted one of Nehru's most damaging mistakes. Now that he himself is dead, his national authority – lustre is not too strong a description – is no longer at the disposal of the national government, and the Indian search for a 'good man' in whom to invest their hopes and trust may well be restricted to the individual states.

If democracy does not now take a new course, with the creation of powerful parties of policy, so that the mass electorate is given a meaningful national choice, then the real contest of policy will move altogether from the centre to the parts, and it will be in the states that a variety of different Indias will be

[1] *Caste and Communication in an Indian Village*, pp. 299–300.

shaped. Such a prospect cannot but excite dismay, for the problems of India are so huge that only a united effort to tackle them can promise a hope of solution. A gradual dissipation of national authority, while the problems merely mount and multiply, must in the end produce the very appetite for centralized authoritarianism which it seems to deny. It was no accident that the totalitarian growth in the Weimar Republic should have assumed the shape of a militant nationalism; it was a response not alone to the seemingly intractable economic problems of Germany, but also to the political disintegration which the different constituent states, with their frequently conflicting policies, represented.

To measure the growing force of regional loyalties, however, is not to ignore the underlying power of the national culture, the unifying call of Hinduism. The really vigorous right-wing movement in India today is not the Swatantra Party, the home of those merchants and industrialists who find Congress too radical for their dispositions, but the Jana Sangh, the party of militant Hinduism. In response to the humiliations that they believed India to have suffered in the border war with China, the leaders of the two parties certainly discussed the possibilities of an alliance, and though no real association has as yet come about, the pressures for one are mounting. One does not have to dig too deeply in the record of Europe to discover the possible consequences of a deal between a substantial section of the business community and the apostles of nationalist resurgence, to meet the dangers of disintegration and Communism within – the Communist Party remains the second strongest party in India and may well benefit electorally from Nehru's death – and Communist power without.

Certainly Communist strength and success were made agonizingly apparent to India during the border crisis. The reputation of the Indian army as a formidable and efficient force received a serious blow, while too many civil administrators in the assaulted areas displayed more anxiety to secure their own speedy escape than to maintain order and morale. To the intellectuals who remember or have learnt of the poverty, corruption and weakness that characterized China before its Communist revolution, the new China cannot but seem an impressive material success, even if the means by which that success was attained are considered disreputable, and to the Indian masses, in village or city, the new China must loom as an intimidating power all the more awesome for being Asian. The debate over means and ends may captivate the intellectuals, but it can be argued not unreasonably that a starving peasant, hopeless of ever changing his condition through the slow and distant processes of Indian government, finds such discussion finally meaningless. He wants food and security, perhaps too a feeling of cultural pride, and if he cannot find them under one system of authority, he will turn to another. The very power that China so closely represents may arouse fear and hostility; but may it not also arouse envy and even imitation? Both China and Japan, in their very different ways, have taken from Western culture, alien and repugnant, what they could not defeat. Success, as the history of nationalism irresistibly records, is infectious; and success is concerned – however regrettable this may be – with ends far more than with means. The traditional Hindu attitude of submission need not disappear because the traditional caste hierarchy does; it may be utilized by Communism on the left – or by a militant communalism on the right, to avoid such an alternative – as a re-enforcement of its authority.

The Indian Communist Party is itself changing rapidly in response to the power that neighbouring China has become. The Sino-Soviet quarrel in the world Communist movement had already caused visible cracks before the border war with China split the whole party wide open. The assistance which the Soviet Union continued giving to India despite the border war seemed to confirm the wisdom of Nehru's non-alignment policy and enabled Indian Communism and nationalism to co-exist contentedly; but the wholesale attachment to the Soviet side by the rank and file of the Indian party, which the war with China and Soviet military aid to India might have been expected to cause, did not in fact occur. The rank and file in West Bengal, the state with the largest Communist representation – nine seats – in the Lok Sabha, broke massively with the pro-Soviet stand taken by the national leadership and even refused a hearing to S. A. Dange, Chairman of the party, when he tried to address a meeting in Calcutta; in Andhra Pradesh and Kerala, the two other states where the Communist Party is strong, the rank and file was split down the middle. Even the national leadership, at first seemingly pro-Soviet, soon displayed a serious division, with E. M. S. Namboodiripad, the former Chief Minister of Kerala, resigning as General Secretary and subsequently attacking Dange, along with the majority behind him in the national committee, as opportunist. The split, it became clear, was far more than a doctrinal one, the taking of sides between Moscow and Peking; it reflected a shift, gradual but drastic, in the whole character of power within the party.

The traditional leaders have come in the main from the middle class, which in India has moved politically up and down the scale, providing the spokesmen both for the group in power and for those groups revolting against it. It is astonishing, for instance, how many of India's senior Communists, the proclaimed leaders in the struggle of the proletarian and peasant masses, speak and indeed think in English rather than the vernacular. One prominent Communist organizer commented wryly: 'We read so many foreign books that we know more about the Italian Communist Party than the French Communist Party does.' And this hiatus between spokesmen and following is emphasized in the similarity of manner and method – a sort of cultural comradeship – between the leaders of Congress, or most other parliamentary parties, and those of the Communist Party itself. It is not only the derivative grandeur common to both the parliament buildings of Britain and India, not even the common ritual of procedure, that makes the two institutions seem so alike; both have the atmosphere of an exclusive association, members of which share the same set of basic assumptions. Where these assumptions are held, as in Britain, by their constituents as well, the parliamentarians may dissent on minor issues with safety. The parliamentary representatives of the Indian Communist Party, however, for all their declared revolutionary resolve, must have seemed to many of their constituents to have had much more in common with other members of parliament than with the factory workers and landless peasants they were supposed to represent, and to have extended this cultural difference – not inevitably, but none the less conclusively – into a fundamental difference of approach to authority and change.

In many of the Indian states, and especially in West Bengal, the clash between the traditional leadership and a new set of leaders, coming from the peasantry itself, constituted the real division within the party that the Sino-Soviet dispute merely tended to reflect. In fact, the division into pro-Soviet and pro-Chinese wings, with which general comment from outside docketed the party quarrel, was a ruthless over-simplification; the split was far more concerned with the whole character of the party's leadership and its policy towards the Nehru administration. The left of the party wanted more militant political and economic action, rejecting the contention of the ruling right that the defence of India's territorial integrity came first and that Communists in India should accept the leadership of Nehru in a united national front, with a moratorium on internal struggle; the identification of the left with support for China in the world Communist dispute, a confusion which the traditional party leadership found it profitable to sustain, was a coincidence that must have wide consequences in the future.

It was staggering, in the period immediately following the border war, how much closer to Nehru's policies the senior leaders of the Communist Party seemed to be than most spokesmen of Congress itself; not a few Communist officials and members of parliament openly claimed that it was Nehru alone who restrained the Congress government from using the war with China as an excuse to crush the Communist Party, and that the soundest hope of accomplishing economic change in the long run, therefore – or, at least, escaping an avalanche of reaction while the war with China lasted – lay in supporting Nehru from outside Congress and so strengthening his hand within. It was the leaders of the party's left wing, and especially the new spokesmen of the peasantry, who complained that Nehru had 'bought off' peasant struggle and, by offering – or promising – reform, delayed revolution. Certainly, now that Nehru is dead, an alliance between the left wing of Congress and the right wing of the Communist Party is going to be difficult, if not impossible, to maintain, and it would be surprising if even the traditional Communist leadership did not now move substantially leftwards, to pose a more militant alternative to Congress policy. The present (August 1964) official Communist campaign of mass action against rising food prices and profiteers, with demonstrations, strikes and civil disobedience, marks the first important Communist initiative since the time of the Namboodiripad government in Kerala over five years ago and promises a new period of internal disturbance and possibly violence.

The aspiring Communist leadership is not the only one which seems closer to village India than the traditional leaders of Congress and most of the opposition; the Jana Sangh, relying on the ageless hold of Hinduism, speaks very differently for and to the peasants, but in an idiom none the less close to their experience. The party's success in the 1962 general election was substantial; the number of its seats rose from 4 to 14 in the Lok Sabha and from 46 to 116 in the state legislatures. Indeed, the Jana Sangh became the main opposition party in Madhya Pradesh with 41 out of 288 seats, to 142 for Congress (a drop from 232), and in Uttar Pradesh, by far the most populous state in India, with 49 seats out of 430, to 249 for Congress (a drop from 286).

The appeal of the party to a nation which seems to have lost its sense of direction is obvious; if the future is bewildering, the past, when properly adjusted, can be made to appear certain and safe. The traditional Hindu social structure appeals not only to the elderly, to whom the world of the ballot box often seems strange and even impious, and to the upper castes whose numerical inferiority has eroded their dominance, but to all those for whom the very rigidity of the caste pattern offered a fixed and known place in society, with comfortably clear rights and responsibilities. A reversion to the past, or rather a past effectively glamorized, conceals the extent of present problems by explaining them in terms of betrayal: the people are poor not because the country's resources are unequally or inade- quately exploited, but because the people themselves have turned their backs on the old ways; the country is weak not because China is stronger or more disciplined, more efficient and resourceful, but because pride and the will to withstand has departed from Hinduism.

Strangely, though in so many ways the living Gandhi proved to be the greatest enemy of Hindu traditionalism with his assault on caste rigidities and discrimination, Gandhi dead may prove to be a powerful ally of the Hindu traditionalists. For Gandhi, too, opposed the establishment of the centralized and industrialized modern state, the society of the machine. His economic philosophy, with its promotion of the self-sufficient village, was as much a reversion, and as impractical a one, as the political philosophy of the Jana Sangh. With the death of Nehru the strongest personal link between Gandhi and Congress has gone, and it would be inept for the Jana Sangh not to claim that it had become the only true exponent of the Mahatma's teachings.

Nothing, however, is more likely to inflame support for the Jana Sangh than a deterioration in India's relationship with Pakistan. Perhaps Nehru's most consistent resolve was the secularism of India, and in the main – doubtless because he pursued it without weakness or wavering – it was a successful policy. Yet it led to the blunders of Kashmir, for it was his refusal to countenance communal choice, a belated attempt at arresting the division of British India into Muslim and Hindu states, that led Nehru to follow not the spirit of Indian independence, but the letter, in his handling of the Kashmir crisis. For a democrat of Nehru's passion to have based the claim of India to Kashmir not on the established will of the area's inhabitants but on the Maharaja's decision to accede in 1947, may have been tenably legal; but it was morally – and who was more aware than Nehru of the distinction between morality and law? – at the very least questionable. To the outsider who has always had far more sympathy with the secular and – if only in declaration – socialist democracy of India than with the military and religious authoritarianism of Pakistan, the Kashmir crisis must be a personal challenge; he cannot but want the state to remain part of India, and cannot but want its future to be decided by its own inhabitants. There can be no doubt that national aggrandizement was never a motive in Nehru's policy towards Kashmir, even if it was the force behind the refusal by many other leaders of Congress to allow a referendum in the territory that might surrender it to Pakistan. It is no more than just to accept that Nehru's own refusal was conditioned by his antagonism to the religious basis of Pakistan and by his belief in the effects that the loss of Kashmir would have, not only upon the security of the huge Muslim minority in India but on the secularism and tolerance of the Hindus themselves.

It may none the less be argued that Nehru's very linking of the Kashmir crisis with the future of India's Muslim minority – a linking to which he gave frequent public expression, if only as a fear, and allowed his government repeatedly to refer – will excite precisely what he aimed to avoid, the descent of the Hindu masses into communal hysteria. The Kashmir crisis has become India's major international embarrassment: it has set the country at loggerheads with the United Nations, though the essence of Indian foreign policy has been and remains the strengthening of that organization's prestige and authority; it has made any final settlement with Pakistan impossible, and driven two natural political enemies of each other – Pakistan and China – into an alliance of hostility against India; and it has provided the Jana Sangh with a device for advancing militant Hinduism. The postponement of any solution has only aggravated the problem, and though the establishment of an independent Kashmir, or even the territory's accession to Pakistan, might fifteen years ago have had manageable effects on Hindu public opinion, the delay has enormously strengthened the forces of intransigence. The status of Kashmir is now a threat not only to the peace of India's frontiers, as it has been for so long, but also, every year increasingly, to the whole future of secularism and democracy in the country.

In some measure it was the Kashmir crisis that led to the border war between India and China. The precise boundaries between the two countries, both in the east, separating Tibet from India's North-East Frontier Agency, and in the west, separating Sinkiang from Ladakh, have been the subject of such intricate dispute that both Chinese and Indian experts are able to produce interminable evidence for the undeniable justice of their conflicting claims. Certainly the disputed border in the west was so remote that China was able to build a road across a corner of Ladakh, to connect Sinkiang with Tibet, and the Indian government is reputed to have known nothing about it until its completion was celebrated, to the astonishment of the Indian ambassador, in Peking. Had the two countries been on better terms, the frontiers might have been much easier to negotiate, and the security and pride of each suitably preserved. By the late 'fifties, however, the two were no longer friends.

Nehru had welcomed the Chinese revolution of 1949, and for

a few years the sentiment of 'Hindi-Chinese bhai-bhai' – the brotherhood of Indians and Chinese – had warmed the air between New Delhi and Peking. Then, in 1956, had come China's absorption of Tibet, a territory which China claimed – not altogether without justification – to be historically hers. The opposition parties to the right of Congress in international affairs, from the Jana Sangh to the Praja Socialists, together with the big business owned national press, shrilly assailed China, and Nehru's own reaction, while carefully unhostile, was – not altogether without justification – less than enthusiastic.

In the belief that the news of Chinese border claims affecting India would needlessly arouse public opinion and so make any settlement more difficult to achieve, Nehru kept the growing disagreement between the two countries as secret as possible, and when late in 1958 an Indian military patrol was arrested by Chinese forces on the Ladakh border, the reports produced all the greater stir in India for being unexpected. A clamour against Chinese aggression arose, which was reinforced when, in March 1959, with the intensification of Chinese control over Tibet, thousands of Tibetan refugees, headed by the Dalai Lama, fled across the border into India. Though Nehru scrupulously offered the refugees, including the Dalai Lama, no more than sanctuary, his formal reception of them, and the sympathy they were accorded by the Indian press and prominent politicians – not all of them outside the ranks of Congress – hardened a Chinese opinion already hostile, in the mounting world-Communist dispute, to the Soviet-supported 'national revolutions' of democracies like India. Excited by the very urban middle-class public opinion which on so many other aspects of his policy he discounted, and nourished by evidence that India's claims to the border areas in dispute were just, Nehru became less hesitant and began both to speak and act as though the Indian case was unanswerable. In doing so, of course, he proceeded to strengthen the very forces in India – and in Congress itself – for which the possession of Kashmir was a symbol of national dignity and power, and for which now the border dispute with China was an affair of national honour all the more important because Ladakh was part of Kashmir. The Indian government demanded the Chinese evacuation of Aksai Chin, the area of Ladakh across which the road had been built, as a prerequisite for negotiation towards a final border settlement, and an open clash between the two countries drew speedily closer.

The Indian Army proposed to follow the same strategy of infiltration by which China had so successfully absorbed the area of Aksai Chin, and on the advice – or in the belief – that the Chinese would, in consequence, be forced to withdraw, Nehru adopted the plan. But this 'forward policy', as it came to be known, depended on a vast miscalculation. The initial Chinese move had been into territory so barren and remote that the supposedly occupying Indian administration had not noticed the building of a road over many miles and months; the Indian forces were moving into an area scattered with Chinese military posts, to take control of a road that the Chinese government considered to be of supreme strategic importance. In the autumn of 1962 the Chinese army, in retaliation, launched massive attacks in both the north-west and north-east, blotting out the Indian border posts established under the 'forward policy' in Ladakh, and overwhelming the Indian Army in the North East Frontier Agency so as to carry Chinese troops to the very edge of the Assam plains. After four weeks of fighting, China all at once declared a cease-fire, but the victory was agonizingly hers: the Indian army had been routed rather than defeated; a large portion of India's sparse resources for economic development were being sluiced off for strengthening the armed forces; and the Indian government, by requesting substantial military assistance from Britain and the United States, would be widely considered to have compromised its policy of non-alignment.

In the wake of the Chinese withdrawal from all but the absorbed border region, it is not only India's plans for economic development and her military prestige that stand severely damaged; much of her foreign policy lies in ruins. While she has not yet concluded a military alliance with the Western powers, she has clearly come to depend on them, and in particular on the United States, for large-scale aid, and though the appearance of non-alignment has been preserved by continuing assistance of a sort from the Soviet Union, the reality is in ever-increasing danger of being sacrificed altogether. There is unlikely to be any crude repayment demanded of her by the

West – American bases on Indian territory, even if they could be obtained under sufficient pressure, would be neither politically prudent nor strategically profitable – but the Indian government will be expected to pursue a foreign policy that does not conflict with the important interests of those states which have come, and may have to come again, to her rescue. Nor would the normally articulate public opinion of India – the national press, the business community, the bulk of the professional politicians and intelligensia – in the main be inclined to view any act by the government of the United States under present circumstances with anything but a grateful sympathy. It was not negligence or apathy that kept the Indian government so silent during the Cuban crisis of late 1962, when the United States, whatever the provocation, acted in open disregard of Cuba's international rights and the peace-keeping prerogatives of the United Nations. More blatantly, it was pressure from the United States and Britain, publicly exercised, that pushed India into a fruitless round of talks with Pakistan over Kashmir during 1963.

An end altogether to the policy of non-alignment – which the death of Nehru, its architect, may effectively advance – would not only be welcomed, but is being strenuously promoted by India's powerful business community. The alternatives are clear, and nowhere more clearly seen than by those in control of India's profitable private sector: if India is to strengthen her armed forces without crippling her economy, she must raise far more revenue for investment from the one domestic source capable of providing it, the business community, in the form of higher and more efficiently gathered taxes, together with restrictions on conspicuous consumption and all profiteering; if more money is not to be raised from a domestic source, it must come from the West on conditions that would irresistibly reduce the political policies and economic organization of India to the requirements of foreign, and especially American, confidence.

The supporters of non-alignment in India have all the greater difficulty in defending it against its detractors for the significant failures which the policy seemed to register during the conflict with China. It is true that the Soviet Union did not support China against India, and though this was partly – it may be supposed – a result of the growing bitterness which marked her own doctrinal quarrel with China, it was also due to her support of Indian non-alignment and her wish to see the policy preserved. Apart from Albania, all the Communist states either rebuked China or meaningfully failed to extend her any support. But in the non-aligned world itself, where her claim for at least moral support against China might properly have been expected to be satisfied, India was dramatically disappointed. No encouragement of any sort came from the governments of such influential non-aligned states as Algeria, Burma, Ceylon, Ghana, Guinea and Indonesia, while the support that India received from the United Arab Republic was so slight as to be hardly worth having. Since India had been the first of the countries freed from colonial rule to expound and pursue a policy of non-alignment, the lack of support and even sympathy that she encountered among her natural allies seemed less a diplomatic reversal than a political disaster.

Yet India should not have been altogether surprised. The failure by other important non-aligned states to rally round her was an implicit criticism of the form which Indian non-alignment had itself taken. When India acquired independence in 1947, her new rulers – and chief amongst them, Nehru himself – saw the success of their own struggle as a prelude to the success of other struggles by other colonial peoples for self-government. Nehru projected the policy of non-alignment not merely because he believed that international peace could best be preserved by keeping India out of any military entanglement with either bloc, and because he was drawn both to the political principles of Western democracy and to the economic principles of Soviet socialism, but also because he wanted a free hand in furthering the escape of captive peoples from the custody of any great power. For a time at the United Nations India took the lead in a diplomatic assault on colonialism, and if her government concentrated upon the liberation of Western colonies rather than the satellite states of Stalinist Russia, it was because India herself had suffered from Western colonialism so that she knew its devastations more nearly, and because the classic colonial empires were all Western. Gradually, however, as India became more absorbed by her own vast economic problems and with mounting anxiety sought substantial aid from the West, the Nehru government grew less concerned about colonial liberation and, not without a measure of self-importance, concentrated its efforts upon securing international peace by attempting to mediate in the quarrels of the great powers.

Although, for instance, there was widespread support in India, even amongst opposition parties to the right of Congress, for the struggle of the Algerian people against France, the Indian government refused to recognize the Provisional Government of the Algerian Republic, in the face of repeated pleas by Algerian representatives that such an act would significantly increase the pressure on France for a settlement. Even the *Times of India*, a newspaper owned by one of India's most prominent industrialists and not itself renowned for radical views, maintained that the Indian government, in the name of moderation, was attempting the grotesque feat of holding the balance evenly over Algeria between the oppressor and the oppressed.[1] When Algeria at last achieved its independence, Nehru duly congratulated the leaders of the new nation, but was careful to congratulate President de Gaulle of France as well for 'his resolve to grant independence to Algeria'. China, on the other hand, isolated by the West and adopting a militant stand against Western colonialism, had given an interest-free loan of 10 million dollars to the Algerians during their fight against France, part of the sum in weapons which the Chinese had trained Algerians to use. In April 1959 China had observed an 'Algeria Week' and had repeatedly received Algerian delegations in a manner that India reserved for the visiting heads of great powers. On the achievement of Algerian independence Chou En-lai congratulated the Algerian leaders on 'the result of the armed struggle waged heroically by the Algerian people'. As an Indian academic himself tartly observed: 'India's cautious attitude on Algeria was not so different from the neutral stand of other non-aligned powers over the India-China conflict.'[2]

[1] *Times of India* editorial, August 18th, 1961.
[2] 'Non-Aligned Radicals' by K. P. Karunakaran, Reader in South Asian History and Institutions at the Indian School of International Studies, in *Seminar* No. 45 (May 1963), p. 19.

When Guinea voted for independence from France in the celebrated de Gaulle referendum of 1958, the French government immediately withdrew all administrators, technicians, economic aid and even such equipment, from office furniture to electrical wiring, as could be removed. The country was threatened with economic collapse, and a few crores of rupees or a small contingent of technicians from India would have been of service out of all proportion to the sacrifice made. But the Indian government offered nothing. In 1960 China, no less resolved on the rapid advance of her own economy than India was, gave Guinea an interest-free loan worth some 25 million dollars and in the following year sent agriculturists to advise on rice-growing. Ghana, anxious to diversify her economy and make it less dependent on the West, signed a friendship treaty with China in 1961 and received from her an interest-free loan of nearly 20 million dollars; during the Sino-Indian border war President Nkrumah wrote to the British Prime Minister expressing his distress at Britain's offer to give India every support and suggesting that peace could best be served 'by refraining from any action that may aggravate the situation'. When Western states blocked Egyptian foreign exchange during the Suez crisis, China gave Egypt five million dollars in Swiss francs; during the Sino-Indian border war President Nasser was careful not to antagonize the Chinese. India's assistance to Ghana and Egypt has at best been verbal.

Both India and China have borders with Burma and have given her economic aid, so that Burma could not properly have been expected to take sides in the Sino-Indian war. Ceylon, however, is a whole India away from China, and she has stronger cultural and historical links with India than with any other country; yet Ceylon not only refused to support India against China, but even prohibited the sending of money by any of her citizens to the Indian Defence Fund. Not irrelevantly, China has for some years been buying rubber from Ceylon at a price higher than that on the world market, and selling rice to her at a lower one; trade between the two countries has risen substantially, and China has eased Ceylon's unfavourable balance by agreeing to accept payment in sterling or goods. India, on the other hand, has done little to help reduce Ceylon's unfavourable balance of trade with her, and the Indian slice of Ceylon's total trade has stayed much the same since 1948. Moreover, while India's relations with the United States have steadily improved, Ceylon's have just as steadily deteriorated, till in February 1963 the United States government suspended all technical and economic assistance to Ceylon on the grounds that she had nationalized American oil companies without paying adequate compensation.

Equally distant from both countries, Indonesia has no cause to consider India's feelings and some to consider China's; India has given her no economic assistance, while China presented her with a low-interest credit of over £14 million in 1958 and has since made every effort to secure friendly relations. More importantly for Indonesia during the last few years than any economic aid, China has shown herself dependable in any struggle with the West, while India has not. At the September 1961 conference of non-aligned nations in Belgrade, President Soekarno declared: 'Prevailing world opinion would have us believe that the real source of international tension and strife is ideological conflict between the great powers. I think that is not true. There is the conflict between the new emergent forces for freedom and justice and the old forces of domination.' Nehru, however, insisted that top priority should be given to the threat of war. 'Imperialism, colonialism, racialism and the rest – things which are vitally important ... are somewhat over-shadowed by the crisis. For if war comes, all else for the moment goes.' Not surprisingly, Africans with their immediate attention on white supremacist regimes within their continent, and Asians concerned with the American military presence in theirs, were more impressed by Soekarno's argument. Then suddenly, in December, Indian troops marched into Portuguese-held Goa and annexed the enclave. While New Delhi trumpeted anti-imperialism as the excuse, the Belgrade non-aligned, on the evidence of Nehru himself, were inclined to suppose that India had been motivated by rather less ideological interests.

The truth is that in foreign policy, no less than in domestic, there has been a great hiatus between what the Indian govern-ment has said and what it has meant, or between what it has meant and what it has done. No one would have been surprised if India had marched into Goa at any time during the early years of independence, and if she had plainly declared her intention to do so beforehand, with the very telling reasons why she should, the West would have done no more than it did in 1961 and said much less. Little, certainly, could be said for a rigid and alien dominion denying to its subjects all prospect of self-determination, and nothing reasonably done except per-suade the United Nations to intervene instead, a course which would have embarrassed London and Washington in their relations with Lisbon even more than mere inaction. India was condemned by Western critics out of her own mouth. For years the Indian government had paid assiduous obeisance to the rule of international law, and the International Court at The Hague had declared that Portugal's title to Goa was legally good. Nehru himself had discouraged periodic invasions by Indian *satyagrahis*, and his government had scrupulously not intervened when the volunteers had been shot down by Portuguese forces. India was committed to keeping the peace, and persuading other countries to do so too, with negotiation as the only instrument of territorial change. Why Nehru should therefore have ordered the invasion of Goa at last, after thirteen years of pious abstention, is not easy to understand: sympathetic criticism claims that he acted on the advice of Krishna Menon, his then Minister of Defence, who believed that militancy over Goa would blunt opposition attacks on the government over sub-missiveness to China and so provide room for manoeuvre and even negotiation in the border dispute; unsubstantiated rumour suggests that the whole expedition was mounted because Menon himself was fighting a crucial by-election in Bombay against a prominent opponent of Congress and the annexation of Goa would have a profitable effect on the polls. But whatever the reason, the move was motivated by expediency and not principle, as Nehru's personal embarrassment made obvious, and con-tradicted the persistent preaching of Nehru himself. The West, unable to find a suitable defence for Portuguese rule, assailed the Indian government – and Nehru especially – instead for sanctimoniousness and deliberate deception.

This hiatus between policy and practice has not been limited to Goa, however; it has been evident in the whole Indian handling of non-alignment. Ceaselessly India has claimed to be supporting the struggle of colonial peoples for independence, but she has done little or nothing to further the struggle's success. Her actions have been a betrayal of the overall meaning which she originally attached to non-alignment herself, and the distrust of the non-aligned has been her inevitable return.

To say that much of Indian foreign policy lies in ruins as a result of the border war with China is perhaps a distortion; for it is doubtful whether India has had a coherent structure of foreign policy at all. In theory, of course, she has, just as she has had, in theory, a coherent structure of economic policy; but in foreign, no less than in economic, affairs, she has displayed only contradiction and confusion, as though the many statements of her leaders on both, with the accompanying grandiose plans and objectives, constituted no more than incidental music. As an anonymous Indian critic has recently put it:

'We have no sustained, long-ranging view on foreign affairs; instead, we have, like instant coffee, an "instant" foreign policy. It is a Nescafé approach to problems. We react to each crisis and stagger because we have not yet fallen.'[1]

India must take a close cool look at herself and her situation. Her international stock is low and falling fast, not because – as so many influential Indians seem to believe – she has lost a border war with China, but because she is losing the far more important war against internal dissipation. She is weak not because her army is smaller than China's or less efficiently equipped, but because her democratic system has grown flabby, because her economic advance has slowed down dangerously and seems even to be lagging behind her population increase, because her people have lost trust in their leaders and the leaders have lost trust in themselves. A foreign policy is as strong as the country behind it; nations, no less than individuals, cannot long spend money that they do not have. Nehru himself saw this – though characteristically he never did enough about it – and referred to it when addressing the Constituent Assembly on December 4th, 1947.

'Ultimately, foreign policy is the outcome of economic policy, and until India has properly evolved her economic policy, her foreign policy will be rather vague, rather inchoate, and will be groping. It is well for us to say that we stand for peace and

---

[1] 'Spinster on the Shelf', by 'Seminarist' in *Seminar* No. 56 (April 1964), p. 39.

freedom and yet that does not convey much to anybody, except
a pious hope.'

Before India directs her attention to the world beyond, she
must direct her attention to herself, to the crisis that exists not
in Moscow and Washington nor even on the borders of Ladakh,
but on the pavements of Calcutta and along the dust tracks of
Uttar Pradesh. To start with, the jingle of the Fool in *Lear*
may with advantage be placed on the desks of government
offices in New Delhi.

> Have more than thou showest,
> Speak less than thou knowest,
> Lend less than thou owest,
> Ride more than thou goest ...

Indian leaders must stop being dazzled by their own words, as
Nehru so frequently was, and ensure instead that the distance
is closed between what they say and what they do. No national
progress is possible without popular participation, and the
people of India have had their mouths crammed with promises
for much too long. The chasm must be bridged between the
rulers and the ruled, and the divisions between the rich in their
tens and the poor in their millions effectively removed. It is
not an easy task and it cannot be accomplished with mere
projects of paper. If Congress believes in democracy and wishes
to avoid the authoritarian alternatives, then it must expel from
its own electoral policies all dependence on caste manipulation
and constituency corruption, exclude from its own ranks the
political profiteers, and concentrate on drawing the masses of
India into the processes of government, not merely because
their confidence is necessary if government is to work, but
because their energies and talents must be of manifest service
in the struggle for self-sufficiency. If Congress believes in
socialism, it must not only proclaim its intention to reduce
economic inequalities, but do so and show that it is doing so.
It must mean what it says and achieve what it pledges. Five
Year Plans less ambitious than those announced would be much
more effective if their aims – not merely in steel tonnage but in
social justice – were accomplished, in the same way that taxes
could be reduced and still provide more revenue if they would
then at least be honestly and efficiently collected. If Congress

believes in a united India, then it must make a united India seem worth preserving; while nationhood offers nothing but frustration and defeat, people will seek an escape in regional allegiances and a sterile communion with the past.

No one will come to the final rescue of India but herself. Even if the West is willing to arm her as she wishes, in order to further the 'containment policy' towards China, it will not feed and clothe her, transform her agriculture and develop her industries on her behalf. To say that she must depend on her own exertions, however, is not to say that she should reject all hope of help and isolate herself from the world around her. She must continue searching for economic aid and take it wherever she finds it unattached to claims on her policy, and the more clearly that she puts such aid to good use, the more of it she is likely to acquire. India has more people than Africa and South America combined, and it is in the ultimate interest of the rich powers, East and West alike, that she should not collapse into anarchy or a desperate militarism. But the world outside is not solely composed of the contending rich. One of the major issues facing humanity – if not, in the long run, the most important of them all – is the division between the rich white nations, with less than a third of the earth's total population, and the poor coloured ones, superior only in their numbers and the abundance of their problems. To accept the truth of this is not to answer the mating call of China, as some influential Indians have suggested; no more radical a figure than Sir Alec Douglas-Home, as Prime Minister of Britain, has said the same. India belongs to the poor and coloured two-thirds of humanity, and her future cannot reasonably be divorced from theirs. She must therefore link her economic struggle with those similarly placed, helping them where she can, being helped by them wherever possible, and working with them – whatever the immediate effects on her own relations with the rich – to reduce the disparities between what are increasingly two worlds. To the extent that a weak state can have a dynamic foreign policy, this should be an integral part of it. It is certainly integral to non-alignment, as almost all the non-aligned have developed the principle, and to further such a form of non-alignment is patently India's duty both to herself and to others trying to escape from the captivity of want.

The non-aligned are not, of course, all coloured, and non-alignment is not solely a struggle to close the ever-widening gap between rich and poor; there are white states of varying wealth, like Yugoslavia and Sweden, which are understandably anxious to reduce the domination of world affairs by the great powers and strengthen instead the authority of the United Nations. Here India has already played a role, in lending troops for United Nations peace-keeping operations, but her general support has been uncreative and, over the Kashmir crisis, spasmodically reticent. She should go further and, in the company of other non-aligned states, offer to sacrifice a degree of sovereignty in a concerted effort to increase the power and prestige of organized international authority. She has little to lose and much to gain by the success of such an initiative, and her example may well stir not only the reluctant non-aligned but even some of the not altogether contented among the aligned themselves, like Poland and Canada.

All this, of course, depends upon her concentrating her energies and resources on an urgent settlement of her internal problems, on making India a society strong because it is just, because it is free from the violence of poverty and superstition no less than from the violence of despotism, because it enjoys the loyalty of all its citizens. At all costs, she must avoid embroilment in a frantic armament programme and wars of national prestige. In so far as she can achieve a reasonable settlement of her borders – perhaps by an exchange of territory, or a political adjustment that responds to the wishes of the inhabitants themselves – with China and Pakistan, she must exert herself as soon as possible to do so. If she cannot succeed, her most formidable defence will lie in the eager sacrifices she can command from her people and in the support she can extract from a thriving economy, not in military postures that cannot intimidate a determined antagonist and will only drain all capacity for progress. The hysterical terms in which many otherwise thinking Indians refer to their frontier disputes are dangerously unrelated to India's present situation.[1] The time

[1] Even the academic world is suffering from extravagant propaganda convulsions:

DELHI UNIVERSITY EXTENSION LECTURES.

Extension Lectures on: Chinese Aggression, Planned Economy,

is past, if it ever existed, when India could attempt to save the world by precept; she must now try and save herself by her own efforts. And the whole world cannot but be concerned in the endeavour. For the 450 millions of India are a large portion of humanity, and humanity itself cannot escape the consequences of their condition.

Indian History, Hindi Literature, English Literature, Child-development and Parent craft, Indian Music, Modern Indian Languages and science, starting from end of February 1963, will be held twice a week between 6–30 and 7–30 p.m. ...

Organising Secretary.

Advertisement in *The Statesman*, Calcutta, January 23rd, 1963.

CHAPTER SIX

CORRUPTION AND THE NEW RAJ

THEY were building blast shelters in New Delhi when I arrived at the end of November 1962 – brick walls at unpredictable intervals in front of shops and houses as a protection against Chinese air raids. Whether the walls would have served any purpose beyond the further darkening of doorways, however, happily did not have to be put to the test. For several of them almost immediately collapsed, under no apparent stress but the brush of passing pedestrians. An inquiry disclosed that the contractors had used an imprudent quantity of sand in adulterating the cement, and this particular experiment in civil defence was relegated to the files, with the contractors themselves officially black-listed.

Indians of widely different classes and occupations were impatient with my astonishment. Even in the mood of heady nationalism that followed the humiliations on the border, the general cynicism remained unmoved. Waiters and industrialists, academics and trade unionists spoke as though they would have been astonished themselves only if the cement in the blast shelters had *not* been adulterated, and the few who objected to my dismay did so not with denials of widespread corruption in India, but with claims that such corruption was no more widespread in India than in Italy or the United States. Hardly anyone felt it necessary to add that Italy and the United States were – in the chronic injustice of this world – rather more able to afford such corruption than India.

The flourishing black market in cement produced a stream of anecdotes at dinner parties and interviews, with those most passionate in their assaults on corruption casually admitting their own purchases of cement at 14 to 18 rupees a bag, or twice the official rate of 8 rupees. An orthopaedic surgeon, who owned a construction company with his brothers, guided me happily through the terrain of market manipulation. Cement factories admit less than their actual production and sell the surplus on the black market. Contractors engaged on public works adulterate their supplies of cement with sand and so accumulate stocks for profitable disposal. The shrewd and experienced save themselves labour and expense by obtaining legal cement at a bribe of one rupee a bag to the relevant official. 'Everyone does it,' the surgeon complained. 'So why shouldn't I?'

Bombay, January 10. The government of Maharashtra late last night sealed all cement godowns of the Bombay Municipal Corporation in a bid to check adulteration of cement, it was officially stated today. The government took the step following the recent report that adulterated cement was used in the construction of a municipal hospital at Borivli, a Bombay suburb. (*The Hindu*, January 11th, 1963.)

Madurai, January 12. One hundred and seventy-seven bags of cement suspected to have been adulterated were seized by the City Police ... last night from four different places in the city. They were found in the possession of persons who were stated not to have either permits or licence to deal in cement. Out of the 90 bags seized from a godown in Chitraikara Street, it is stated, 76 were found adulterated with white granite power (Kolapodi). The owner of the godown, it is stated, took to his heels and is now absconding.   (*The Hindu*, January 13th, 1963.)

If only half the scandal that the visitor hears is to be believed – and there is ample confirmation in the newspapers – the adulteration of scarce commodities is a national neurosis. Milk in India has a taste and colour nowhere else encountered, and the stranger is easily led into assuming an exotic variety of cow. In the weird world of professional saints and homespun politics, there is very little that would seem out of place. But the explanation is soon enough provided: the milk is anything up to three-quarters water. The Communist trade-union organizer who stirred the milk in angry witness at my Delhi hotel had served on the city council. 'We put up check-posts to examine the milk, but we found that the more check-posts we had, the more water entered the city. You see, the bribes had to be made up somehow.'

Roads rot because the wrong materials have been used. Huge dams crack and even collapse. A few years ago a sudden crack appeared in the Punjab's Bhakara Nangal dam, the highest in India, and the power station was submerged. There were many accusations of corruption, but no inquiry has yet been held. No one in authority has even bothered to explain why the recently completed Panchet earth dam gave way in 1961 under the monsoon rains. It is just safely assumed that corruption of one sort or another was responsible. One would not suppose that voters were a scarce commodity in India, but doubtless that depends on the objective of anyone in an appropriate position to adulterate them.

New Delhi, February 11. The Congress High Command proposes to take drastic action against the Bihar Pradesh (State) Congress which has two million bogus members on its rolls. These bogus members said to be larger in number than in any other State have been enrolled by interested persons to capture positions of authority in the organization.

(*Hindustan Times*, February 12th, 1963.)

Bribery – or what is delicately called 'grease money' – is ubiquitous, for important licences, building permission, civil service appointments, agricultural aid, liquor permits, for almost anything that requires administrative sanction – even for school examination results. In New Delhi I met an American academic, with several books on India to his credit, who was preparing a paper on the constructive character of corruption. Without bribery, he maintained, commerce and industry would be suffocated by controls, and production would be restricted to the infinite procreation of administrative files. He himself never entered a government office without flourishing a few rupee notes in his fingers.

Certainly, the practice is so general that officials require compensation not to speed an application, but merely to desist from unduly delaying its progress. It takes thirty days, gossip claims, for a file to travel from one table to another in Mysore, unless an acceptable bribe helps to propel it. The head of a large publishing and printing house in Bangalore brushed aside my scepticism. His firm had applied for a sales tax exemption on tickets to a charitable function and received verbal permission from the Commercial Tax Officer. But the official notification was unaccountably delayed, while the date of the charitable function drew remorselessly nearer. At last, with only a few days left, the firm dispatched a messenger with 'grease' for all the relevant clerks, and the official notification slipped into the post at once.

No one can accurately measure the extent of corruption in India, and certainly the assessments of rumour seem improbable. But whether or not corruption is as widespread as is commonly supposed matters relatively little. Of far more importance, everyone believes that it is widespread and claims that it is increasing. A political structure can support an almost limitless weight of corruption, as one state after another has displayed. What it cannot for long support is an equivalent or greater weight of cynicism, a common withdrawal of trust, especially when the structure advertises itself as democratic socialism. And in India poor and rich alike proclaim the dictatorship of money.

Travelling by car through Rajasthan, economically and politically perhaps the most depressed of the states in the Indian Union, we turned off the main road – my driving companion liked to experiment with maps – and stopped at a small scrubby village. As we sat drinking tea at the single shop, villagers gathered round to stare suspiciously, then question and at last ply us with answers. The local Bania was not popular. He lent money at an interest rate of one anna a month for every rupee, about 72 per cent a year. My shock must have been absurd, because there was an outburst of laughter along the benches and beyond, amongst the crowd in the road. I suggested that there were laws against such rates, and there was another outburst. The old villager sitting next to me puffed at his *bidi* and then smiled compassionately. 'Who is the government? The Bania pays at election time. And he charges interest on his money.' A clap of agreement from the crowd accompanied his shrug of helplessness.

Such comments, of course, are blunt. For the more intricate details one must go to the rich themselves. The editor of one of India's largest circulation newspapers, with a rigid right-wing line, was entertaining me to a lush lunch at a restaurant in Bombay. At tables around us sat gentlemen in Gandhi caps and *khadi*, the home-spun simplicity of resistance to the British raj, swilling down apple-juice – for Bombay is dry – and assaulting sole in cheese sauce. I heard all about one of India's foremost millionaire industrialists, who ran his cars, his houses, his entertainment, his travel, all on his various companies. 'Oh no, he pays no expenditure tax. He draws a personal salary of 5,000 rupees (about £385) a month.'

Tax evasion is so spectacular that Nicholas Kaldor, the British economist, who was invited by the Indian government to advise on the tax structure of the country, suggested that if taxes were reduced and just strictly collected the revenues would appreciably rise. Some 200 crores, or £150 million escape the government through tax evasion every year, and yet tax evasion remains an offence generally punishable by fines and not by imprisonment. Film stars notoriously pay tax on only 10 per cent of their incomes, receiving perhaps 50,000 rupees in salary and 450,000 in secret transaction. When S. A. Dange, Chairman of the Communist Party, told me that every self-respecting Indian merchant and industrialist keeps three account books – one for the government, one for the lawyer he trusts, and one for himself – I assumed a partisan exaggeration. Yet industrialists and merchants themselves subsequently paraded the story in interviews, with a kind of coy relish. The head of a large investment corporation in Bombay explained distastefully that India was facing a crisis of character, and then looked pleased. The abstraction clearly comforted him.

Sporadic scandals lift the lid from the very biggest of big business.

New Delhi, January 23. In a sensational inquiry report, presented to Parliament today, five of India's top industrialists, collectively known as the Dalmia–Jain group, have been held responsible for serious offences including fraud, manipulation of accounts, promoting personal gain at the expense of the investors as well as the Exchequer, and avoidance of taxes ... The commission [of inquiry] has described at length how its progress was impeded because of repeated petitions before the High Court and the Supreme Court, because of the refusal or failure of the people concerned to give evidence, and because of destruction of books and records... In considerable detail the commission has set out the numerous methods of the various Dalmia–Jain companies to avoid income tax liability. These include manipulation of accounts; extinguishing of reserves and accumulated profits before taking the companies into liquidation; introduction of secret profits under cover of share money by allotting shares to non-existing persons; and transfer of assets and liabilities to companies taken into liquidation. (*The Statesman*, January 24th, 1963.)

The special commission of inquiry under the chairmanship of Vivian Bose, a former Supreme Court judge, took more than six years to unravel the affairs of the Dalmia–Jain companies and issue its intricate 800-page report. By then Ram Krishna Dalmia, described by the commission as the 'master mind behind all the various malpractices', was already in jail serving sentences for other offences, and an undiscoverably huge amount of money had been lost by small investors all over the country. Labelled by the commission as a 'key man, second only to Dalmia', and held to have been 'actively associated' with at least four cases of fraud, was Shanti Prasad Jain, India's most powerful press millionaire, whose interests extend from jute, sugar, paper and cement to a chain of newspapers and magazines that include the *Times of India*, dailies in Hindi and Marathi, and Bombay's *Evening News* and *Economic Times*.

The Vivian Bose Report reveals a record of manipulation that must stagger lay belief. Funds of public concerns, banks and insurance companies were employed to seize control of companies with large accumulated resources, which were then 'squeezed dry', till 'the husks' could be 'discarded and destroyed'. Loans and advances, totalling many millions of pounds, were extracted without security and at a low rate of interest from public companies by the Dalmia–Jain group, and assets juggled between balance-sheets. Dividends were passed to depress the shares, and then suddenly declared, to nourish profitable speculation on the stock exchange. Managing agencies under the control of the group were given long-term contracts by public companies also under the control of the group and heavily compensated for the sudden termination of their contracts. One such agency had its twenty-year agreement terminated within sixteen days of appointment, and received more than 11,900,000 rupees, or over £900,000, in compensation. As a final recourse, when the funds of public companies had been exhausted, the companies themselves were placed under voluntary liquidation with co-operative officials and all books and records destroyed to remove the traces of fraud.

On this occasion, no important member of the government was apparently involved. In February 1958 a previous scandal had broken over the purchase by the government Life Insurance Corporation of stock to the value of £1 million from another Marwari millionaire, H. D. Mundhra, at an allegedly inflated price. The report by Mr Justice Chagla on the transaction had described Mundhra as 'a financial adventurer' and declared that the Minister of Finance, T. T. Krishnamachari, 'must fully and squarely accept responsibility' for the purchase. The Minister attempted to shift the blame on to his Permanent Secretary, and Nehru attempted to ride the sharp criticism in parliament. But at last he dismissed the Minister, to appoint him subsequently Minister without Portfolio, then Minister for Defence and Economic Co-ordination, and once more Minister of Finance in the Cabinet reshuffle of July 1963.

There might be some aesthetic – if there could be no other – excuse for the corruption of the Indian business community if riches occasionally resorted to the patronage of art. The Medici, after all, would not have welcomed a modern judicial inquiry into their business practices. But the Indian rich must be counted amongst the most culturally sterile in history. They employ no painters, sculptors, writers or architects who exhibit the slightest sign of original merit; they promote no publishing houses without a cast-iron promise of profit; they support neither theatre nor concert-hall; the only musicians they encourage are those required by tradition at weddings; with discreet exceptions, they do not even collect books or antiques. It is the government which temperately stimulates painting with purchases and exhibitions; literature, with prizes; architecture, with such initiatives as the city of Chandigarh in the Punjab. It is the economically depressed lower middle class which keeps the Bengali theatre so alive, and the peasantry in Kerala which allows a Malayalam theatre to exist at all. The rich collect cars and refrigerators and drawing-room decorations; build echoing ornate houses in a style that can best be described as viceregal baroque; hold lavish parties, especially to celebrate weddings; and, where prohibition operates, serve seemingly limitless quantities of foreign liquor. The small *avant-garde* visits night-clubs and costly restaurants; the traditional seem hardly to emerge from their homes at all, except to conduct business or enjoy for a while the shared security of relatives and friends.

Much of the consumption, however, is not conspicuous at all, but furtive: the accumulation of easily negotiable assets like foreign currency, precious stones, gold in jewellery and bullion. Perhaps India has endured too many invasions and conquests; perhaps Indian poverty is so stark and ubiquitous that it has sapped all sense of security in the rich; perhaps the custom that a woman's jewellery is safe even from the hands of her husband has become a national refuge. Certainly, whatever the reason, India seems to require a constant supply of portable reassurance. The appetite for gold, whether as an essential ingredient in dowries or a visible comfort in the safe, is insatiable. Only in the nineteen thirties, when the peasantry was hard hit by agricultural depression, did India export any gold, and then little more than £200 million worth. For the rest India has bought, feverishly, smuggling whenever the government intervened, pushing the internal price to twice the international market value. No one knows how much gold the country now has in private hands, but estimates by reputable economists place the sum at somewhere between 3,000 and 5,000 crores, or between £2,250 and £3,750 million. Even the lower figure – over twice the Sterling Area's total reserves – would provide sufficient capital, if gainfully employed, for a major industrial advance. But the gold is carefully concealed in safe deposit boxes and wardrobes, disclosed only to be swollen further.

At the height of the emergency, the government attempted to extract some of it by bribery. Much of the gold in the hands of the business community was solid evidence of tax evasion and profiteering. The then Minister of Finance, Morarji Desai, in his Gandhi homespun, offered a bargain. All gold surrendered to the government at the international price could purchase gold bonds, redeemable and carrying an annual interest of $6\frac{1}{2}$ per cent, with no questions asked. In fifteen years, black money could become white. The response was dismal. In the first hectic few weeks, with every newspaper pulsating patriotism, hardly £250,000 emerged. At last, in January 1963, the government decided to get tough and issued a decree that all future ornaments manufactured in India were not to exceed a gold purity of 14 carat. Since gold ornaments in India are traditionally 22 carat, some reaction might have been expected. But if Nehru had been right in assuming for India the spirit of Dunkirk, few would have predicted the scenes that followed. I was in Madras at the time, and every jeweller's shop was besieged by near-frantic families. Necklaces, ear-rings, bracelets, brooches were snatched, in seeming disregard of their appearance, with all the bustle of a bargain basement. Showcases were stripped clear in a flashing of hands. It was difficult to believe that the goods were not drastically reduced summer clothes but heavy gold ornaments at specially inflated prices. It was even more difficult to believe that India was at intermittent war with China – as the press and radio proclaimed – for its very survival. Before I left India at the end of February there was much talk of how the regulations on gold purity were to be evaded. All the suggestions I heard seemed ludicrously feasible.

It was in Madras that an industrialist proclaimed to me the predicament of the rich. He took me to his club, a shabby-genteel, hard-drinking, bridge-playing, crowded and yet somehow desolate souvenir of the British raj, and entertained me on his alcoholic's liquor permit. 'You see,' he said embroidering the air with his plump but delicate fingers, 'it's different in England. If you die, the government will look after your family. Your children will get free medicine and free schooling and they won't starve in the streets. You have been in India – how long? Two months? Six weeks?' I nodded my head, and he stared at me with his large liquid eyes. 'Still, it is enough. If I die here, what will happen to my children? They will sleep on the pavements, like they do in Calcutta and Bombay, unless I leave them a … a protection. I have two sons and three daughters. You must meet them before you go. Who will marry my daughters without dowries?' 'I thought there was a law about dowries,' I interrupted in embarrassment. 'A law, a law,' he scoffed, washing it away with a quick ripple of his fingers. 'Who pays any attention to the law! I must have a lakh of rupees – you know what a lakh is? One hundred thousand! – a lakh for each of my daughters, and a business worth several lakhs for my sons. They talk of an emergency now, suddenly, because of the Chinese. Isn't there always an emergency in India? What would you do if you were in my place?' The phrases leapt from my mouth, but he only smiled at me in a kind of supplication. 'Let the government show the social responsibility, let the government show me that it will look after my children, and I'll pay my taxes, I'll stop what you call this fiddling.' I didn't believe him, but all the same, I suppose he had a point.

The government's Planning Commission was reported late in January 1963 to have been busy investigating how long it would take, at current rates of economic growth and population increase, before every Indian had at least enough to eat. The Commission's examination revealed that the poorest 10 per cent of the country's 439 million people earned less than 2½ per cent of the national income and consumed less than 3 per cent of the goods available to the nation; in absolute terms they earned less than 7 rupees – or about 10s. 6d. – a head each month. The next 10 per cent earned less than 10 rupees a head each month, and the 10 per cent after that less than 12 rupees. Some 131,400,000 people, therefore, lived on less than £1 each a month. For a further 10 per cent of the population, the average monthly income was below 15 rupees; for the next 10 per cent below 18 rupees; and for the 10 per cent after that, below 22 rupees. In other words, some 262,800,000 people, or 60 per cent of the population, earned less than an average monthly income of £2 a head, and hardly two-thirds of the 35 rupees a month required to be spent on food alone, if – in the view of nutritional experts – minimum standards of health were to be attained.

The Planning Commission gloomily concluded that, at the present pace of progress, something like a third of the Indian people would be living below the bread-line by the year A.D. 2000. It seems a desperate enough prospect. But it is, in fact, wildly optimistic. For though the Commission did not contradict the view of nutritional experts on the necessary consumption of 35 rupees' worth of food, it assumed that anyone enjoying a monthly income of 25 rupees in the year A.D. 2000 would have enough to eat. It apparently ignored the possibility of fast-rising prices for food in the intervening years, and dismissed altogether the cost of clothing, fuel, the most primitive housing, furniture and travel. It is rather to be asked whether, at the present pace of progress, there will not be far more starvation in the year A.D. 2000 than there is already.

At the other end of the scale, the top 10 per cent of the population enjoys at present more than a third of the entire national income and accounts for a quarter of the country's aggregate consumption (*The Statesman*, January 29th, 1963). And there is sufficient evidence that the disparity between rich and poor has actually grown, not diminished, in the years of economic planning since independence for the government itself to have initiated a special inquiry. Indian independence, for so long the promise of the poor, has become instead the reward of the rich. Why should the rich themselves show any greater sense of responsibility than the government encourages them to have? If Congress rule denounces the pursuit of profit and in practice not merely permits but even promotes it, why should the business community display an isolated virtue?

Despite its commitment to socialism, the government has reserved but a small – and expensive – portion of the industrial sector for public ownership and control. It is precisely those fields which, in the special circumstances of India, require the most massive investment of capital and the longest wait for a return, which carry a risk as considerable as the need, that the government has claimed for its own. Transport and communications, new steel mills and old mines, constitute the backbone of the public sector, which in its turn supports the often flabby limbs of private industry. The successive five-year plans determine the objectives and priorities, and then set out to remove all impediments by providing private industry with the needed material and financial resources. The government shoulders the responsibility, and the private industrialist shoulders the profits. The licensing of industrial concerns limits the competition from within, while the control over foreign trade prevents competition from without. Import permits ensure an exclusive supply of capital goods to begin with, and then exclusive supplies of spare parts and raw materials. State institutions help with finance, and where necessary, the government itself stands guarantor, while collaboration with private industry abroad is assiduously encouraged. Where the government fixes prices, it does so after providing liberal margins of profit for the industrialist, and direct taxation – even when it is effectively collected – is kinder to the rich than in supposedly less socialist societies.

Under this protective regime, the major cost of which is carried by the consumer, the Indian capitalists have been enabled to parcel out the vast and fast-expanding terrain of private industry, acquiring individual control of scarce resources. The industrial empires of the Birla and Tata families, for instance, command between them the entire production of cars and trucks in the country. They do not even compete with each other, since the demand is consistently greater than the supply. The easy success of the private industrialist is a direct consequence of government policy and is maintained at public cost. Yet the government makes no attempt to acquire direct control over the most profitable portion of the private sector or even introduce a substantial element of public ownership. Instead, ever-increasing incentives are offered to private industry. Capitalists already nourished and sheltered by government action are encouraged to export by further opportunities of adding to the resources under their control. Moreover, since the government has ceaselessly proclaimed its reliance on savings in the private sector for industrial expansion, it inevitably adjusts prices and protection so as to provide industrialists with a substantial savings margin. It not only reduces competition and risk for the individual capitalist – it assures him a more than reasonable profit. Congress leaders may babble about socialism, but the government nourishes the profit of the Indian capitalist, with the rapidly increasing concentration of economic resources and power in his hands, as deliberate policy.

The usual excuse offered by government apologists is contained in the call, 'Production before Distribution'. Addressing the Convocation of Nagpur University on January 20th, 1962, Professor D. R. Gadgil, Director of the Gokhale Institute of Politics and Economics at Poona, examined the call.

That you can distribute only what you have produced is not truer than that the hen lays the egg. However, equally as the hen itself comes out of the egg, so production cannot be maintained or increased without adequate maintenance in health and well-being of human labour and of natural resources and capital equipment, which is the aim of a proper system of distribution. 'Production before Distribution' is, therefore, no more than a plausible cliché used as a cloak for a policy which its protagonists find it difficult to avow openly. What it conveys, in fact, is that immediate attention should be concentrated on policy which speeds up production, and all other objectives especially that of distributive justice shall be laid aside. To put it bluntly, it is a plea for allowing concentration of the ownership of means of production and turning a blind eye to the need for improvement of standards of living, with perhaps the added implication that such a policy will be transitional and can, in due time, be reversed.

Yet many new states have found it possible to pursue rapid industrialization without surrendering control over the means of production to a small group of ravenous and socially irresponsible private capitalists. Few states, however, which have allowed the concentration of economic power in the hands of a small group, have subsequently found it easy to take the power back and submit it to public control. One may wave the red flag or a copy of the *Wall Street Journal*, but to wave both together betrays a dangerous schizophrenia. If the Indian government is sincere in its protestations of socialism, then it must be seen to be arming those whom it proclaims to be its enemies and with whom it will sooner or later have to do battle. It hardly seems a reasonable policy to pursue.

Several of the more powerful merchants and industrialists are already dissatisfied with the degree of power they have achieved and are groping for more through the ballot box. Led, according to common gossip, by some of the administrators of the Tata empire, and allied with a few of the still-ambitious princely houses, like that of Jaipur, they formed the Swatantra Party as a right-wing, anti-socialist, pro-Western contender in the 1962 general election. Campaigning under the tattered genius of C. Rajagopalachari, the new group emerged from the polls with some 8,700,000 votes, or 6·8 per cent of the total cast for the Lok Sabha, and won sufficient State Assembly seats to

become the official opposition in Bihar, Gujarat, Rajasthan, and
– after its merger with the Ganatantra Parishad – Orissa. But
in five states it won no seats at all, and the overall dominance
of Congress – with some 51,500,000 votes and 353 seats out of
494 in the Lok Sabha – remained unshaken. Even worse, despite
the border conflict with China, the Communist Party won 29
seats in the Lok Sabha, to stay the largest opposition party, and
mustered 11,400,000 votes, or nearly 10 per cent of the total
cast.

The shrewder – and more grateful – merchants and industrialists prefer to exercise pressure through the press and in
parliament through Congress itself. Ceaselessly they bombard
the government with their propaganda, salvo after salvo of
plea and protest, moving it steadily rightwards. It was they
rather than the vociferous opposition in parliament who forced
the dismissal of Krishna Menon as Minister of Defence during
the emergency and engineered the resignation in June 1963
of K. D. Malaviya, Minister for Mines and Fuel, leaving Nehru
himself the sole committed socialist in office. And if some of the
less far-sighted had had their way, Nehru too would have gone
at the height of the emergency.

In New Delhi at the beginning of December 1962, when I
arrived in India, it was easy to believe that the whole country
was raging against 'inefficiency' and 'corruption' in the Ministry of Defence. Some old India hands in London had compla-
cently predicted the downfall not only of Krishna Menon,
whom they proclaimed with absurd earnestness to be a Kremlin
agent, but also his muddle-headed dupe, Nehru, as well, and
with them both the whole Congress policy of socialism and
international non-alignment. The army, I had been told,
would not stand for any further humiliations, and public
opinion was behind it. The middle class in New Delhi seemed
to seethe with confirmation of such gossip, and the views of
leading conspirators against Nehru's rule were endlessly
discussed. India's English-language newspapers – S. P. Jain's
Times of India, the Goenka family's *Indian Express*, and above
all the *Hindustan Times*, owned by the country's richest industrialist, G. D. Birla – were battering the administration.

Yet India, I was soon to discover, was not New Delhi, and
public opinion was not the English-language press. Less than

two days' driving away, on the barren road through Rajasthan, my companion – a young Punjabi just down from Oxford – and I stopped at a mica mine. One of the workers lounging in the road turned suddenly and fled, and only stopped and looked back at us, suspiciously, when Ashok shouted at him in Hindi, 'Why are you running away?' 'Who is that white man with you?' the worker called back. 'Has he come to find men for the war?' Ashok laughed, and the worker came a little closer. 'No, he writes books. And what do you think of the war?' The worker grunted in disgust. 'What war! To hell with the war! I've got a field to plough and a family to feed, and I'm going off to have something to eat.' And with that he bowed ironically in our direction and set off down the road. He, it seemed to me, with his shrug at the war as of no concern to him, was more typical of India's multitude than the shrill New Delhi press or the Bombay industrialists, who wanted the Indian army to liberate Tibet and march on Peking – with the help, of course, of American forces. For the worker at the mica mine, as for the many millions of Indians, India and its security would assume a meaning when India was seen to be doing something for them, and not merely for their rulers, when the preservation of the present became at last their self-interested concern.

There may be cities more disembodied than New Delhi in the world, but I have never visited any. To me it seemed ecto-plasmic, as though it were an effusion of some spiritual contact with the dead British raj. Its menacing ornate red administrative buildings, its long empty roads, its competitively splendid embassies, its houses and gardens and lawns, its vast Children's Playground in a corner of which small clusters of well-dressed children can sometimes be seen to play, its clean and regulated spaciousness, bear as much relation to the teeming squalor and poverty of the India all around as a Byzantine court would have done to the streets of Constantinople and the villages a thousand miles away. And, indeed, there is something Byzantine about New Delhi, a feverish obsession with form, with the intricacies of power, an atmosphere of conspiracy and intrigue, an absolute remoteness. A few miles away stretch the suffocating streets of Old Delhi, with their shrill cross-legged shopkeepers, their beggars and open drains, and the festering slums on their fringes. But from the windows of the air-conditioned govern-

ment offices and luxury hotels in New Delhi, they are scrupulously invisible. And New Delhi is mirrored in miniature in
most of the state capitals. The government occupies an island
of lawns and flower-beds and massive administrative monuments. Nor is it true – as is occasionally canvassed in excuse –
that the heirs of the British raj had no reasonable economic choice
but to utilize the facilities already there. The splendour has
been maintained with the structures, and where the structures
themselves did not exist, they have been imitatively built. The
new headquarters of the Mysore state government in Bangalore
is unreticently imperial. An enormous building of grey stone,
with costly doors of inlaid teak and insulating expanses of grass
and tarmac all around, it is rumoured to have squandered two
crores, about £1,500,000, before scandal called a halt. The
responsible Chief Minister resigned and is now a member of
the Lok Sabha.

The state governors perform in the main little more than a
decorative function, but the cost to the public purse of their up-
keep must be staggering. They command vast Raj Bhavans which
are run like luxury hotels and which all require armies of largely
ornamental servants. There is even in several states a second
residence for the summer, to which the governor and retinue
carefully withdraw from the heat. The whole institution of state
governorships may, after all, be useful. It provides a system of
political rewards and a method of promoting political embarrass-
ments from power to prestige. More constructively, perhaps, it
promotes some continuity of contact between central and state
governments, and the sporadic adjudication of expert advice.
But convenience must not be confused with ceremonial, and
anyone who has visited a few of the state Raj Bhavans will know
the extravagant difference. State governors could do their work
efficiently and doubtless with much greater public effect if they
concerned themselves less with polishing the silver of the raj.
The garden parties, the banquets, the display to cow the natives
and impress the visitor from abroad are as much an illustration
of India's court government as the whispering corridors of New
Delhi. All are part of the still living legacy of British rule.

A colonial government selects the site and style of its official
residences, promotes pomp and measures of security to maintain a sense of separateness – the distance between ruler and

ruled – and convey an intimidating impression of power. Separation, especially under a British regime, becomes inseparable from the retention of rule, and the alien governors hide their inescapable weaknesses in their own clubs, at their own dances and swimming-pools, in their own sealed residential suburbs. In British India, as in British Africa, social distance was a categorical imperative, the remoteness of command secured by a rejection of all but the most necessary contact. Officialdom held itself aloof, with the gradations of class and the rigidity of caste organization. The civil service, with a close recruitment pattern, monopolized all the higher posts, while other administrative personnel were firmly placed in an inferior position and excluded from taking any part in the determination of policy. Within the civil service itself, the topmost rungs were scrupulously reserved for the British, and such Indians as were permitted to occupy the lower ones were expected to – and generally did – wear the same uniform, if a shabbier version, of distant authority as their superiors. The comfort and interests of the civil servants were pursued to the neglect of the general welfare, and the provision of public amenities pivoted round administrative convenience. Simla and the other hill stations, the seasonal retreat from the sun, picturesquely flouted the condition of the governed. An aristocracy, almost entirely British but with a few Indian imports on the lower levels, maintained its distance at considerable expense and some little exercise of imagination.

It is this distance which has survived the change of governors, to substitute for the old raj merely a new one. The withdrawal of the British was not accompanied by any substantial alteration in the appearance of power. The new raj may have discarded the dress of the old, but it has remained as remote in homespun as its predecessor was in braid and feathers. The pomp, the trappings of exclusion persist in ceremony and setting – in the commanding architecture of the numerous New Delhis, the appointments of security, the retinue of 'peons' in constant attendance on officials, the whole display and arrogance of authority. Administrative convenience still determines much of public policy, and the government does more to maintain the prestige of high officials than to encourage a mutual confidence and common agreement on objectives between ruler and ruled.

Endless complaints suggest to the observer that the difficulties experienced by the poor and uninfluential in approaching and receiving attention from officialdom are no less formidable under the new raj than they were under the old. In the very projects of change themselves, the programmes of welfare and reform, the administering personnel reflect the same attitudes of bestowal and employ the same dignified pace as their British predecessors did. There is little effort at stimulating popular enthusiasm by a joint emotional investment of guided and guides. The mood is one of directive. And the directive more often than not lacks the virtue of example. Ministers are permitted to live in glaring extravagance while they make impassioned appeals for popular sacrifice. Socialism in a Mercedes Benz may be eloquent, but it seldom conveys an impression of sincerity.

The political acrobatics of Jayaprakash Narayan, one of the more self-troubled heirs of Gandhi, may be dizzying. But many of his assaults on the new raj are well-mounted. Addressing a public meeting at New Delhi in December 1963, he questioned the slogans of the war for national survival. What, he asked, did the struggle against the Chinese set out to preserve? The profits of the great industrialists? The scramble for power, and the manipulations of patronage within the governing party? One need only note, he declared, the differences in the way the Chinese and the Indian leaders lived. The Congress government called for national sacrifice, but where was the example that it should give?

Professor Gadgil, in his Convocation Address to Nagpur University of January 1962, had struck the same strings: '... Among the special features noted about Communist China by most observers are the plain living of its leaders, the absence of wasteful consumption, the focus of administrative arrangements on helping the poor and the backward, the emphasis on utilizing idle manpower and on the dispersal of industry. I attach importance to all these. It is true that little effective attention is paid to any of them in the Indian Plan.'

Jayaprakash Narayan and Professor Gadgil – neither of whom can reasonably be discounted as an undercover Communist – are not alone in using China as the main measure of comparison with India. Less knowledgeably and articulately, but none the less vigorously, peasants and industrial workers will increasingly make the comparison themselves and draw their own conclusions. It is, of course, undeniable that the corruption and the remoteness of the new Indian raj dwindle when contrasted with some regimes in Latin America or, much closer, in Asia itself. But it is not with such regimes that most Indians will want, after all, to compare their own government. By size, significance, proximity and conflict, it is China that will provide the standard for approval or censure.

Corruption in India has an ancient lineage; it is sanctified by tradition. The author of the *Arthaśāstra* – a Mauryan manual of government, rather like Machiavelli's *The Prince* in its untroubled cynicism – might have been writing for the merchants and industrialists of modern Bombay. 'There are about forty ways of embezzlement: what is realized earlier is entered later on; what is realized later is entered earlier; what ought to be realized is not realized...' Certainly his remarks on Mauryan officials can properly be applied to many servants of the Indian Republic.

> Just as it is impossible not to taste the honey or the poison that finds itself at the tip of the tongue, so it is impossible for a government servant not to eat up, at least, a bit of the King's revenue. Just as with fish moving under water it cannot possibly be discerned whether they are drinking water or not, so it is impossible to detect government servants employed on official duties when helping themselves to money. It is possible to mark the movements of birds flying high up in the sky; but it is not possible to ascertain the secret movements of government servants.[1]

Two thousand years later, with the advent of the British, another empire brought stability to a distracted India. Disraeli's *Sybil*, published in 1845, carried a portrait of the 'Nabob'.

> One of the most fortunate of this class of obscure adventurers was a certain John Warren. A few years before the breaking out of the American war, he was a waiter at a celebrated club in St. James' Street; a quick, yet steady young fellow; assiduous, discreet, and very civil. In this

[1] *Oxford History of India*, 3rd ed., pp. 111–12.

capacity, he pleased a gentleman who was just appointed
to the government of Madras, and who wanted a valet.
Warren, though prudent, was adventurous; and accepted
the opening which he believed fortune offered him. He
was prescient. The voyage in those days was an affair of six
months. During this period, Warren still more ingratiated
himself with his master. He wrote a good hand, and his
master a very bad one. He had a natural talent for accounts;
a kind of information which was useful to his employer. He
arrived at Madras, no longer a valet, but a private secretary.

His master went out to make a fortune; but he was in-
dolent, and had indeed none of the qualities for success,
except his great position. Warren had every quality but that.
The basis of the confederacy therefore was intelligible; it
was founded on mutual interests and cemented by reci-
procal assistance. The governor granted monopolies to the
secretary, who apportioned a due share to his sleeping
partner. There appeared one of those dearths not unusual
in Hindostan; the population of the famished province
cried out for rice; the stores of which, diminished by nature,
had for months mysteriously disappeared. A provident
administration it seems had invested the public revenue
in its benevolent purchase; the misery was so excessive that
even pestilence was anticipated, when the great forestallers
came to the rescue of the people over whose destinies they
presided; and at the same time fed, and pocketed, millions.

This was the great stroke of the financial genius of
Warren. He was satisfied. He longed once more to see St
James' Street, and to become a member of the club where
he had once been a waiter. But he was the spoiled child of
fortune, who would not so easily spare him. The governor
died, and had appointed his secretary his sole executor. Not
that his Excellency particularly trusted his agent, but he
dared not confide the knowledge of his affairs to any other
individual. The estate was so complicated, that Warren
offered the heirs a good round sum for their quittance, and
to take the settlement upon himself. India so distant, and
Chancery so near, the heirs accepted the proposition. Wind-
ing up this estate, Warren avenged the cause of plundered
provinces; and the House of Commons itself, with Burke

and Francis at its head, could scarcely have mulcted the
late governor more severely.

Disraeli does not leave his Nabob rich but unrespectable.
Warren buys a large estate in the north of England, and with it,
a rotten borough, becomes a member of the House of Commons,
is made a baronet and then an Irish baron, and dies as Lord
Fitz-Warene, an English peer of Norman origin. Disraeli, of
course, was writing fiction, but his corrupt official, the ennobled
Nabob, had countless precedents among the shapers of the
empire. India's initial encounter with British rule was not an
edifying one.

Later officers of the raj, fired by a belief in the rectitude of
British rule, attempted to stamp out corruption, but never
altogether succeeded. The Revenue Department, which enjoyed
discretionary powers, was widely considered amenable to
presents – *nagranas* – as were the police and excise officials.
In the main, the top civil servants were not corrupt, and it was
they who gave the raj such reputation as it had for disinterested
authority. Partly this resulted from the studied remoteness of
the raj. Senior British officials kept their distance from the whole
business community and in particular from the Indian one.
Even in the cities the relations between administrator and
merchant or industrialist were seldom close. And partly this was
a consequence of the high incomes which the officials received.
Members of the civil service were amongst the best-paid men
in India, and although there were already a few Indian businessmen of considerable wealth, they constituted no more than a
minute proportion of their community. Senior officials had
neither the need nor the proper opportunity – even if they had
the taste – for wide-scale corruption.

A change in the relationship between business and government was, however, in the making, even in the very struggle
against British rule. From its earliest days, the Indian Congress
was led by men from the professional and commercial classes,
and though protest and petition gave way, under Gandhi's
leadership from 1919 onwards, to more militant forms of
opposition – *hartals* and *satyagraha*, strikes and civil disobedience
– the participation of businessmen in Congress increased rather
than diminished. Nationalism, of course, was the most powerful

force in forging the strange alliance between industrialist and peasant, but it was not the only one. The general desire of all Indians to be free was accompanied by the particular desire of some to enrich themselves in the process. There were many merchants and manufacturers who saw *swaraj*, self-government, as an opportunity for profitable employment as well as the restoration of national dignity.

Session after session of Congress passed, in addition to protests against political repression, demands for the promotion of industrial development, with – to quote the resolution of the 33rd session, held at Delhi on December 26th, 1918 – encouragement given to Indian capital and enterprise, and protection against foreign exploitation. The British government was understandably determined to sell, through the manipulation of tariffs, as much as possible of its industrial output to India, and the Indian industrialists were no less understandably determined to secure the sale and export of their own products. The struggle was a national one, for the development of Indian manufacture and trade would enrich India as a whole, but such development was none the less an especially dear objective of the industrialists themselves, who stood to gain rather more than anyone else. In the early years of the century, the *swadeshi* movement, with its mammoth demonstrations and burning of foreign cloth in Bengal, must have warmed the heart of every aspiring textile manufacturer in the country. And the progress of Congress policy provided constant encouragement. The special Calcutta session of the Congress, held from September 4th to 9th, 1920, adopted the programme of non-cooperation for which Gandhi had fought, and as part of that programme called for a boycott of foreign goods.

And inasmuch as Non-co-operation has been conceived as a measure of discipline and self-sacrifice without which no nation can make real progress, and inasmuch as an opportunity should be given in the very first stage of Non-co-operation to every man, woman and child for such discipline and self-sacrifice, this Congress advises adoption of Swadeshi in piece-goods on a vast scale, and inasmuch as the existing mills of India with indigenous capital and control do not manufacture sufficient yarn and sufficient cloth for the requirements of the Nation, and are not likely to do so for a long time to come, this Congress advises immediate stimulation of further manufacture on a large scale by means of reviving hand-spinning in every house and hand-weaving on the part of the millions of weavers who have abandoned their ancient and honourable calling for want of encouragement.[1]

Significantly, the resolution posed hand-spinning and weaving as an alternative to foreign manufactured textiles but not to domestic ones. When there were sufficient mills of indigenous capital and control, the whole cult of *khadi* would, it seemed, no longer be needful. The mill-owners, of course, never thought of *khadi* as even a potentially serious rival. It would be an ally in disposing of the real competition – British textiles – and could then be relegated to the museums or the wardrobes of cranks. In the event, *khadi* became the Gandhian uniform, and most self-respecting Congress political bosses, whatever their textile interests and financial character, wear it in public as a kind of chastity belt. Today the richer streets of Ahmedabad, the textile capital of India, are white with homespun. But happily for the mill-owners, there are not many Congress political bosses, relatively, and hardly more manufacturers and merchants who feel the need for a disguise, while the true Gandhians would not keep a small-sized factory of home-spinners occupied with supplying their requirements. The flag of the Indian Republic has a spinning-wheel in the centre. A textile mill would be rather more in place.

It is no libel on the independence struggle itself to declare that the motives of some participants were mixed. Certainly, the stories of the merchant-industrialist who took advantage of the *swadeshi* movement to sell his huge stocks of Japanese textiles by stamping them – with the knowledge of several top Congress leaders – 'Made in India', are too often encountered to be casually dismissed. The connection between the Congress leadership and the business community was far too close not to provide opportunities of profit to the corrupt, and the association of Gandhi himself with G. D. Birla, India's foremost

[1] B. Pattabhi Sitaramayya, *The History of the Indian National Congress*, 1935, p. 342.

capitalist, made the connection generally acceptable. There were, of course, criticisms, but Gandhi, whatever his private thoughts may have been, proclaimed them unwarranted. His statement that the rich were 'trustees', holding their possessions 'in trust' for the poor, almost sanctified the connection.

Perhaps, despite his proved political acumen, Gandhi was innocent. So, at least, one political figure who was of some significance in the struggle against British rule and now holds an important post in the government of the Republic described him. The Congress leaders used to meet sometimes at the home of a prominent industrialist, and the stock exchange would echo their secret decisions on the following day. 'Jawaharlal and others went to see Gandhiji and complained. But Gandhiji just stared at them and said that they must be mistaken. Their host would never be a party to such manoeuvres. It was mere co-incidence. And I'm sure,' my informant added, 'that he thought it was.'

Time and again, after the departure of the British, the Congress leadership, at last in power, bribed the business community into allegiance or simply succumbed to its pressures. During the war the Ahmedabad mill-owners, many of whom had organized secret shifts, had amassed vast undeclared profits, and they displayed a natural anxiety that their affairs should not be subjected to close examination by the new government. They need not have agitated themselves. At a conference in Mussoorie soon after the assassination of Gandhi, Sardar Vallabhbhai Patel, Home Minister and disciple of Gandhi, the first and greatest of the Congress party bosses, promised that substantial contributors to the Gandhi Memorial Fund would escape too zealous a scrutiny by the income tax inspectors. It was a not unfitting comment on the equivocal role of the Gandhian in modern India. Because of business opposition, the Congress government avoided – and still avoids today – taking any effective steps to combat inflation and artificial shortages by freezing prices and rationing scarce consumer commodities. Even during the emergency, with India fighting by official account for its very life, the government introduced no price controls, but contented itself with asking the country's one million merchants voluntarily to keep prices from rising. Britain under a Conservative-dominated administration during the Second World War placed rather less trust in the patriotism and capacity for self-denial of its business community.

It is this close association of government and business in India that is more than any other factor responsible for the corruption of the new raj. The rulers remain remote from the ruled, but the rulers are now merchants and manufacturers as well as administrators. Together they constitute a new kind of caste, the members of which visit, marry and assist each other while shunning intimate contact with those of different castes. The relationship of official and businessman has radically changed since the days of British rule. The salaries paid to officials are much the same, but inflation has constantly eroded their real value; the rupee today buys only a fifth of what it did before the outbreak of the Second World War. Businessmen, on the other hand, have acquired considerable economic power, with the range of their activities so expanded that they now comprise by far the most important group of employers offering high salaries. In consequence, of course, those who wish to earn high salaries – and India's acute endemic poverty places a special premium on wealth – no longer aspire to the senior ranks of government service, but struggle towards the upper reaches of the technician and managerial class in private business. A senior employee of a foreign-owned company like Burmah Oil or an indigenous concern like Tata Industries earns far more than a senior civil servant. Inevitably the relatives of administrators and prominent politicians are just as vulnerable to the greater economic inducements of industry and commerce as anyone else, and their possible employment must influence the conduct of their fathers and uncles, brothers and cousins in positions of authority. Moreover, the fathers and uncles, brothers and cousins are themselves aware of the problems posed by eventual retirement. Under the old raj, officials retired on relatively comfortable pensions; they did not generally seek further employment, and if they did, they almost invariably avoided employment with Indian business. Under the new one, however, senior administrators find after their retirement profitable positions in commerce and industry, and the consideration with which they are then treated by the government bestows official sanction on the process. The same civil servants, therefore, who enjoy wide powers of discretion in regulating

business activity, look upon businessmen as potential employers
of themselves or their relatives. The opportunities for favours
and consequent rewards are countless and manifest. Even
where administrators and politicians – Cabinet Ministers
amongst them – lead lives of irreproachable simplicity, their
sons and nephews have often achieved far more success in
business far more rapidly than any reasonable assessment of
their talents would warrant.

The very increase in the economic terrain over which the
government exercises authority has led to an increase in the
opportunities for corruption. The more that imports are restricted by permits in order to preserve foreign exchange, the
more bribes are offered to the responsible officials. The more
that the number of those engaged in any one field of industrial
activity is limited by licences in order to prevent costly competition, the more considerable are the rewards of obtaining such
licences and the greater are the inducements dangled by businessmen before those who issue them. At this level of official decision
Professor Gadgil declared in an interview, 'corruption is
terrifying'. And all the economists I met in India confirmed his
description. Controls are not corrupting in themselves. A
properly planned economy cannot exist without them. But
when they are allied to a pampered and protected free enterprise, when they are employed to nourish and not sap the power
of the private sector, they further rather than reduce economic
injustice. The muddle of socialism and capitalism that is modern
India is less the best of both worlds than the worst.

The bribing of officials, with money or offers of employment,
does not exhaust the resources of the business community.
For in addition to the pressure of the newspapers that they own,
the merchants and industrialists exercise a powerful influence
on politics through their contributions to party funds. In a
democracy where voters are counted in their tens of millions,
political campaigning is a very expensive process, and no party
without funds to spend on advertising, on posters and pamphlets,
the hiring of halls and transmission facilities, the dispatch of
speakers over vast distances and the employment of professional
organizers, can hope to reach a meaningful proportion of the
electorate with a statement of its policies. Congress, as the main
movement in the struggle against British rule and the achieve-

ment of independence, above all as the party still linked in the public mind with the Mahatma, might reasonably expect to win elections on the mere memory of the past if all its opponents were naked of resources for hostile propaganda. But the principal opposition parties have in varying degrees acquired the means with which to communicate their programmes, and a competition for the resources of propaganda has inevitably ensued. Moreover, elections are not won or lost by policies and propaganda alone. There must be few democracies in the world from which the bribing of voters at election time is altogether absent, and India, by common account, is not amongst them. Though gossip undoubtedly exaggerates the extent of the practice, votes are certainly bought with liquor and money, especially in the urban constituencies. The corruption in government office and company board-room extends to the polling booth as well.

Congress has only itself to blame for the consequences of its economic policy. The Congress government has given the business community the means by which to hold the Congress party to ransom. The richer and more powerful the business community becomes, the richer and more powerful it demands to be, and the greater are the resources with which it is able to pursue its demands. Inevitably, the very nature of Congress has changed in the process. The determination of policy has fallen further and further into the hands of the party bosses, the political entrepreneurs who collect the contributions of the business community, transmitting its desires along with its gifts, and then organize the constituencies for battle. It is they who man the political machine of Congress, and it is the political machine which manufactures electoral victory. Sardar Patel, the first of the party bosses, was a great administrator as well, who used his power to promote business interests, but, when he felt it necessary for the kind of India he wanted to build, showed himself prepared to ignore and even flout them. His successors, however, are in the main little men, who pursue power and not policy, and who have made their party, together with themselves, the client of wealth.

More and more it is the businessmen who deserve to be called the ultimate rulers of India today. It is on their patronage that the professional class – the doctors, the lawyers, the engineers, those who exercised so considerable an influence in the struggle for independence – now depends. They are the heirs to the priests, the princes and the landlords who traditionally stood at the apex of Indian society and have lost so much of their power and prestige. And these rulers of the new raj, the men behind the men in authority, are not for the most part pioneers, ready to risk their resources in exploration, determined to develop, in however ruthless a way, the economic strength of their country. There are, of course, a few who have displayed imgination and courage. The Tatas, on the whole, have cultivated as they fed, and India is the richer – as perhaps disproportionately are they – for their activities. But in general the businessman is more a speculator than a builder, a pirate rather than a pioneer. His base is not in industry, though he will exploit industry to his profit, but in commerce and finance. He has none of that sense of national responsibility which characterized the Japanese businessman in the first flush of his country's economic expansion. Still less has he the moral disposition of the Quaker industrialist. For him the production and sale of goods – within the law if possible, and outside whenever profit demands – is an opportunity to advance himself, his family and his caste in an accumulation of alliances and wealth. He is an empire-builder with the vision of a chartered accountant, and a chartered accountant skilled at cooking his books. The greater his power, the smaller are the uses to which he puts it. And it is he who governs the mood of the new raj.

Corruption, like sacrifice, starts at the top and, percolating down, colours the whole society. The clerk who knows that his superior has taken a bribe for propelling an import permit in the right direction, demands his own repayment for failing to lose a file. The clerk is at least able to offer the excuse that he cannot support his family on what he legally earns. A small contractor, reading in the press about industrialists whose frauds run into many crores of rupees, feels entitled to engage in a little profitable fraud himself by adulterating his cement supplies and selling a few bags on the black market. The secondary school teacher earning 120 rupees – or just over £9 – a month considers himself more justified in taking a bribe to adjust the examination results of a pupil than a civil servant who earns more than ten times as much and connives at the false tax returns of an industrialist in return for an appropriate reward.

Were corruption widespread only in the towns and cities, it would be critical enough, but not calamitous. For India is a country of villages, and over 80 per cent of the Indian people live in them. It is by the integrity of the officials with whom the ordinary villager comes into contact that India as a whole must judge its government and the political system behind. In the nineteen fifties, research workers from Lucknow University, with financial help from the Ford Foundation, undertook a detailed study of life in Mohana, a medium-sized village in Uttar Pradesh. From their findings it appears that corruption is as commonplace in Mohana as in Calcutta and Bombay.

> Bribery is on the increase not only in cities but in villages also ... For instance, anyone wanting any information regarding his lands can get it from the *Lekhpal* (village accountant) who goes to the village once a week or so. The *Lekhpal* demands three to four rupees to show the land records. The villagers realise that it is wrong to give any gratification to the *Lekhpal*, for they know that he is paid by the Government for this work, but then, if they do not give the *Lekhpal* a bribe, he will not show them the records, and they will have to go to the Tehsil (district) headquarters to see the records for themselves, and to go there they will have to spend more than four rupees. Most of the villagers are poor. So they would rather pay four rupees to the *Lekhpal*. Many are the officials besides the *Lekhpal* who take bribes from the villagers. There is the *Pradhan* (head) of the Gram Sabha (village council) with whom is left the Register of Agricultural Taxes. The tax-collector himself exploits the ignorant villagers and if, desiring to know the implications of the tax or the rate of tax levied on them, they approach the *Pradhan*, he charges them another rupee or two. The *Pradhan* himself confesses that he takes bribes, but adds that the money he gets thus is just sufficient for him to buy betel and cigarettes, but others opine that he makes good money by this means.
>
> Police constables, whose duty it is to prevent corruption of any sort, show no hesitation in accepting bribes. Many

cases are hushed up because the criminal presses a few rupees into the palms of a police constable. When the villagers take their melons to Lucknow in carts, they usually go at night, and often they fail to have lights on their carts. This is against traffic rules, but the police let them pass after taking a few melons from each cart.[1]

Poor as they are, the villagers are required to pay taxes of three different kinds, into the collection of which corruption inevitably enters. The agricultural tax varies from two to ten rupees a *bigha* – a rural land-measure that varies from state to state but is equivalent in Uttar Pradesh to some two-thirds of an acre – according to the fertility of the land. If the tax-collector fails to deposit the calculated total at the relevant office on the due date, his pay is withheld, and so he resorts to various expedients – including the confiscation of property for auction – in order to realize the tax. But he is not without resources, and for an appropriate bribe will usually find some loop-hole in the law to provide a defaulter with temporary escape. The irrigation tax – varying from four and a half to nine rupees a *bigha* – is collected by the *Patraul* or canal-guard.

The villagers can escape paying the canal tax, or at least a part of it, if they are willing to bribe the *Patraul*. In May, 1954, it was alleged that the *Patraul* went to the village and took a bribe of Rs. 2 to Rs. 5 from every farmer, assuring them that they will not have to pay a mite as Irrigation Tax for the melon crop, and that he would make some concession in the same tax for the other crops also. Such an attractive proposal could not be turned down by the villagers who are eager to save money. In this way the *Patraul* earned about a thousand rupees. Besides receiving the bribe he was entertained to a good feast by the prominent villagers. But in September, at the time when irrigation taxes are collected, the villagers realised the big blunder they had committed, for the *Patraul* whom they bribed was no longer in the Canal Department, and a new man had taken his place. The villagers could not escape paying the tax.[2]

[1] Dr D. N. Majumdar, *Caste and Communication in an Indian Village* (Asia Publishing House, 1962), pp. 146–7.
[2] Ibid., pp. 177–8.

A third tax of 9·37 rupees is levied on every bicycle and bullock cart, though payment can be postponed and mistakes rectified by bribing the relevant officials. The villagers complain bitterly, but 'have to pay all the taxes imposed by the Government in addition to gratifying the officials concerned now and then.'[1]

'He was not a great tyrant,' Edgar Snow has written of Chiang Kai-shek, 'only a petty one; he failed not because he was Caesar or killed too many people but because he killed too few of the right people; he never understood that his worst enemies were inside his own camp. Chiang was not resolute, only obstinate; not wise, only obsolete; not disciplined, only repressed; not original, only a scavenger among the relics of the past; and not ruthless, merely vain – as none knew better than the greedy parasites who surrounded and finally consumed him.'[2]

As a comment on the late Jawaharlal Nehru – humanist and humane, cultured and complex and profound, for some seventeen years the leader of a free and secular India in its struggle against poverty and violence and superstition and greed – this would be absurd.

Superficially there can be little resemblance between the generalissimo who achieved power through the army and had undisguised contempt for democratic forms, and the prime minister who reached rule after years of imprisonment, through his association with a saint and his leadership of a passive resistance movement, who believed with passion in democracy and socialism. Chiang Kai-shek was not concerned with change; he wanted solely to preserve. Nehru was obsessed with change, with prising India free from the squalor and resignation of its past. Yet the comparison, in its very antagonisms, betrays a resemblance. Chiang Kai-shek never possessed the imagination to lead his impoverished people out of their despair; hostile to the alternative of Communism, he none the less offered no escape himself. Nehru possessed too much imagination rather than too little, and his capacity to act was constantly paralysed by his vision of alternatives. Hamlet never ascended the throne. If he had, he would probably have made a less effective ruler than his uncle.

---

[1] *Caste and Communication in an Indian Village*, p. 179.
[2] *Journey to the Beginning* (Victor Gollancz Ltd, London, 1960), p. 137.

Nehru never wished to be a tyrant, but he became one – not a great one but a petty one, and not through will but through vacillation. He reigned but did not rule, he commanded but did not conduct, he arbitrated where he should have resolved. His Cabinet consisted in the main of courtiers, chosen for their personal loyalty or influence or political past, for everything but their policies. And because, inevitably, they did not promote his own ideas, he governed by intervention, not control. His was the tyranny of confusion and caprice. He failed, not because he antagonized too much, but because he was afraid to antagonize enough. He never realized that his worst enemies were in his own party, undermining his policies, debasing the coinage of his thought. He was not resolute, only obstinate. He retained Ministers whom he should have dismissed for corruption or incompetence or flagrant disloyalty, because he regarded criticism of them as a reflection on himself, and he dismissed Ministers whom he should have retained for their allegiance to his own beliefs, because his support of them did not in itself still the carefully mounted campaigns of criticism. He said and did more than any Indian in modern history to secularize his people, yet he allowed his spokesmen to inflame religious feelings by threatening calamitous consequences for the Muslim minority if Kashmir were surrendered to Pakistan. He fought the power of caste, yet permitted his party to deploy it in electoral tactics. He reverenced the rule of law, yet detained political opponents without trial. He despised corruption and recognized its dangers, but he sat by, silent, while political colleagues, and even relatives, openly engaged in it. He was brilliant, but he was not wise, for the wise have the ability not just to perceive, but also to adopt and pursue the best means for accomplishing an end. He was embarrassed by a richness of ends and a poverty of means. He was not disciplined, he was a romantic repressed. He was impatient with detail – he pursued policy in swoops – and the intricacies of administration merely irritated him. He was lustrously original, but originality must be based in the present if it is to achieve any change. Nehru was wrapped in visions of the future so tightly that he lost sight of the disorder and dismay everywhere around him. Above all, he was not ruthless and he was vain – as none knew better than the parasites who surrounded and threatened to consume him.

With the death in 1950 of Sardar Patel, his one-time rival for leadership, Nehru enjoyed an absolute ascendancy over Congress. His rule within the party was unquestioned; he was opposed from without by mediocrities; he could have moulded Congress, and much of India, into any shape that he sufficiently willed. But he allowed dedication to decay into lassitude, enthusiasm into despair. One political economist complained to me with bitterness: 'A ruler must rule! The British did!' In countless interviews with journalists and academics, trade unionists and artists, I heard the lament: 'There is no ruthlessness at the top. The government is weak.' From almost all of them the cry arose, different in language, in meaning the same – 'If only Nehru would act, rid Congress of the party bosses and throw corrupt officials and businessmen in jail. If only he showed that he could be ruthless, if only he would rule, if he would make a start somewhere, the enthusiasm would come again and the trust, and for fear or shame or pride Indians would begin to dig India out of the centuries.' For the want of a nail...

Now Nehru is dead, and his legacy is the lost and distracted Congress that does not so much govern India as preside over its survival. His successor, Lal Bahadur Shastri, is a man of the centre, dedicated to keeping Congress from fragmentation, the executor of Nehru's estate. Will the possession of power at last produce in him the determination to use it? Will India have an Indian government ruthless enough to rule in the interests of the still silent masses? And if it will not, how much longer will the masses stay silent?

To what end, to what vision of the future, the Kuomintang progressed, no one really knew. Not many of its members cared. The short-term prospect, the rewards and spoils of office, the ambition of high command, all these things were eagerly sought and fiercely contested, but when it was asked where all was tending... all was uncertain ... The intellectuals withdrew from politics; the careerists controlled the party and strove to secure the favour of the Generalissimo, upon whom all depended... Chiang Kai-shek never really controlled China; he could not prevent Japanese infiltration, he could not crush the Communists ... he juggled with the factions of the Kuomintang, but only ruled by playing off one against the other. A military ruler to command respect must be successful in war; a civilian autocrat must, like Stalin, construct an instrument of government both efficient and loyal. Chiang was an unsuccessful general; his party was neither loyal nor efficient.[1]

The disease from which the Kuomintang collapsed has already infected Congress. It is a far cry from the one-time chaos of Nanking to the present-day splendours of New Delhi. But the alarm has begun to sound.

[1] C. P. Fitzgerald, *Revolution in China* (Cresset Press, 1953), pp. 71–2.

BIBLIOGRAPHY

THIS selection of books on India for further reading is necessarily limited by my own small acquaintance with the vast literature that exists, and has been further limited by the omission of all those, however useful on particular points I have found them to be, which are of specialist rather than general service. Those books which have been of especial value to me in writing my own study of India – books from which I have freely borrowed in formulating my own ideas and from which I have taken crucial quotations – are marked with an asterisk.

The seven divisions of the list that follows are not sharp. There are books in one of them that might reasonably have been placed in another. I have merely provided a guide for readers interested in studying a particular aspect of an enormous – indeed overwhelming – subject.

POLITICS

*Jawaharlal Nehru: An Autobiography. The Bodley Head, London, and the John Day Company Inc., New York, 1958

*The Discovery of India by Jawaharlal Nehru. Meridian Books Ltd, London, 1960

*An Autobiography by M. K. Gandhi. Navajivan Publishing House, Ahmedabad, India, 1959

*India – The Most Dangerous Decades by Selig S. Harrison, Princeton University Press and Oxford University Press, 1960

*The Constitution of India by G. N. Joshi. Macmillan & Co. Ltd, London, 1961

*The Politics of Scarcity by Myron Weiner. Asia Publishing House, Bombay, 1963

India's Foreign Policy, Selected Speeches by Jawaharlal Nehru. Government of India, Delhi, 1961

Communism in India by Gene D. Overstreet and Marshall Windmiller. The Perennial Press, Bombay, 1960

India and Pakistan by Hugh Tinker. Pall Mall Press, London, 1962

Party Politics in India by Myron Weiner. Princeton University Press, 1957

Village Government in India by Ralph H. Retzlaff. Asia Publishing House, Bombay, 1962

ECONOMICS

*_Indian Economy – Its Nature and Problems_ by Alak Ghosh. The
World Press, Calcutta, 1962

*_Indian Economy Since Independence_ by H. Venkatasubbiah. Asia
Publishing House, Bombay, 1961

* _The Food Problem of India_ by N. C. Agrawal. K. K. Vora, Vora
& Co., Bombay, 1961

The Economic Development of India by Vera Anstey. Longmans,
Green & Co., London, 1957

The Indian Middle Classes by B. B. Misra. Oxford University
Press, 1961

Land and Labour in India by Daniel and Alice Thorner. Asia
Publishing House, Bombay, 1962

Towards Non-Violent Socialism, Selected writings of M. K.
Gandhi. Edited by Bharatan Kumarappa, Navajivan
Publishing House, Ahmedabad, 1957

SOCIOLOGY AND PSYCHOLOGY

* _The Twice Born_ by G. Morris Carstairs. Hogarth Press, London,
1961

*_Blossoms in the Dust_ by Kusum Nair. Gerald Duckworth & Co.,
London, 1961

*_Caste in Modern India and Other Essays_ by M. N. Srinivas. Asia
Publishing House, Bombay, 1962

* _The Hindu Woman_ by Margaret Cormack. Asia Publishing
House, Bombay, 1961

*_Caste Today_ by Taya Zinkin. Oxford University Press, 1962

*_Caste and Communication in an Indian Village_ by D. N. Majumdar.
Asia Publishing House, Bombay, 1962

She Who Rides a Peacock (Indian Students and Social Change) by
Margaret Cormack. Asia Publishing House, Bombay, 1961

The Myth of the Caste System by Narmadeshwar Prasad. Samjna
Prakashan, Patna, India, 1957

Hindu Society – An Interpretation by Irawati Karve, Deccan
College, Poona, India, 1961

India's Urban Future, edited by Roy Turner. Oxford University
Press, 1962

The Sikhs Today by Khushwant Singh. Orient Longmans, India,
1959

RELIGION AND PHILOSOPHY

Hinduism, edited by Louis Renou. Prentice-Hall International, London, 1961

History of Philosophy Eastern and Western, with Dr Sarvepalli Radhakrishnan, now President of India, as Chairman of the Editorial Board. Sponsored by the Indian Ministry of Education and published by Allen & Unwin, London, 1952 (Volume I) and 1953 (Volume II)

Hinduism by K. M. Sen. Penguin Books, Harmondsworth, 1961

The Essentials of Indian Philosophy by M. Hiriyanna. Allen & Unwin, London, 1959

HISTORY

Prehistoric India by Stuart Piggott. Penguin Books, Harmondsworth, 1950

The Oxford History of India, Third Edition. Oxford University Press, 1961

India Wins Freedom by Maulana Abul Kalam Azad. Orient Longmans, India, 1959

The History of the Congress by B. Pattabhi Sitaramayya. Published by the Working Committee of Congress on the occasion of the 50th anniversary, Allahabad, India, 1935

The Transfer of Power in India by V. P. Menon. Orient Longmans, India, 1957

The Story of the Integration of the Indian States by V. P. Menon. Orient Longmans, India, 1961

Nehru: A Political Biography by Michael Brecher. Oxford University Press, 1953

Rulers of India Series. Published by the Clarendon Press, Oxford, in the 1890s

The Indian Awakening and Bengal by N. S. Bose. Firma Mukhopadhyay, Calcutta, 1960

My Days with Gandhi by Nirmal Kumar Bose. Nishana, Calcutta, 1953

In the Shadow of the Mahatma by G. D. Birla. Orient Longmans, India, 1955

The Communist Party of India and its Formation Abroad by Muzaffar Ahmad. National Book Agency, Calcutta, 1962

STATISTICAL REFERENCE BOOKS AND PERIODICALS

The *Times of India Directory and Year Book, 1962–63*. Bennett,

Coleman & Co., Bombay and London

India 1961. Indian Ministry of Information and Broadcasting, Publications Division

Statistical Outline of India, 1961. Produced by Tata Industries and published by Vora & Co., Bombay

Census of India, 1961. Government of India, Delhi

Statistical Yearbook, 1963. United Nations

The *Eastern Economist,* Annual Number, 1963. New Delhi

Seminar. Published monthly from Malhotra Building, Janpath, New Delhi

LITERATURE

The novels, plays and poems of Rabindranath Tagore, published by Macmillan & Co., London. See especially the novel, *The Wreck*

The novels of R. K. Narayan, among them:

Waiting for the Mahatma, first published by Methuen, London 1955

Mr. Sampath, first published by Eyre & Spottiswoode, London 1949

The Guide, first published by Methuen, London, 1958

The Bachelor of Arts, first published by Eyre & Spottiswoode, London, 1937

The novels of Mulk Raj Anand, among them:

Coolie, first published by Hutchinsons, London, 1947

The Village, first published 1939. Kutub Publishers, Ltd, Bombay

The novels of R. Prawer Jhabyala, among them:

The Householder, John Murray, London, 1960

Get Ready for Battle, John Murray, London, 1962

A novel by Balwant Singh Anand, *Cruel Interlude,* for the gruesomely factual picture that it gives of the partition terror. Asia Publishing House, Bombay, 1961

And of course, for a picture of the British raj and much else, *A Passage to India* by E. M. Forster. First published by Edward Arnold, London, 1924

Many of the books listed are available in other editions. I have quoted those editions which I have myself used, so that quotations in the text with their page references can easily be traced.

INDEX

WITHDRAWN